DATA MINING USING GRAMMAR BASED GENETIC PROGRAMMING AND APPLICATIONS

GENETIC PROGRAMMING SERIES

Series Editor

John Koza
Stanford University

Also in the series:

GENETIC PROGRAMMING AND DATA STRUCTURES: Genetic Programming + Data Structures = Automatic Programming! *William B. Langdon*; ISBN: 0-7923-8135-1

AUTOMATIC RE-ENGINEERING OF SOFTWARE USING GENETIC PROGRAMMING, *Conor Ryan;* ISBN: 0-7923-8653-1

The cover image was generated using Genetic Programming and interactive selection. Anargyros Sarafopoulos created the image, and the GP interactive selection software.

DATA MINING USING GRAMMAR BASED GENETIC PROGRAMMING AND APPLICATIONS

by

Man Leung Wong
Lingnan University, Hong Kong

Kwong Sak Leung
The Chinese University of Hong Kong

SPRINGER SCIENCE+BUSINESS MEDIA, LLC

Library of Congress Cataloging-in-Publication Data

Wong, Man Leung, 1966-
Data mining using grammar-based genetic programming and applications / by Man Leung Wong, Kwong Sak Leung.
p. cm. -- (Genetic programming series ; GPEM 03)
ISBN 978-1-4757-8421-3 ISBN 978-0-306-47012-7 (eBook)
DOI 10.1007/978-0-306-47012-7
1. Data mining. 2. Genetic programming (Computer science) I. Leung, Kwong Sak, 1955- II. Title. III. Series

QA76.9.D343 W66 2000
006.3--dc21

99-089334

Originally published by Kluwer Academic Publishers in 2000
Softcover reprint of the hardcover 1st edition 2000

Printed on acid-free paper.

Contents

List of figures

List of tables

Preface

Data mining is an automated process of discovering knowledge from databases. There are various kinds of data mining methods aiming to search for different kinds of knowledge. Genetic Programming (GP) and Inductive Logic Programming (ILP) are two of the approaches for data mining. GP is a method of automatically inducing S-expressions in Lisp to perform specified tasks while ILP involves the construction of logic programs from examples and background knowledge.

Since their formalisms are very different, these two approaches cannot be integrated easily although their properties and goals are similar. If they can be combined in a common framework, then their techniques and theories can be shared and their problem solving power can be enhanced.

This book describes a framework, called GGP (Generic Genetic Programming), that integrates GP and ILP based on a formalism of logic grammars. A system in this framework called LOGENPRO (The LOgic grammar based GENetic PROgramming system) is developed. This system has been tested on many problems in knowledge discovery from databases. These experiments demonstrate that the proposed framework is powerful, flexible, and general.

Experiments are performed to illustrate that knowledge in different kinds of knowledge representation such as logic programs and production rules can be induced by LOGENPRO. The problem of inducing knowledge can be formulated as a search for a highly fit piece of knowledge in the space of all possible pieces of knowledge. We show that the search space can be specified declaratively by the user in the framework. Moreover, the formalism is powerful enough to represent context-sensitive information and domain-dependent knowledge. This knowledge can be used to accelerate the learning speed and/or improve the quality of the knowledge induced.

Automatic discovery of problem representation primitives is one of the most challenging research areas in GP. We have illustrated how to apply LOGENPRO to emulate Automatically Defined Functions (ADFs) proposed by Koza (1992; 1994). We have demonstrated that, by employing various knowledge about the problem being solved, LOGENPRO can find a solution much faster than ADFs and the computation required by LOGENPRO is much smaller than that of ADFs.

LOGENPRO can emulate the effects of Strongly Type Genetic Programming (STGP) and ADFs simultaneously and effortlessly (Montana 1995).

Data mining systems induce knowledge from datasets which are huge, noisy (incorrect), incomplete, inconsistent, imprecise (fuzzy), and uncertain. The problem is that existing systems use a limiting attribute-value language for representing the training examples and induced knowledge. Furthermore, some important patterns are ignored because they are statistically insignificant. LOGENPRO is employed to induce knowledge from noisy training examples. The knowledge is represented in first-order logic programs. The performance of LOGENPRO is evaluated on the chess endgame domain. Detailed comparisons with other ILP systems are performed. It is found that LOGENPRO outperforms these ILP systems significantly at most noise levels. This experiment indicates that the Darwinian principle of natural selection is a plausible noise handling method which can avoid overfitting and identify important patterns at the same time.

We apply the system to two real-life medical databases for limb fracture and scoliosis. The knowledge discovered provides insights to the clinicians and allows them to have a better understanding of these two medical domains.

Chapter 1

INTRODUCTION

Databases are valuable treasures. A database not only stores and provides data but also contains hidden precious knowledge, which can be very important. It can be a new law in science, a new insight for curing a disease or a new market trend that can make millions of dollars. Conventionally, the data are analyzed manually. Many hidden and potentially useful relationships may not be recognized by the analyst. Nowadays, many organizations are capable of generating and collecting a huge amount of data. The size of data available now is beyond the capability of our mind to analyze. It requires the power of computers to handle it. Data mining, or knowledge discovery in database, is the automated process of sifting the data to get the gold buried in the database.

In this chapter, section 1.1 is a brief introduction of the definition and the objectives of data mining. Section 1.2 states the research motivations of the topics of this book. Section 1.3 lists the contributions of this book. The organization of this book is sketched in section 1.4.

1.1. Data Mining

The two terms Data Mining and Knowledge Discovery in Database have similar meanings. *Knowledge Discovery in Database* (KDD) can be defined as the nontrivial process of identifying valid, novel, potentially useful, and ultimately understandable patterns in data (Fayyad et al. 1996). The data are records in a database. The knowledge discovered from the KDD process should not be obtainable from straightforward computation. The knowledge should be novel and beneficial to the user. It should be able to be applied to new data with some degree of certainty. Finally the knowledge should be human understandable. On the other hand, the term *Data Mining* is commonly used to denote the finding of useful patterns in data. It consists of applying data analysis and discovery algorithms to produce patterns or models from the data.

KDD is an interactive and iterative process with several steps. In Fayyad et al. (1996), KDD is divided into several steps. Data Mining can be considered as one of the steps in the KDD process. It is the core of the KDD process, and thus the two terms are often used interchangeably. The whole process of KDD consists of five steps:

1. *Selection* extracts relevant data sets from the database.
2. *Preprocessing* removes the noise and handles missing data fields.
3. *Transformation* (or *data reduction*) is performed to reduce the number of variables under consideration.
4. A suitable data mining algorithm of the selected model is employed on the prepared data.
5. Finally, the result of data mining is interpreted and evaluated.

If the discovered knowledge is not satisfactory, these steps will be iterated. The discovered knowledge can then be applied in decision making.

Different data mining algorithms aim to find different kinds of knowledge. Chen et al. (1996) grouped the techniques for knowledge discovery into six categories.

1. *Mining of association rules* finds rules in the form of "$A_1 \wedge \ldots \wedge A_m \Rightarrow B_1 \wedge \ldots \wedge B_n$", where A_i and B_j are attributes values. This association rule tries to capture the association between the attributes. The rule means that if A_1 and ... and A_m appear in a record, then B_1 and ... and B_n will usually appear.
2. *Data generalization and summarization* summarize the general characteristics of a group of target class and present the data in a high-level view.
3. *Classification* formulates a classification model based on the data. The model can be used to classify an unseen data item into one of the predefined classes based on the attribute values.
4. *Data clustering* identifies a finite set of clusters or categories to describe the data. Similar data items are grouped into a

cluster such that the interclass similarity is minimized and the intraclass similarity is maximized. The common characteristics of the cluster are analyzed and presented.

5. *Pattern based similarity search* tries to search for a pattern in temporal or spatial-temporal data, such as financial databases or multimedia databases.
6. *Mining path traversal patterns* tries to capture user access patterns in an information providing system, such as World Wide Web.

Machine learning (Michalski et al. 1983) and data mining share a similar objective. Machine learning learns a computer model from a set of training examples. Many machine learning algorithms can be applied to databases. Rather than learning on a set of instances, machine learning is performed on data in a file or records from a database (Frawley et al. 1991). However, databases are designed to meet the needs of real world applications. They are often dynamic, incomplete, noisy and much larger than typical machine learning data sets. These issues cause difficulties in direct application of machine learning methods. Some of the data mining and knowledge discovery techniques related to this book are covered in chapter 2.

1.2. Motivation

Data mining has recently become a popular research topic. The increasing use of computers result in an explosion of information. These data can be best used if the knowledge hidden can be uncovered. Thus there is a need for a way to automatically discover knowledge from data. The research in this area can be useful for a lot of real world problems. For example, the medical domain is a major area for applying data mining. With the computerization in hospitals, a huge amount of data has been collected. It is beneficial if these data can be analyzed automatically.

Most data mining techniques employ search methods to find novel, useful, and interesting knowledge. Search methods in Artificial Intelligence can be classified into weak and strong methods. Weak methods encode search strategies that are task independent and consequently less efficient. Strong methods are rich in task-specific knowledge that is placed explicitly into the search mechanism by programmers or knowledge engineers. Strong methods tend to be narrowly focused but fairly efficient in their abilities to identify domain-specific solutions. Strong methods often use one or more weak methods working underneath the task-specific knowledge. Since the knowledge to solve the problem is usually represented explicitly within the problem solver's knowledge base as search strategies and heuristics, there is a direct relation between the quality of knowledge and the performances of strong methods (Angeline 1993; 1994).

Different strong methods have been introduced to guide the search for the desired programs. However, these strong methods may not always work because they may be trapped in local maxima. In order to overcome this problem, weak methods or backtracking can be invoked if the systems find that they encounter troubles in the process of searching for satisfactory solutions. The problem is that these approaches are very inefficient.

The alternatives are evolutionary algorithms, a kind of weak methods, which conducts parallel searches. Evolutionary algorithms perform both exploitation of the most promising solutions and exploration of the search space. It is featured to tackle hard search problems and thus it is applicable to data mining. Although there are a lot of researches on evolutionary algorithms, there is not much study of representing domain-specific knowledge for evolutionary algorithms to produce evolutionary strong methods for the problems of data mining.

Moreover, existing data mining systems are limited by the knowledge representation in which the induced knowledge is expressed. For example, Genetic Programming (GP) systems can only induce knowledge represented as S-expressions in Lisp (Koza 1992; 1994). Inductive Logic Programming (ILP) systems can only produce logic programs (Muggletion 1992). Since the formalisms of these two approaches are so different, these two approaches cannot be integrated easily although their properties and goals are similar. If they can be combined in a common framework, then many of the techniques and theories obtained in one approach can be applied in the other one. The combination can greatly enhance the overall problem solving power and the information exchange between these fields.

These observations lead us to propose and develop a framework combining GP and ILP that employs evolutionary algorithms to induce programs. The framework is driven by logic grammars which are powerful enough to represent context-sensitive information and domain-specific knowledge that can accelerate the learning of programs. It is also very flexible and knowledge in various knowledge representations such as production rules, decision trees, Lisp, and Prolog can be induced.

1.3. Contributions of the Book

The contributions of the research are listed here in the order that they appear in the book:

- We propose a novel, flexible, and general framework called Generic Genetic Programming (GGP), which is based on a formalism of logic grammars. A system in this framework called LOGENPRO (The LOgic grammar based GENetic PROgramming system) is developed. It is a novel system developed to combine the implicitly parallel search power of GP and the knowledge representation power of first-order logic. It takes the advantages of existing ILP and GP systems while avoids their disadvantages. It is found that knowledge in different representations can be expressed as derivation trees. The framework facilitates the generation of the initial population of individuals and the operations of various genetic operators such as crossover and mutation. We introduce two effective and efficient genetic operators which guarantee only valid offspring are produced.
- We have demonstrated that LOGENPRO can emulate traditional GP (Koza 1992) easily. Traditional GP has a limitation that all the variables, constants, arguments for functions, and values returned by functions must be of the same data type. This limitation leads to the difficulty of inducing even some rather simple and straightforward functional programs. It is found that knowledge of data type can be represented easily in LOGENPRO to alleviate the above problem. An experiment has been performed to show that LOGENPRO can find a solution much faster than GP and the computation required by LOGENPRO is much smaller than that of GP. Another advantage of LOGENPRO is that it

can emulate the effect of Strongly Type Genetic Programming (STGP) effortlessly (Montana 1995).

- Automatic discovery of problem representation primitives is one of the most challenging research areas in GP. We have illustrated how to apply LOGENPRO to emulate Automatically Defined Functions (ADFs) proposed by Koza. ADFs is one of the approaches that have been proposed to acquire problem representation primitives automatically (Koza 1992; 1994). We have performed an experiment to demonstrate that, by employing various knowledge about the problem being solved, LOGENPRO can find a solution much faster than ADFs and the computation required by LOGENPRO is much smaller than that of ADFs. This experiment also shows that LOGENPRO can emulate the effects of STGP and ADFs simultaneously and effortlessly.
- Knowledge discovery systems induce knowledge from datasets which are frequently noisy (incorrect), incomplete, inconsistent, imprecise (fuzzy) and uncertain (Leung and Wong 1991a; 1991b; 1991c). We have employed LOGENPRO to combine evolutionary algorithms and a variation of FOIL, BEAM-FOIL, in learning logic programs from noisy datasets. Detailed comparisons between LOGENPRO and other ILP systems have been conducted using the chess endgame problem. It is found that LOGENPRO outperforms these ILP systems significantly at most noise levels.
- An approach for rule learning has been developed. This approach uses LOGENPRO as the learning algorithm. We have designed a suitable grammar to represent rules, and we have investigated how the grammar can be modified in order to learn rules with different formats. New techniques have been employed in LOGENPRO to facilitate the learning: seeds are used to generate better rules, and the operator 'dropping condition' is used to generalize rules. The evaluation function is designed to measure both the accuracy and significance of the rule, so that interesting rules can be learned.
- The technique token competition has been employed to learn multiple rules simultaneously. This technique effectively

maintains groups of individuals in the population, with different groups evolving different rules.

- We have applied the data mining system to two real-life medical databases. We have consulted domain experts to understand the domains, so as to pre-process the data and construuct suitable grammars for rule learning. The learning results have been fed back to the domain experts. Interesting knowledge are discovered, which can help clinicians to get a deeper understanding of the domains.

1.4. Outline of the Book

Chapter 2 is an overview on the different approaches of data mining related to this book. The approaches are grouped into decision tree approach, classification rule learning, association rule mining, statistical approach and Bayesian network learning. Representative algorithms in each group will be introduced.

In chapter 3, we will first introduce a class of weak methods called evolutionary algorithms. Subsequently, four kinds of these algorithms, namely, Genetic Algorithms (GAs), Genetic Programming (GP), Evolution Strategies (ES), and Evolutionary Programming (EP), will be discussed in turn.

We will describe another approach of data mining, Inductive Logic Programming (ILP), that investigates the construction of logic programs from training examples and background knowledge in chapter 4. A brief introduction to inductive concept learning will be presented first. Then, two approaches of the ILP problem will be discussed followed by an introduction to the techniques and the methods of ILP.

A novel, flexible and, general framework, called GGP (Generic Genetic Programming), that can combine GP and ILP will be described in chapter 5. A high-level description of LOGENPRO (The LOgic grammar based GENetic PROgramming system), a system of the framework, will be presented. We will also discuss the representation method of individuals, the crossover operator, and the mutation operator.

Three applications of LOGENPRO in acquiring knowledge from databases will be discussed in chapter 6. The knowledge acquired can be expressed in different knowledge representations such as decision tree, decision list, production rule, and first-order logic. We will illustrate how to apply LOGENPRO to emulate GP in the first application. In the second application, LOGENPRO is used to induce knowledge represented in decision trees from a real-world database. In the third application, we apply LOGENPRO to combine genetic search methods and a variation of FOIL to induce knowledge from noisy datasets. The acquired knowledge is represented as a logic program. The performance of LOGENPRO has been evaluated on the chess endgame problem and detailed comparisons to other ILP systems will be given.

Chapter 7 will discuss how evolutionary computation can be applied to discover rules from databases. We will focus on how to model the problem of rule learning such that LOGENPRO can be applied as the learning algorithm. The representation of rules, the genetic operators for evolving new rules, and the evaluation function will be introduced in this chapter. We will also describe how to learn a set of rules. The technique token competition is employed to solve this problem. A rule learning system will be introduced, and the experiment results on two machine learning databases will be presented in this chapter.

The data mining system has been used to analyze real-life medical databases for limb fracture and scoliosis. The applications of this system and the learning results will be presented in chapter 8.

Chapter 9 is a conclusion of this book. The research work will be summarized, and some suggestions for future research will be given.

Chapter 2

AN OVERVIEW OF DATA MINING

There are a large variety of data mining approaches (Ramakrishnan and Grama 1999, Ganti et al. 1999, Han et al. 1999, Hellerstein et al. 1999, Chakrabarti et al. 1999, Karypis et al. 1999, Cherkassky and Mulier 1998, Bergadano and Gunetti 1995), with different search methods aiming at searching for different kinds of knowledge. This chapter reviews some of the data mining approaches related to this book. Decision tree approach, classification rule learning, association rule mining, statistical approach, and Bayesian network learning are reviewed in the following sections.

2.1. Decision Tree Approach

A decision tree is a tree like structure that represents the knowledge for classification. Internal nodes in a decision tree are labeled with attributes, the edges are labeled with attribute values and the leaves are labeled with classes. An example of a decision tree is shown in figure 2.1. This tree is for classifying whether the weather of a Saturday morning is good or not. It can classify the weather into the class P (positive) or N (negative). For a given record, the classification process starts from the root node. The attribute in the node is tested, and the value determines which edge is to be taken. This process is repeated until a leaf is reached. The record is then classified as the class of the leaf. Decision tree is a simple knowledge representation for a classification model, but the tree can be very complicate and difficult to interpret. The following two learning algorithms, ID3 and C4.5, are commonly used for mining knowledge represented in decision trees.

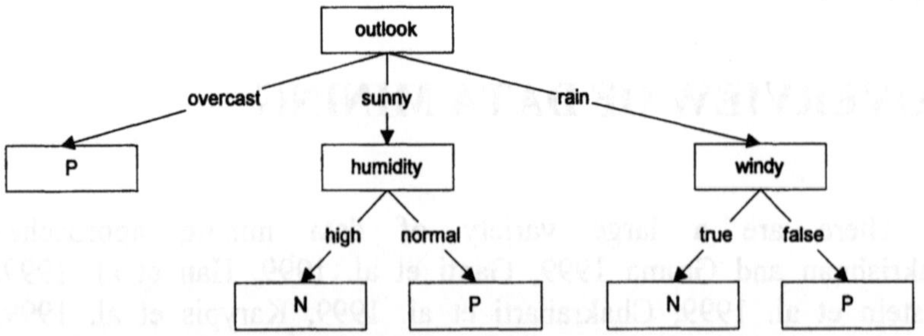

Figure 2.1: *A decision tree*

2.1.1. ID3

ID3 (Quinlan 1986) is a simple algorithm to construct a decision tree from a set of training objects. It performs a heuristic top-down irrevocable search. Initially the tree contains only a root node and all the training cases are placed in the root node. ID3 uses information as a criterion for selecting the branching attribute of a node. Let the node contains a set T of cases, with $|C_j|$ of the cases belonging to one of the pre-defined class C_j. The information needed for classification in the current node is

$$info(T) = -\sum_j \frac{|C_j|}{|T|}\log_2\left(\frac{|C_j|}{|T|}\right) \tag{2.1}$$

This value measures the average amount of information needed to identify the class of a case. Assume that using attribute X as the branching attribute will divide the cases into n subsets. Let T_i denotes the set of cases in subset i. The information required for the subset i is $info(T_i)$. Thus the expected information required *after* choosing attribute X as the branching attribute is the weighted average of the subtree information:

$$info_X(T) = \sum_i \frac{|T_i|}{|T|} \times info(T_i) \tag{2.2}$$

Thus the information gain will be

$$gain(X) = info(T) - info_X(T) \tag{2.3}$$

As a smaller value in the information corresponds to a better classification, the attribute X with the maximum information gain is selected for the branching of the node.

After the branching attribute is selected, the training cases are divided by the different values of the branching attribute. If all examples in one branch belong to the same class, then this branch becomes a leaf labeled with that class. If all branches are labeled with a class, the algorithm terminates. Otherwise the process is recursively applied on each branch.

ID3 uses the chi-square test to avoid over-fitting due to the noise. In a set T of cases, let o_{C_j,x_i} denote the number of records in class C_j with $X = x_i$. If attribute X is irrelevant for classification, the expected number of cases belonging to class C_j with $X = x_i$ is

$$e_{C_j,x_i} = |C_j| \times \frac{|T_i|}{|T|} \tag{2.4}$$

The value of chi-square is approximately

$$\chi^2 \approx \sum_i \sum_j \frac{(o_{C_j,x_i} - e_{C_j,x_i})^2}{e_{C_j,x_i}} \tag{2.5}$$

In choosing the branching attribute for the decision tree, if χ^2 is lower than a threshold, then the attribute will not be used. This can avoid creating unnecessary branches that make the constructed tree complicate.

2.1.2. C4.5

C4.5 (Quinlan 1992) is the successor of ID3. The use of information gain in ID3 has a serious deficiency that favors tests with many outcomes. C4.5 improves this by using a gain ratio as the criterion for selecting the branching attribute. A value *split* $info_X(T)$ is defined with a similar definition of $info_X(T)$

$$split\ info_X(T) = -\sum_{i=1}^{n} \frac{|T_i|}{|T|} \log_2\left(\frac{|T_i|}{|T|}\right) \tag{2.6}$$

This value represents the potential information generated by dividing T into n subsets. The gain ratio is used as the new criterion

$$gain\,ratio(X) = gain(X) / split\ info_X(T) \tag{2.7}$$

The attribute with the maximum value on *gain ratio*(X) is selected as the branching attribute.

C4.5 abandoned the chi-square test for avoiding over-fitting. Rather, C4.5 allows the tree to grow and prunes the unnecessary branches later. The tree pruning step replaces a subtree by a leaf or the most frequently used branch. The decision on whether a subtree is pruned depends on an estimation of the error rate. Suppose that a leaf gives an error of E out of N training cases. For a given confidence level CF, the upper limit of the error probability for the binomial distribution is written as $U_{CF}(E, N)$. The upper limit is used as the pessimistic error rate of the leaf. The estimated number of errors for a leaf covering N training cases is thus $N \times U_{CF}(E, N)$. The estimated number of errors for a subtree is the sum of errors of its branches.

Pruning is performed if replacing a subtree by a leaf or a branch can give a lower estimated number of errors. For example, for a subtree with three leaves, which respectively covers 6, 9, and 1 training cases without errors, the estimated number of mis-classification with the default confidence level of 25% is

$$6 \times U_{25\%}(0, 6) + 9 \times U_{25\%}(0, 9) + 1 \times U_{25\%}(0, 1) =$$
$$6 \times 0.206 + 9 \times 0.143 + 1 \times 0.750 = 3.273.$$

If they are combined to a leaf node, it mis-classifies 1 out of 16 training cases. The estimated number of mis-classifications of this leaf is

$$16 \times U_{25\%}(1, 16) = 16 \times 0.157 = 2.512.$$

This number is better than that of the original subtree and thus the leaf can replace the subtree.

2.2. Classification Rule

A rule is a sentence of the form "if *antecedents*, then *consequent*". Rules are commonly used in expressing knowledge and are easily understood by human. Rules are also commonly used in expert systems for decision making. Rule learning is the process of inducing rules from a set of training examples. Many algorithms in rule learning try to search for rules to classify a case into one of the pre-specified classes. Three commonly used classification rule learning algorithms are given as follows:

2.2.1. AQ Algorithm

AQ (Michalski 1969) is a family of algorithms for inductive learning. One example is AQ15 (Michalski et al. 1986a). The knowledge representation used in AQ is the decision rules. A rule is represented in Variable-valued Logic system 1 (VL_1). In VL_1, a *selector* relates a variable to a value or a disjunction of values, e.g. color = red $\vee$ green. A conjunction of selectors forms a *complex.* A *cover* is a disjunction of complexes describing all positive examples and none of the negative examples. A cover defines the antecedents of a decision rule. The original AQ can only construct exact rules, i.e. for each class, the decision rule must cover only the positive examples and none of the negative examples.

AQ algorithm is a covering method instead of the divide-and-conquer method of ID3. The search algorithm is described as follows (Michalski 1983):

1. A positive example, called the *seed*, is chosen from the training examples.
2. A set of complexes, called a *star*, that covers the seed is generated by the star generating step. Each complex in the star must be the most general without covering a negative example.
3. The complexes in the star are ordered by the lexicographic evaluation function (LEF). A commonly used LEF is to maximize the number of positive examples covered.
4. The examples covered by the best complex is removed from the training examples
5. The best complex in the star is added to the cover.
6. Steps 1-5 are repeated until the cover can cover all the positive examples.

The star generating step (step 2) performs a top down irrevocable beam search. This step can be summarized as follows:

1 Let the partial star be the set containing the empty complex, i.e. without any selector.

2 While the partial star covers negative examples,

(a) Select a covered negative example.

(b) Let *extension* be the set of all selectors that cover the seed but not the negative example.

(c) Update the partial star to be the set $\{x \wedge y \mid x \in$ partial star, $y \in$ *extension*$\}$.

(d) Remove all complexes in the partial star subsumed by other complexes.

3 Trim the partial star, i.e. retain only the *maxstar* best complexes, where *maxstar* is the beam width for the beam search.

In the star generating step, not all the complexes that cover the seed are included. The partial star will be trimmed by retaining only *maxstar* best complexes. The heuristics used is to retain the complexes that "maximize the sum of positive examples covered and negative examples excluded".

2.2.2. CN2

CN2 (Clark and Niblett 1989) incorporates ideas from both AQ and ID3 algorithms. AQ algorithm cannot handle noisy examples properly. CN2 retains the beam search of AQ algorithm but removes its dependence on specific training examples (the seeds) during the search. CN2 uses a decision list as the knowledge representation. A decision list is a list of pairs (ϕ_1, C_1), (ϕ_2, C_2), …, (ϕ_r, C_r), where ϕ_i is a complex, C_i is a class, and the last description ϕ_r is the constant true. This list means "if ϕ_1 then C_1 else if ϕ_2 then C_2 … else C_r".

Each step of CN2 searches for a complex that covers a large number of examples of class C and a small number of other classes. Having found a good complex, say ϕ_i, the algorithm removes those examples it covers from the training set and adds the rule "if ϕ_i then predict C" to the end of the rule list. This step is repeated until no more satisfactory complexes can be found.

The searching algorithm for a good complex performs a beam search. At each stage in the search, CN2 stores a *star* S of "a set of best complexes found so far". The star is initialized to the empty complex. The complexes of the star are then specialized by intersecting with all possible selectors. Each specialization is similar to introducing a new branch in ID3. All specializations of complexes in the star are examined and ordered by the evaluation criteria. Then the star is trimmed to size *maxstar* by removing the worst complexes. This search process is iterated until no further complexes that exceed the threshold of evaluation criteria can be generated.

The evaluation criteria for complexes consist of two tests for testing the prediction accuracy and significance of the complex. Let $(p_1,\ldots,p_n)$ be the probability of covered examples in class $C_1,\ldots C_n$. CN2 uses the information theoretic entropy

$$info = -\sum_i p_i \log_2(p_i) \tag{2.8}$$

to measure the quality of a complex (the lower the entropy, the better the quality). The likelihood ratio statistic is used to measure the significance of the complex:

$$2\sum_{i=1}^{n} f_i \log(f_i / e_i) \tag{2.9}$$

where $(f_1,\ldots,f_n)$ is the observed frequency distribution and $(e_1,\ldots,e_n)$ is the expected distribution. A complex with a high value of the ratio means the high accuracy is not obtained by chance.

2.2.3. C4.5RULES

Other than being able to produce a decision tree as described in section 2.1.2, a component of C4.5, C4.5RULES (Quinlan 1992), can transform the constructed decision tree into production rules. Each path of the decision tree from the root to the leaf equals to a rule. The antecedent part of the rule contains all the conditions of the path, and the consequent is the class of the leaf. However this rule can be very complicate and a simplification is required. Suppose that the rule gives E errors out of the N covered cases, and if condition X is removed from the rule, the rule will give E_{X-} errors out of the N_{X-} covered cases. If the pessimistic error $U_{CF}(E_{X-}, N_{X-})$ is not greater than the original pessimistic error $U_{CF}(E, N)$, then it makes sense to delete the condition X. For each rule, the pessimistic error for removing each condition is calculated. If the lowest pessimistic error is not greater than that of the original rule, then the condition that gives the lowest pessimistic error is removed. The simplification process is repeated until the pessimistic error of the rule cannot be improved.

After this simplification, the set of rules can be exhaustive and redundant. For each class, only a subset of rules is chosen out of the set of rules classifying it. The subset is chosen based on the Minimum Description Length principle. The principle states that the best rule set should be the rule set that required the fewest bits to encode the rules and their exceptions. For each class, the encoding length for each possible subset of rules is estimated. The subset that gives the smallest encoding length is chosen as the rule set of that class.

2.3. Association Rule Mining

Association rule mining (Agrawal et al. 1993) focuses on discovering knowledge between items in a large database of sales transactions. Association rule is a rule of the form "if X then Y", where X and Y are items in a transaction. Association rule mining is different from classification, as there is no pre-specified classes in the consequent. An association rule is valid if it can satisfy the threshold requirement on confidence factor and support. The rule is required to have at least c% of records that satisfy X and Y, where c is the confidence threshold. It is also required that the number of records satisfying both X and Y has to be larger than s% of the records, where s is the support threshold.

The problem of mining association rules from a database can be solved in two steps. The first step is to find the sets of attributes that have enough support. These sets are called *large itemsets* as 'large' is used to denote having enough support. The second step is from each large itemset, association rules with confidence larger than the threshold are searched. The attributes are divided into antecedents and consequent and the confidence is calculated. The main researches (Agrawal et al. 1993, Mannila et al. 1994, Agrawal and Srikant 1994, Han and Fu 1995, Park et al. 1995) consider Boolean association rules, where each attribute must be Boolean (e.g. have or have not bought the item). They focus on developing fast algorithms for the first step, as this step is very time consuming. They can be efficiently applied to large databases, but the requirement of Boolean attributes limited their uses. The following two commonly used association rule mining algorithms are given as examples:

2.3.1. Apriori

Apriori (Agrawal and Srikant 1994) is an algorithm for generating large itemsets, the sets of attributes that have enough support, in Boolean association rule mining (i.e. the first step). The support of an itemset has a characteristic that the subsets of a large itemset must be large, and the supersets of a small (i.e. not large) itemset cannot be large. Apriori makes use of this characteristic to drastically reduce the search space. The outline of the Apriori algorithm is listed as follows:

1 Count the support of itemsets with 1 element.

2 L_1= the set of size 1 itemsets that are large.

3 For (*k*=2; *k*<*no_of_attributes*; *k*++)

(a) generate extensions of each size *k*-1 large itemset by adding one more attribute;

(b) C_k= the set of extensions of size *k*-1 large itemsets;

(c) for each itemset in C_k, if one of its size *k*-1 subset is not in L_k, delete it from C_k;

(d) for each itemset in C_k, count the support and check whether it is large;

(e) L_k = the set of large itemsets in C_k.

Apriori first searches for large itemsets with one attribute. Then other large itemsets are searched from the itemsets known to be large. The large itemsets are extended by adding one attribute. If one subset of the extended itemset is not known to be large, this itemset is removed because the subset of a large itemset must be large. The supports of these extended itemsets are counted to check whether they are still large. Once a large itemset is found to be not large, further extension of it is no longer necessary because its superset must be small.

2.3.2. Quantitative Association Rule Mining

Quantitative association rules do not restrict the attributes to be Boolean. Quantitative or categorical attributes are allowed. In Srikant and Agrawal (1996), the problem of mining quantitative association rules is mapped into a Boolean association rule problem. Intervals are made for each quantitative attribute. A new Boolean attribute is created for each interval or category. This attribute is set to 1 if the original attribute is in that interval or category. For example, a record with age equals 23 will have 1's in the new interval attributes 'Age:(20-29)' and 'Age:(15-30)', and have 0's in the new interval attribute 'Age:(30-39)'. However, this mapping will face two new problems:

- **Execution Time:** The number of attributes is hugely increased, and greatly affects the execution time.
- **Many Rules:** If an interval of a quantitative attribute has minimum support, any range containing this interval will also has minimum support. Thus the number of rules increase greatly. Many of them just differ in the ranges of the quantitative attributes and in fact refer to the same association.

To tackle the first problem, a "maximum support" parameter is required from the user. The new Boolean attributes are not created for all possible intervals. If the support of an interval exceeds the maximum support, it will not be considered as the rule will be too general and should already be covered by other rules having a smaller interval. To tackle the second problem, an "interesting level" parameter is required from the user. An interesting measure is defined to measure how much the support and/or the confidence of a rule are greater than expected. Those rules with interest measures lower than the user requirement are pruned.

2.4. Statistical Approach

Statistics and data mining both try to search knowledge from data. Statistical approach focuses more on quantitative analysis. A statistical perspective on knowledge discovery has been given in Elder IV and Pregibon (1996). Statisticians usually assume a model for the data and then look for the best parameters for the model. They interpret the models based on the data. They may sacrifice some performance to be able to extract the meaning from the model. However, in recent years statisticians have also moved the objective to the selection of a suitable model. Moreover, they emphasize on estimating or explaining the model uncertainty by summarizing the randomness to a distribution. The uncertainties are captured in the standard error of the estimation. Some of the typical statistical approaches are briefly described below.

2.4.1. Bayesian Classifier

The Bayesian probability theorem can be used to classify an object into one of the classes $\{c_1, c_2, \ldots, c_m\}$. Let the object be described by a feature vector F which consists of attributes $\{f_1, f_2, \ldots, f_l\}$. The probability of this object belonging to class c_i is given by

$$p(c_i \mid F) = \frac{p(F \mid c_i)p(c_i)}{p(F)} \tag{2.10}$$

The use of this theorem can provide probabilistic knowledge for classifications of unseen objects. The object with a feature vector F can be classified into the class c_i which gives the maximum value on this probability. Since the denominator $p(F)$ appears in every probability, it is actually a normalizing factor and can be ignored in the calculation. The probability $p(c_i)$ can be estimated as the occurrence of c_i over the total number of existing objects. Thus the main concern is on how to estimate $p(F| c_i)$.

This probability can be estimated by making assumptions. The simplest assumption is that each feature in F is statistical independence, that is

$$p(F \mid c_i) = \prod_{k=1}^{l} p(f_k \mid c_i) \tag{2.11}$$

the value $p(f_k|c_i)$ can be estimated as the occurrence of objects in class c_i having f_k over the occurrence of objects in class c_i. Another assumption given in Wu et al. (1991) is that the probability can be under a normal distribution, that is

$$p(F \mid c_i) = \frac{1}{(2\pi)^{n/2} \mid C_i \mid^{1/2}} \exp\left(-\frac{1}{2}(F - M_i)' C_i^{-1} (F - M_i)\right) \tag{2.12}$$

where C_i is the covariance matrix and M_i is the mean vector over n unseen cases. Thus the problem is reduced to the measurement of the two parameters C_i and M_i.

2.4.2. FORTY-NINER

FORTY-NINER (Zykow and Baker 1991) is a system for discovering regularities in a database. It searches for significant regularities compared to the null distribution hypothesis. The search is divided into two phases. The first phase is a search for two-dimensional regularities (i.e. regularities between two variables). The second phase generalizes the two-dimensional regularities to more dimensions. Either phase can be repeated many times with human interventions.

In the first phase, each attribute is transformed by using aggregation, slicing, and projection. The search is performed on partitions of the database. The user can reduce the search space by limiting the number of independent variables and the depth of partitioning. The regularity is represented in a contingency table and in the best linear fit. An example of a contingency table is shown in table 2.1, where o_{c_1,a_1} is the actual number of occurrence of $C=c_1$ and $A=a_1$. This value is compared with $e_{c_1,a_1} = {o_{c_1} \times o_{a_1}}/{N}$ (where N is the total number of records), and χ^2 is calculated to measure the significance of the regularity. The best liner fit between C and A is a linear regularity $C=mA+b$ obtained by using the least squares method, where m is the slope and b is the intercept. A value r^2 measures the significance of the linear regularity. It is calculated over all data points (X_i, Y_i) using the formula:

$$r^2 = 1 - \frac{\sum_{i=1}^{n}(Y_i - \widetilde{Y}_i)^2}{\sqrt{\sum_{i=1}^{n}(Y_i - \overline{Y})^2}} \qquad (2.13)$$

where $\overline{Y}$ is the average value of Y over the n data points, and $\widetilde{Y}_i$ is the value of Y_i predicated by the linear regularity.

	$A=a_1$	$A=a_2$	Total
$C=c_1$	o_{c_1,a_1}	o_{c_1,a_2}	o_{c_1}
$C=c_2$	o_{c_2,a_1}	o_{c_2,a_2}	o_{c_2}
Total	o_{a_1}	o_{a_2}	

Table 2.1: A contingency table for variable A vs. variable C.

In the second phase, the user selects the 2-D regularities for expansions. The regularity expansion module adds one dimension at a time and the multi-dimension regularity is formed. This module can be applied recursively. Since the search space would be exponential if all possible multi-dimensional regularities are considered, user intervention is required to guide the search.

2.4.3. EXPLORA

EXPLORA (Hoschka and Klosgen 1991) is an integrated system for helping the user to search for interesting relationships in the data. A statement is an interesting relationship between a value of a dependent variable and values of several independent variables. Various statement types are included in EXPLORA, e.g., rules, changes and trend analyses. The value of the dependent variable is called the *target group* and the combination of values of independent variables is called the *subgroup*. For example, the sufficient rule pattern

```
48% of the population are CLERICAL.
However, 92% of AGE > 40,
SALARY < 10260 are CLERICAL
```

is a relationship between the target group CLERICAL and the independent variables AGE and SALARY. The user selects one statement type, identifies the target group and the independent variables, and inputs the suitable parameters. EXPLORA calculates the statistical significance of all possible statements and outputs the statements with significance above the threshold.

The search algorithm in EXPLORA performs a graph search. Given a target group, EXPLORA search for the subgroup for regularities. It first uses values from one variable, then combinations of values from two variables, and then combination of values from three variables, and so on until the whole search space is exhaustively explored. The search space can be reduced by limiting the number of combinations of independent variables and by the use of redundancy filters. Depending on the type of the statements, different redundancy filters can be used. For example, for the sufficient rule pattern "if subgroup then target group", the redundancy filter is "if a statement is true for a subgroup a, then all statements for the subgroup $a \wedge$ other values are not interesting". For the necessary rule pattern "if target group then subgroup", the redundancy filter is "if a statement is true for subgroup $a \wedge b$, then the statement for subgroup a is true".

2.5. Bayesian Network Learning

Bayesian network (Charniak 1991) is a formal knowledge representation supported by the well-developed Bayesian probability theory. A Bayesian network captures the conditional probabilities between attributes. It can be used to perform reasoning under uncertainty. A Bayesian network is a directed acyclic graph. Each node represents a domain variable, and each edge represents a dependency between two nodes. An edge from node A to node B can represent a causality, with A

being the cause and B being the effect. The value of each variable should be discrete. Each node is associated with a set of parameters. Let N_i denote a node and $\prod_{N_i}$ denote the set of parents of N_i. The parameters of N_i are conditional probability distributions in the form of $P(N_i \mid \prod_{N_i})$, with one distribution for each possible instance of $\prod_{N_i}$. Figure 2.2 is an example Bayesian network given in Charniak (1991). This network shows the relationships between whether the family is out of the house (*fo*), whether the outdoor light is turned on (*lo*), whether the dog has bowel problem (*bp*), whether the dog is in the backyard (*do*), and whether the dog barking is heard (*hb*).

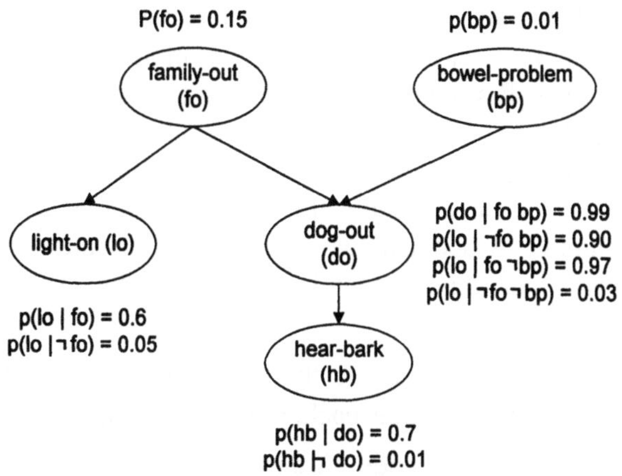

Figure 2.2: *A Bayesian network example.*

Since a Bayesian network can represent the probabilistic relationships among variables, one possible approach of data mining is to learn a Bayesian network from the data (Heckerman 1996; 1997). The main task of learning a Bayesian network is to automatically find directed edges between the nodes, such that the network can best describe the causalities. Once the network structure is constructed, the conditional probabilities are calculated based on the data. It has been shown that the problem of Bayesian network learning is believed to be computationally intractable (Chickering et al. 1995). However, Bayesian networks learning can be implemented by imposing limitations and assumptions. For instance, the algorithms of Chow and Liu (1968) and Rebane and Pearl

(1987) can learn networks with tree structures, while the algorithms of Herskovits and Cooper (1990), Cooper and Herskovits (1992), and Bouckaert (1994) require the variables to have a total ordering. More general algorithms include Heckerman et al. (1995), Spirtes et al. (1993) and Singh and Valtorta (1993). More recently, evolutionary algorithms have been used to induce Bayesian networks from databases (Larranaga et al. 1996a; 1996b, Wong et al. 1999).

One approach for Bayesian network learning is to apply the *Minimum Description Length* (MDL) principle (Lam and Bacchus 1994, Lam 1998). In general there is a trade-off between accuracy and usefulness in the construction of a Bayesian network. A more complex network is more accurate, but computationally and conceptually more difficult to use. Nevertheless, a complex network is only accurate for the training data, but may not be able to uncover the true probability distribution. Thus it is reasonable to prefer a model that is more useful. The MDL principle (Rissanen 1978) is applied to make this trade-off. This principle states that the best model of a collection of data is the one that minimizes the sum of the encoding lengths of the data and the model itself. The MDL metric measures the *total description length DL* of a network structure *G*. A better network has a smaller value on this metric. A heuristic search can be performed to search for a network that has a low value on this metric.

Let $U=\{X_1,\ldots, X_n\}$ denote the set of nodes in the network (and thus the set of variables, since each node represents a variable), Π_{X_i} denote the set of parents of node X_i, and D denote the training data. The total description length of a network is the sum of description lengths of each node:

$$DL(U,G,D) = \sum_{X_i \in U} DL(X_i, \Pi_{X_i}) \tag{2.14}$$

This length is based on two components, the *network description length* DL_{net} and the *data description length* DL_{data}:

$$DL(X_i, \Pi_{X_i}) = DL_{net}(X_i, \Pi_{X_i}) + DL_{data}(X_i, \Pi_{X_i}) \tag{2.15}$$

The formula for the network description length is

$$DL_{net}(X_i, \Pi_{X_i}) = k_i \log_2(n) + d(s_i - 1) \prod_{j \in \Pi_{X_i}} s_j \tag{2.16}$$

where k_i is the number of parents of variable X_i, s_i is the number of values X_i can take on, s_j is the number of values a particular variable in $\prod_{X_i}$ can take on, and d is the number of bits required to store a numerical value. This is the description length for encoding the network structure. The first part is the length for encoding the parents, while the second part is the length for encoding the probability parameters. This length can measure the simplicity of the network.

The formula for the data description length is

$$DL_{data}(X_i,\Pi_{X_i}) = \sum_{X_i,\Pi_{X_i}} M(X_i,\Pi_{X_i})\log_2 \frac{M(\Pi_{X_i})}{M(X_i,\Pi_{X_i})} \qquad (2.17)$$

where $M(.)$ is the number of cases that match a particular instantiation in the database. This is the description length for encoding the data. A Huffman code is used to encode the data using the probability measures defined by the network. This length can measure the accuracy of the network.

2.6. Other Approaches

Some other data mining approaches (such as regression methods for predicting continuous variables, unsupervised and supervised clustering, fuzzy systems, neural networks, nonlinear integral networks (Leung et al. 1998), and semantic networks) are not covered here since they are less relevant to the main themes of this book. However, the inductive logic programming approach to be integrated with genetic programming in the following chapters is detailed separately in chapter 4. Genetic programming is introduced in the next chapter, which is one of the four types of evolutionary algorithms.

Chapter 3

AN OVERVIEW ON EVOLUTIONARY ALGORITHMS

The problem of data mining can be formulated as conducting a search for novel, useful, and interesting knowledge. The search can be accomplished by various techniques including general weak methods and domain-specified strong methods. In this chapter, we first introduce a class of general weak methods called evolutionary algorithms. Subsequently, four kinds of evolutionary algorithms, namely, Genetic Algorithms (GAs), Genetic Programming (GP), Evolution Strategies (ES), and Evolutionary Programming (EP), are discussed in turn.

3.1. Evolutionary Algorithms

Evolutionary algorithms are weak search and optimization techniques inspired by natural evolution (Angeline 1993; 1994). Weak methods are a category of problem solving methods studied in the field of Artificial Intelligence (AI). In contrast to strong methods, weak methods are more general and widely applicable in different domains (Nilson 1980, Newell and Simon 1972). Weak methods do not employ problem-dependent search operators and make no commitment to specific *credit assignment methods*.

Problem solving methods conduct their tasks by traversing the search space of the problem. They should identify blame and/or credit (credit assignment) on the components of each search point encountered in the search space (Minsky 1963). This information evaluates the qualities of all components of a search point, their interaction, and their impact on the overall quality of the search point. Problem solving methods apply this information to determine how to combine and manipulate different components from the current and previous search points to produce the next search point. Thus, good credit assignment methods direct the future search towards promising regions (Angeline 1993; 1994). An efficient problem solving method has an excellent credit assignment method for the problem and manipulates components of various search points to traverse the search space. However, it is often difficult to design an appropriate credit assignment method for a particular problem.

Nevertheless, strong methods employ domain-dependent credit assignment techniques, search strategies, and heuristics to strengthen the efficiency and ability of problem solving. They contain a significant amount of domain-specific knowledge. This knowledge can be represented procedurally or declaratively. A procedural problem solver finds an analytic solution for a problem by executing a sequence of hard-wired instructions. Thus, its knowledge is represented procedurally. A knowledge-based system (Buchanan and Shortliffe 1984) solves a problem by performing inferences. The inferences are carried out by the inference engine of the system according to the knowledge stored declaratively in the knowledge base of the system. The knowledge usually takes the forms of heuristic rules, frames, semantic nets and first-order logic (Leung and Wong 1990). This specific knowledge allows the problem solvers to find accurate solutions quickly.

Traditional weak methods are inspired by observations of human performance (Newell and Simon 1972, Pearl 1984). They include depth-first search, breadth-first search, best-first search, generate and test, hill climbing, mean-ends analysis, constraint satisfaction, and problem reduction.

On the other hand, evolutionary algorithms are inspired from the idea of achieving intelligent behavior of humans through a search and learning method (Angeline 1993; 1994). They employ the principle of natural selection and evolution to achieve the goals of function optimization and machine learning. In general, evolutionary algorithms include all population-based algorithms that use selection and recombination operators to generate new search points in a search space. They include genetic algorithms (Holland 1992, Goldberg 1989, Davis 1991, Michalewicz 1996, Mitchell 1996), genetic programming (Koza 1992; 1994, Koza et al. 1999, Kinnear 1994, Angeline and Kinnear 1996, Banzhaf et al. 1998, Langdon 1998), evolutionary programming (Fogel et al. 1966, Fogel 1992; 1999), and evolution strategies (Schewefel 1981, Bäck et al. 1991, Bäck 1996).

The various kinds of evolutionary algorithms differ mainly in the evolution models applied, the evolutionary operators employed, the selection methods and the fitness functions used (Fogel 1994). Genetic Algorithms (GAs) and Genetic Programming (GP) model evolution at the level of genetic. They emphasize the acquisition of genetic structures at the symbolic level and regularities of the solutions. On the other hand, the idea of optimization is used in Evolution Strategies (ES) and the structures being optimized are the individuals of the population. Various behavioral properties of the individuals are parametrized and their values evolved as an optimization process. Evolutionary Programming (EP) uses the highest level of abstraction by emphasizing the adaptation of behavioral properties of various species. The following sections describe the four kinds of evolutionary algorithms.

3.2. Genetic Algorithms (GAs)

Genetic algorithms (GAs) are general search methods that use the analogies from natural selection and evolution. These algorithms encode a potential solution to a specific problem in a simple string of alphabets called a chromosome and apply reproduction and recombination operators to these chromosomes to create new chromosomes. The applications of GAs include function optimization, problem solving, and machine learning (Goldberg 1989). The elements of a genetic algorithm are listed in table 3.1.

- an encoding mechanism for solutions to the problem,
- a population of chromosomes representing the solutions,
- a mechanism to generate the initial population of solutions,
- an evaluation function that evaluates the fitness values of the solutions,
- a probabilistic selection mechanism that models Darwin's survival of the fittest principle,
- genetic operators, such as crossover and mutation, that modify the composition of the offspring during reproduction, and
- parameter values such as the population size, and the probabilities of applying genetic operators that control a GA.

Table 3.1: The elements of a genetic algorithm.

3.2.1. The Canonical Genetic Algorithm

Consider a parameter optimization problem where we must optimize a set of variables either to maximize some targets such as profits, or to minimize costs or some measures of errors. The goal is to maximize or minimize some functions, say $F(X_1, X_2, ..., X_n)$, by varying the parameters. In genetic algorithms, the encoding mechanism is essential because it determines the means of representing the variables of the optimization problem. In the Canonical Genetic Algorithm (CGA), binary bit strings are used to represent values of various parameter variables being optimized. Thus, the variables are discretized and the range of the discretization corresponds to some power of 2. The discretization should have enough resolution to represent the solution precisely. The binary codes of all variables are concatenated to form a binary string. This binary string is also called the chromosome or the genotype while the set of encoded parameters is called the phenotype of the individual.

The CGA for solving optimization problems is shown in table 3.2. The algorithm starts with an initial population Pop(0). Each chromosome of the population is a binary string of length L (Holland 1992, Schaffer 1987). The initial population is usually generated randomly using a uniform distribution.

Each chromosome in Pop(0) is then evaluated and assigned a fitness value by a fitness function. The fitness function is sometimes called the evaluation function or the objective function. It provides a measure of performance (fitness value) of a chromosome by evaluating the set of parameters represented in the chromosome. The fitness function first decodes the parameter values encoded in the chromosome to form the phenotype of the individual. The problem-dependent phenotype is then evaluated by the fitness function to determine the fitness value of the corresponding chromosome. In the CGA, *relative fitness* is defined as $f_i / \bar{f}$ where f_i is the fitness value associated with chromosome *i* and $\bar{f}$ is the average fitness of all the chromosomes in the population.

Each generation of the CGA is a three stage process which starts with the current population Pop(t). Selection is applied to the current population to create an intermediate population Pop(t'). Recombination (crossover) is then applied to the Pop(t') to create another intermediate population Pop(t"). Then mutation is employed to create the next population Pop(t+1) from the intermediate population P(t"). The process starting from the current population Pop(t) to the next population Pop(t+1) establishes one generation in the execution of the genetic algorithm. This basic implementation of genetic algorithms is also referred to as a Simple Genetic Algorithm (SGA) by Goldberg (1989). For the first generation, the current population Pop(t) is also the initial population Pop(0). It produces the next population Pop(1) and the execution proceeds to the next generation. This process iterates until the termination function is satisfied. During each generation, the relative fitness values $f_i / \bar{f}$ of all chromosomes are first evaluated, and then selection is carried out.

```
•  Assign 0 to generation t.
•  Initialize a population of chromosomes
   Pop(t).
•  Evaluate the fitness of each chromosome in
   the Pop(t).
•  While the termination function is not true do
      •  Select chromosomes from Pop(t) and
         store them into Pop(t') according to a
         scheme based on the fitness values.
      •  Recombine the chromosomes in Pop(t')
         and store the produced offspring into
         Pop(t").
      •  Perform simple mutation to the
         chromosomes in Pop(t") and store the
         mutated chromosomes into Pop(t+1).
      •  Evaluate the fitness of each individual
         in the next population P(t+1)
      •  Increase the generation t by 1.
•  Return an individual as the answer. Usually,
   the best individual will be returned.
```

Table 3.2: *The canonical genetic algorithm.*

The selection process models Darwin's survival of the fittest principle. In the CGA, a fitter chromosome reproduces a higher number of offspring and thus has a higher chance of propagating its genetic materials to the subsequent generation. In *fitness proportionate selection*, a chromosome with a relative fitness value $f_i / \bar{f}$ is allocated $f_i / \bar{f}$ offspring. Thus a chromosome with a fitness value higher than the average is allocated more than one offspring, while a chromosome with a fitness value smaller than the average is allocated less than one offspring. The relative fitness value represents the expected number of offspring of a chromosome. Since it is impossible to produce fractional numbers of offspring, some chromosomes have to produce a higher number of offspring than their relative fitness values and some less than their relative fitness values. The current population Pop(t) can be viewed as a mapping onto a roulette wheel, where each chromosome is represented by a slice of the roulette wheel that corresponds proportionally to its relative fitness value. By repeatedly spinning the roulette wheel, chromosomes are chosen using stochastic sample with replacement to fill the intermediate population Pop(t'). The spinning process iterates until it has generated the entire Pop(t'). Thus, fitness proportionate selection is also called the *roulette wheel selection*. This method generates a large sampling error because the final number of offspring allocated to a chromosome may vary significantly from its relative fitness. The allocated number of offspring approaches the expected number only if the population size is very large.

After selection has been carried out, the construction of the intermediate population Pop(t') is completed and recombination can occur. This can be viewed as generating another intermediate population Pop(t") form Pop(t'). Crossover is applied to randomly paired chromosomes with a crossover probability denoted as p_c.

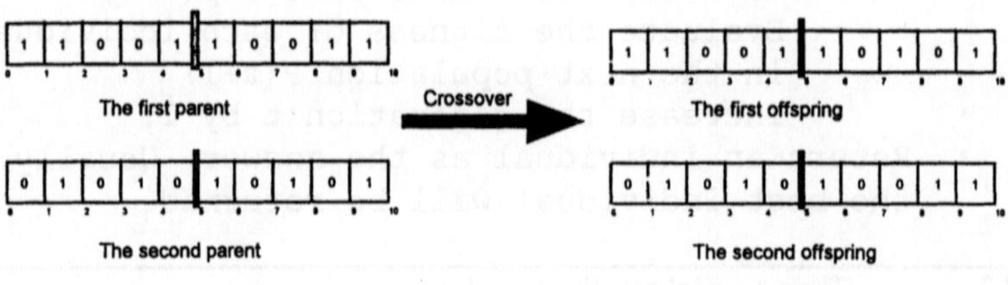

Figure 3.1: *Crossover of CGA. A one-point crossover operation is performed on two parent, 1100110011 and 0101010101, at the fifth crossover location. Two offspring, 1100110101 and 0101010011 are produced*

Consider the two chromosomes 1100110011 and 0101010101. For one-point crossover, a single crossover location is selected randomly. Since the length L of the chromosomes in this example is 10, a crossover location can assume values in the range between 1 to 9 (L-1 locations in total). Assume the fifth location of chromosomes is chosen as the crossover location. By swapping the fragments between the two parents, the crossover operator produces the two offspring 11001:10101 and 01010:10011 where the symbol ":" is used here to denote the crossover location (figure 3.1).

After recombination is performed, other genetic operations are applied to the intermediate population Pop(t") to generate the next population Pop(t+1). In the CGA, only simple mutation can be applied. For each bit of each chromosome in the Pop(t"), it is mutated with some low probability p_m. There are two different implementations of mutation. The first mutation flips the bit value from 1 to 0 or vice versa, while the second one randomly selects a value from 0 and 1 to fill the mutated bit. Thus, for the latter one, there is only 0.5 probability that the bit value is really modified even if it has been selected for mutation. The mutated chromosome is then placed in the Pop(t+1). Figure 3.2 depicts that the chromosome 1100110101 is modified to 0100110100 by flipping the first and the last bits.

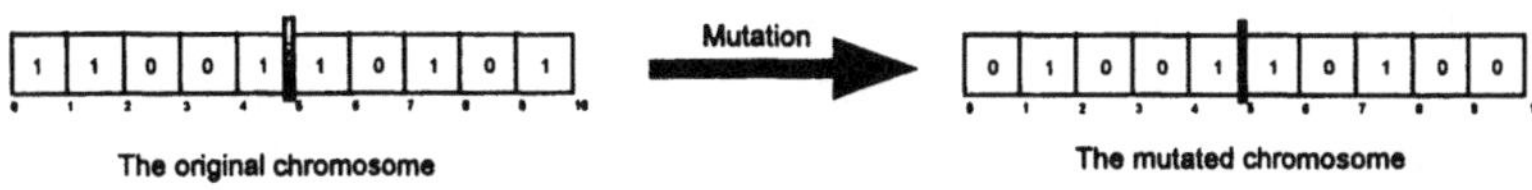

Figure 3.2: *Mutation of CGA. A mutation operation is performed on a parent 1100110101 at the first and the last bits. The offspring 0100110100 is produced.*

The about evolution process iterates until a fixed number of generations are attempted, the available computational resources are consumed, or satisfactory solutions are found.

GAs can be viewed as performing both exploration of new regions in the search space and exploitation of already sampled regions. The question is then on the balance between these two competing methods. The performance of GAs is significantly affected by the choice of different parameter values such as the crossover and mutation probabilities and the population size. The optimal choice of parameter values was investigated extensively using empirical and analytical techniques. Grefenstette (1986), DeJong and Spears (1990) respectively proposed two different sets of parameter values that are competent in general.

In addition to fitness proportionate selection, one-point crossover, and simple mutation described above, other techniques have been investigated in other genetic algorithms. The following sub-sections present these techniques.

3.2.1.1. Selection Methods

Because the expected number of offspring is usually not an integer, but only integer numbers of offspring can be allocated in fitness proportionate selection, there is an intrinsic discrepancy between the allocated and the expected number of offspring. The *remainder stochastic sampling method* was proposed to achieve a distribution of offspring very close to the corresponding expected number of offspring.

Remainder Stochastic Sampling Method

In the remainder stochastic sampling method, the relative fitness value $f_i / \bar{f}$ of each chromosome i is evaluated first. If this value is greater than 1.0, the integer portion of this number indicates how many copies of that chromosome are directly placed in the intermediate population Pop(t'). All chromosomes (including those with relative fitness less then 1.0) then place additional copies of themselves in the intermediate population Pop(t') with a probability corresponding to the fractional portion of their relative fitness values. This selection method is unbiased and is efficiently implemented using a technique known as Stochastic Universal Sampling (Baker 1987).

Fitness proportionate selection has other problems. In the first few generations, the population typically has a low average fitness value, but it is common to have a few extraordinary chromosomes. Fitness proportionate selection allocates a large number of offspring to these chromosomes. These dominant chromosomes cause premature convergence. A different situation appears in the later stages when the population average fitness value is close to the best fitness value. There may be significant diversity within the population, but approximately equal numbers of offspring are allocated to all chromosomes because the variance in their fitness values is very small. *Fitness scaling techniques*, *rank-based selection*, and *tournament selection* can overcome these problems.

Fitness Scaling Techniques

Fitness scaling techniques readjust fitness values of chromosomes (Grefenstette 1986, Goldberg 1989). Forrest (1990) presented a survey of current scaling techniques including linear scaling, sigma truncation, and power law scaling.

Linear scaling computes the scaled fitness value as $f_i' = af_i + b$ where f_i is the fitness value of the ith chromosome, f_i' is the scaled value, and a and b are appropriate constants. In each generation, a and b are calculated to ensure that the maximum value of the scaled fitness values is a small number, say 1.5 or 2.0 times of the average fitness value of the population. Sometimes the scaled fitness values may become negative for chromosomes that have fitness values far smaller than the average fitness value of the population. In this case, a and b must be recomputed to avoid negative fitness values.

Sigma truncation calculates the scaled fitness value as $f_i' = f_i - (\bar{f} - c\sigma)$ where $\bar{f}$ is the average fitness value of the population, σ is the standard derivation of the fitness values in the population, and c is a small constant typically ranging from 1 to 3. Chromosomes whose fitness values are less than c standard deviations from the $\bar{f}$ are discarded.

Power law scaling finds some specified power of the fitness f_i. The scaled fitness is $f_i' = f_i^k$. The k value is in general problem-dependent and may be modified during a run to stretch or shrink the range of fitness values.

Rank Based Selection

Baker (1985) proposed rank-based selection that is non-parametric. In this method, the chromosomes of a population are sorted according to their fitness values. Each chromosome is allocated the number of offspring that is a function of its rank. Usually, the number of offspring varies linearly with the rank of a chromosome. Whitley (1989) showed that significant improvements could be obtained with the selection method.

Tournament Selection

Tournament selection approximates the behavior of ranking. In an *m*-ary tournament, *m* chromosomes are selected randomly using a uniform distribution from the current population after evaluation. The best of the *m* chromosomes is then placed in the intermediate Pop(t'). This process is repeated until Pop(t') is filled. Goldberg and Deb (1991) showed analytically that 2-ary tournament selection is the same in expectation as ranking using a linear 2.0 bias. If a winner is chosen probabilistically from a tournament of 2, then the ranking is linear and the bias is proportional to the probability with which the best chromosome is selected.

3.2.1.2. Recombination Methods

Two-point and Multi-point Crossovers

The CGA uses one-point crossover. However, many other crossover mechanisms have been devised, often involving more than one crossover location. In *two-point crossover* and *multi-point crossover*, chromosomes are regarded as rings formed by joining the two ends together. To exchange a segment from one ring with that from another one requires the selection of two or multiple crossover locations as depicted in figure 3.3.

One-point crossover can be viewed as two-point crossover with one of the crossover locations fixed at the beginning of the chromosome. Hence two-point crossover is more general than one-point crossover. Researchers now agree that two-point crossover is generally better than one-point crossover.

Uniform Crossover

Uniform crossover exchanges bits of a chromosome rather than fragments. A crossover mask is first randomly generated. At each position in the offspring, the genetic material is obtained from either one of the parents. If there is a 1 in the crossover mask, the genetic material is copied from the first parent, otherwise it is obtained from the second parent. The process is repeated with the parents exchanged to produce the second offspring (figure 3.4).

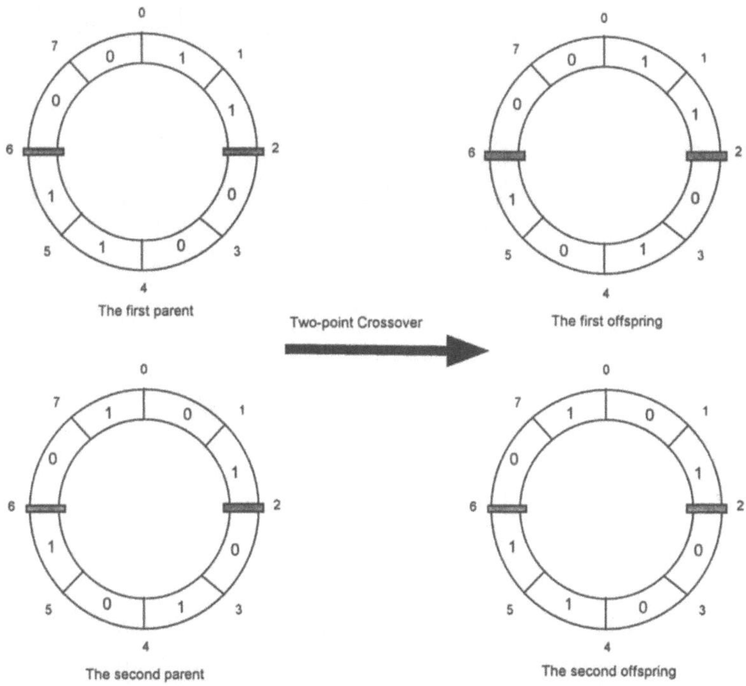

Figure 3.3: ***The effects of a two-point (multi-point) crossover. A two-point crossover operation is performed on two parent, 11001100 and 01010101, between the second and the sixth locations. Two offspring, 11010100 and 01001101, are produced.***

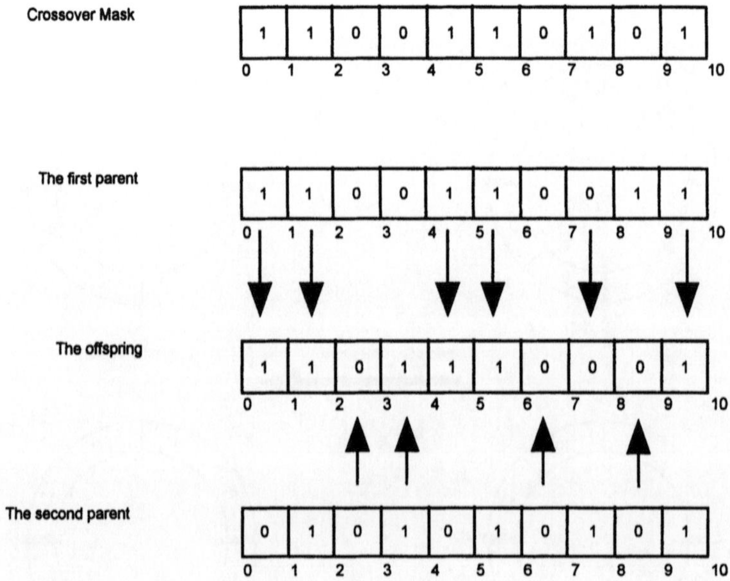

Figure 3.4: *The effects of a uniform crossover. A uniform crossover operation is performed on two parenst, 1100110011 and 0101010101, and two offspring will be generated. This figure only shows one of them (1101110001).*

An extensive comparison of different crossover methods was performed (Eshelman et al. 1989). One-point, two-point, multi-point, and uniform crossover were theoretically analyzed in terms of positional and distributional bias, and empirically evaluated on several problems. A crossover method has *positional bias* if the probability that a bit is swapped depends on its position in the chromosome. The crossover method has *distributional bias* if the distribution of the number of bits exchanged by the method is non-uniform. One-point crossover exhibits the maximum positional bias and the least distributional bias. At the other extreme, uniform crossover has the least positional bias and the maximum distributional bias. The empirical experiments showed that there was no more than about 20% difference in performances among the methods.

Order-based Crossover Operators

In an order-based problem, such as the traveling salesman problem, gene values are fixed and the fitness value depends on the order in which gene values appear. The above crossover techniques cannot be used because they will produce invalid offspring. Goldberg (1989) described *Partially Matched crossover* (PMX) for this kind of problems. In PMX, it is the orders in which gene values appear are exchanged. Offspring have genes which inherit ordering information from each parent. This avoids the generation of offspring that violate problem constraints. Syswerda (1991b) and Davis (1991) described other order-based operators including enhanced edge recombination, order crossover, cycle crossover, and position-based crossover. Starkweather et al. (1991) compared these operators using the traveling salesman problem and the job shop scheduling problem. They found that the effectiveness of different operators is problem-dependent.

Many other techniques have also been suggested. Several methods use the idea of biasing the crossover locations at some more probable chromosome positions (Schaffer and Morishma 1987, Holland 1987, Davidor 1991, Levenick 1991, Louis and Rawlins 1991). The GAs learn which sites should be favored for crossover. The information is stored in a punctuation string as part of the chromosome, which is crossed over and propagated to offspring. Thus, good punctuation strings that lead to fit offspring will be propagated through the population.

3.2.1.3. Inversion and Reordering

The purpose of reordering is to attempt to find gene orderings which have better evolutionary potential (Goldberg 1989). Inversion (Holland 1992) works by reversing the order of genes between two randomly selected positions in a chromosome. The operation of an inversion is illustrated in figure 3.5.

Goldberg and Bridges (1990) analyzed a reordering operator on a very small task and showed that it has advantages. Reordering also greatly expands the search space because GAs must also find good gene orderings. Thus, much more time is required for finding the solutions of the problem.

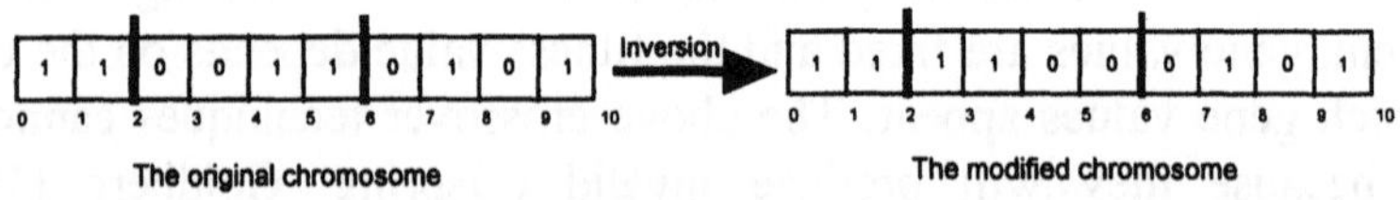

Figure 3.5: The effects of an inversion operation. An inversion operation is performed on the parent, 1100110101, between the second and the sixth locations. An offspring, 1111000101, is produced.

Meta-GAs (Grefenstette 1986) can be used to learn gene orderings. A meta-GA has a population where each member is a GA. Each individual GA is configured to solve the same problem, but using different gene orderings. The fitness of each individual is determined by running the GA, and examining the time required to converge. Meta-GAs are very computationally expensive to run and are worthwhile only if the results obtained can be reused many times.

3.2.2. Steady State Genetic Algorithms

A *steady state genetic algorithm* selects two parents for recombination and produces only one offspring at a time. The offspring is then placed immediately back into the population. Moreover, offspring replaces some relatively less fit members of the population rather than its parents. Steady state genetic algorithms are more susceptible to sampling error and genetic drift. The advantage is that the best chromosomes found in the search space are maintained in the population. The search conducted by these algorithms is more aggressive and effective (Syswerda 1989; 1991a, Holland 1992).

Genitor (Whitley 1989) is an implementation of a steady state genetic algorithm. In Genitor, the worst chromosome in the population is replaced by the offspring just created. The accumulation of improved chromosomes in the population is thus monotonic. Goldberg and Deb (1991) showed that the method of replacing the worst member in the population resulted in a much higher selective pressure than the method of random replacement. Genitor applies rank-based selection rather than fitness proportionate selection. The advantage of rank-based selection is that it maintains a stable selective pressure over the course of search.

3.2.3. Hybrid Algorithms

Although genetic algorithms are robust and general problem solving methods, they are usually not the most effective ones on any particular domain (Davis 1991). Therefore, combining genetic algorithms and other problem-specific strong methods may result in some general, robust, and effective problem solving systems. Many researchers use non-binary encoding and problem-specific recombination operators to strengthen the capability of traditional genetic algorithms (Davis 1991, Michalewicz 1996). Muhlenbein (1991; 1992) described a parallel genetic algorithm that employed local hill-climbing techniques to speed up the search.

A *hybrid genetic algorithm* typically performs well on optimization and other search problems because it is performing local hill-climbing from multiple points in the search space. Unless the problem to be solved is highly irregular or the function to be optimized is severely multi-modal, it is likely that some points are in the basin of attraction of the global solution. In this case, hill-climbing is a fast and effective form of search. In general, the local search methods can find a number of significant improvements of a point without dramatically modify its structure. Thus, a hybrid algorithm takes the benefits of both the problem-specific search methods and the implicit parallelism of genetic algorithms.

3.3. Genetic Programming (GP)

Genetic Programming (GP) is an extension of GAs (Koza 1992; 1994, Koza et al. 1999). The main difference between them is the representation of the structure they manipulate and the meanings of the representation. GAs usually operate on a population of fixed-length binary strings. GP typically operate on a population of parse trees which usually represent computer programs. A parse tree is represented as a rooted, point-labeled tree. Since GP concerns with the behavior of computer programs, the definition of phenotype in GP is more abstract than that in GAs.

3.3.1. Introduction to the Traditional GP

Most computer programs can be easily understood as performing a sequence of functions to the arguments. Most language compilers first translate a given program into a parse tree and then generate a sequence of machine instructions that can be executed on a computer (Aho and Ullman 1977). Thus, parse trees are natural representations of computer programs and GP induces Lisp programs represented as parse trees (Koza 1992).

In Lisp, a program is also called an S-expression and all its operations are implemented as function calls. A function call consists of a list of elements enclosed by parentheses. The first element within the list is the name of the function and the other elements are arguments to the function. To represent a function call as a parse tree, the function name is the root of the parse tree while the arguments are the children at the next level down the parse tree. The arguments may be variables, constants, or other function calls. In the latter case, these function calls are again represented as parse trees and they form sub-trees of the parental parse tree. For example, the program `(* (+ X (/ Y 1.5)) (- Z 0.3))` can be represented as the parse tree in figure 3.6.

There are two sets of nodes in a parse tree. The internal nodes are called primitive functions while the leaf nodes are called terminals. In figure 3.6, the sets of primitive functions and terminals are {+, –, *, /} and {X, Y, Z, 1.5, 0.3}, respectively. The terminals can be viewed as the inputs to the program being induced. They might include the independent variables and the set of constants. The primitive functions are combined with the terminals or simpler function calls to form more complex function calls. The above procedure of combination iterates to produce a program. The arity of a function *f*, arity(*f*), is its number of arguments.

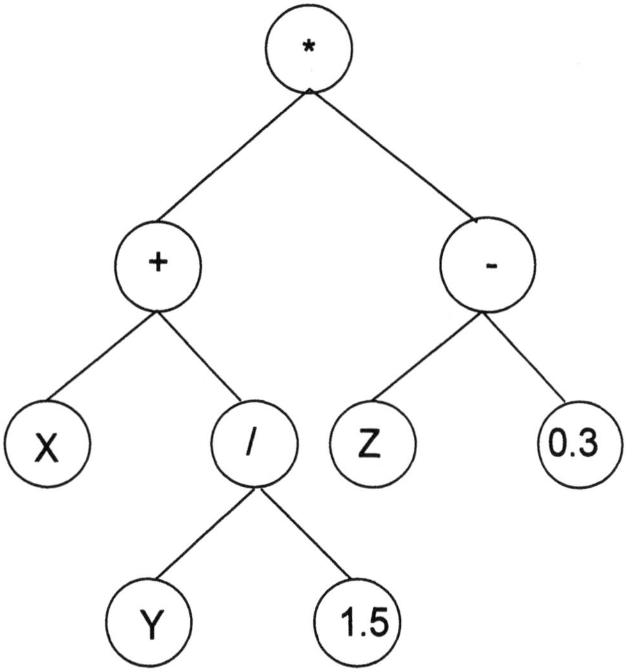

Figure 3.6: *A parse tree of the program* `(* (+ X (/ Y 1.5)) (- Z 0.3))`.

The set of primitive functions might include arithmetic operators and transcendental functions. In fact, there is no limit to the complexity of the primitive functions used. Koza (1992; 1994) also used iteration, functions with side-effect, and a wide variety of problem-specific functions. It is important that the function set has the *closure property*. That is, each primitive function should be able to accept any terminal or the output from any function as inputs. To apply GP to a problem, the user must determine:

- the set of primitive functions ***F***,
- the set of terminals ***T***,
- the fitness function,
- the parameters for controlling the run,
- the method for designating a result, and

- the termination function.

```
• Assign 0 to generation t.
• Initialize a population Pop(t) of programs
  composed of the primitive functions and
  terminals.
• Evaluate the fitness of each program in the
  Pop(t).
• While the termination function is not
  satisfied do
      • Create a new population Pop(t+1) of
        programs by employing the selection,
        crossover, mutation, and other genetic
        operations.
      • Evaluate the fitness of each individual
        in the next population P(t+1)
      • Increase the generation t by 1.
• Return the program that is identified by the
  method of result designation as the solution
  of the run
```

Table 3.3: *A high-level description of GP.*

The fitness function, the controlling parameters, the method for designating a result, and the termination function are similar to those of GAs. GP usually generates an initial population of programs randomly. Programs in the population are then manipulated by various genetic operators to produce a new population of programs. These operations include crossover, mutation, permutation, editing, encapsulation, and decimation (Koza 1992). The whole process of proceeding from one population to the next population is called a generation. A high level description of the algorithm of GP is given in table 3.3.

The creation of an initial random population is a random search of the search space for computer programs. A parse tree is generated randomly by first selecting a function from $\boldsymbol{F}$ to be the label for the root of the tree. Whenever a node of a tree is labeled with a function f from $\boldsymbol{F}$, arity(f) nodes are generated as the children of that node and an element from $\boldsymbol{F} \cup \boldsymbol{T}$ is randomly selected to be the label for each child. If a function is selected, the above process continues recursively. Otherwise, the generation process is terminated for that node because it is a leaf node of the tree.

Each program in the population is evaluated in terms of how well it performs in the particular problem. In GP, three measures of fitness are used as follows:

The *raw fitness* is the measurement of fitness that is stated in the natural semantics of the program. For example, raw fitness in a classification program can be either the number of examples that are classified correctly or the number of mis-classified examples. Which one should be used depends on the nature of the problem (Koza 1992). Raw fitness is usually evaluated over a set of fitness cases. They provide a basis for evaluating the performance of a program over a number of representative cases.

The *standardized fitness* transforms the raw fitness so that smaller value is always a better value. Transformation can be achieved by different methods. Since the standardized fitness may not lie between 0 and 1, adjustment is performed to converse it into the *adjusted fitness* in the desired range.

The *adjusted fitness* is obtained by $a_i = 1/(1+s_i)$ where s_i is the standardized fitness of the program i and a_i is the corresponding adjusted fitness. The adjusted fitness has the benefit of strengthening the selective pressure when the population converges. The same effects can be achieved by using tournament and rank-based selection methods. Hence, the adjusted fitness is not used for these methods.

The evolution process of GP is similar to that of GAs. Another key difference between them is the details of the genetic operations because the GP operations must now manipulate parse trees rather than fixed-length strings in GAs. Crossover of two parental trees in GP is achieved by creating two duplications of the trees first to form two intermediate offspring. Then two crossover points are selected randomly from the two intermediate offspring, respectively. The final offspring are obtained by exchanging sub-trees under the selected crossover points at the intermediate sub-trees. The produced offspring are usually different in sizes and shapes from their parents and from one another. The effects of the crossover operation are depicted in figure 3.7.

The syntactic correctness of the offspring is guaranteed because of the closure property of the set of primitives. However, the generated programs may be meaningless because they may perform invalid (such as division by zero), redundant, or useless operations. The semantics of the primitives is redefined to avoid the problem of executing invalid operation. For example, the primitive, protected division `%`, normally returns the quotient. However, if division by zero is attempted, the function returns 1.0.

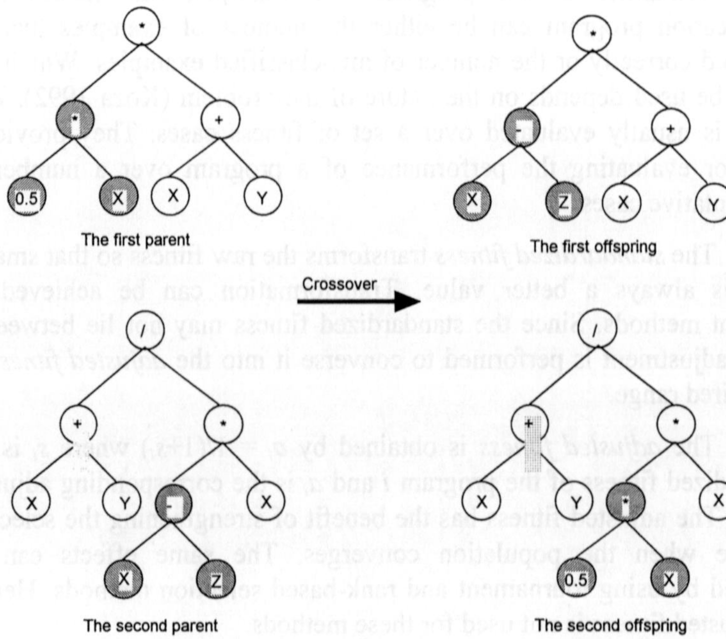

Figure 3.7: ***The effects of crossover operation. A crossover operation is performed on two parental programs,*** `(* (* 0.5 X) (+ X Y))` ***and*** `(/ (+ X Y) (* (- X Z) X))`***. The shaded areas are exchanged and two offspring generated are:*** `(* (- X Z) (+ X Y))` ***and*** `(/ (+ X Y) (* (* 0.5 X) X))`***.***

In GP, mutation is considered to be of relatively less important operation. First, a copy of a single parental tree is made. Then a mutation point is randomly selected from the copy, which will be either a leaf node or a sub-tree. The leaf node or sub-tree at the mutation point is replaced by a new leaf node or sub-tree generated randomly. The effects of the mutation operation are depicted in figure 3.8.

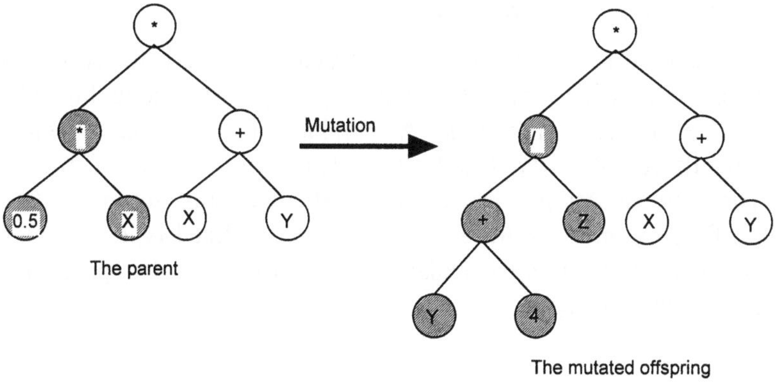

Figure 3.8: *The effects of a mutation operation. A mutation operation is performed on the program* `(* (* 0.5 X) (+ X Y))`*. The shaded area of the parental program is changed to a program fragment* `(/ (+ Y 4) Z)` *and the offspring program* `(* (/ (+ Y 4) Z) (+ X Y))` *is produced.*

3.3.2. Strongly Typed Genetic Programming (STGP)

One limitation of GP is the requirement of the closure property of the set of primitive functions. In *Strongly Typed Genetic Programming* (STGP), all the variables, constants, arguments, and returned values can be of any data type provided that these data types have been defined by the user (Montana 1995). One of its applications is to generate a program that uses both scalars and vectors.

STGP requires the output from each function or terminal to be given a data type and the inputs of each function to take certain types. The implementation differences between GP and STGP are the generation methods of the initial population and the crossover operators. In STGP, the generation method of the initial population must comply to the type restrictions and the crossover operator must occur between functions and/or terminals of the same type.

Programs in the initial population are generated in such a way that the arguments of each function in each tree have the required data types.

Crossover is implemented by randomly selecting a node from one parental tree and then randomly selecting node from the second parental tree until it is of the same type as the first selected node.

An extension to STGP that makes it easier to use is the concept of generic functions, which are not true strongly typed functions, but rather templates for classes of functions. A template of a function can take a variety of different data types and return values of a variety of different types. The only constraint is that for any particular set of argument types, a generic function must return a value of a well-defined type. A generic function is instantiated to a particular instance of function by specifying a set of input argument types.

3.4. Evolution Strategies (ES)

In *Evolution Strategies* (ES), the individual model of evolution is typified (Rechenberg 1973, Schwefel 1981, Bäck et al. 1991, Bäck 1996). In these techniques, the emphasis is on the improvement of a behavior that is rated well by the fitness function rather than on the acquisition of building blocks with high fitness values. By concentrating on optimizing the behavior, the representation and reproduction heuristics must create objects that are behaviorally similar to their parents but not necessarily structurally similar. However, the acquisition of an appropriate behavior should be easier since the effects on behavior have been modeled in the reproduction operators.

ES consider an individual to be composed of a set of features. The interaction among the features is typically unknown. ES use fixed-length, real-valued strings to represent individuals. Each position marks a separate behavioral trait. The adherence to fixed-length strings eases the problem of how to manipulate the structure in order to preserve behavioral similarity between offspring and their parents. Different operators have been defined to manipulate the contents of strings to create offspring that are behaviorally similar (Bäck et al. 1991).

ES originate from Germany for applications in real-valued function optimization (Rechenberg 1973, Schwefel 1981). The problem is defined as finding the real-valued vector **X** with L numbers that minimizes or maximizes an objective function F(**X**): $R^L \rightarrow R$. There are various evolution strategies that are different in their models of evolution. The one called (μ+1)-ES is presented in table 3.4.

1. An initial population Pop(0) of μ members is created. Each member e_i, $1 \le i \le \mu$, is an ordered pair $(\mathbf{X}_i, \sigma_i)$ where $\mathbf{X}_i$ is a real-valued vector storing the object variables $x_{i,j}$, $1 \le j \le$ L, for the objective function F, σ_i is also a real-valued vector containing L independent strategy variables $\sigma_{i,j}$, $1 \le j \le$ L. The value of each object variable $x_{i,j}$ is selected randomly from a feasible range. The values of $\sigma_{i,j}$, $1 \le j \le$ L are usually equal for all elements e_i, $1 \le i \le \mu$.
2. Set t to 0.
3. Create an intermediate population Pop(t') with μ+1 elements. The first μ elements are obtained from Pop(t).
4. Create a new offspring $e'_{\mu+1}$ using a recombination operator r on Pop(t), i.e. $e'_{\mu+1} = (\mathbf{X}'_{\mu+1}, \sigma'_{\mu+1}) = \mathrm{r}(\mathrm{Pop(t)})$.
5. Create an offspring $e''_{\mu+1}$ using a mutation operator m on $e'_{\mu+1}$, i.e. $e''_{\mu+1} = (\mathbf{X}''_{\mu+1}, \sigma''_{\mu+1}) = \mathrm{m}(e'_{\mu+1})$.
6. Store $e''_{\mu+1}$ to Pop(t').
7. Select the best μ elements from Pop(t') using the selection operator s and store them to the new population Pop(t+1). Thus it contains only μ elements.
8. Increase t by 1.
9. If the termination function is not true, goto step 3.
10. Return an element of the last population as the result of the run.

Table 3.4: The algorithm of (μ+1)-ES.

Different recombination methods have been proposed (Schewefel 1981). They can be classified into non-global and global. In the former class, two elements $e_a = (\mathbf{X}_a, \sigma_a)$ and $e_b = (\mathbf{X}_b, \sigma_b)$ are selected from the current population Pop(t) using a uniform distribution. For the simplest recombination, no actual crossover will be performed. In other words, $\mathbf{X}'_{\mu+1} = \mathbf{X}_a$ and $\sigma'_{\mu+1} = \sigma_a$.

For the *discrete recombination operator*, a number of uniform random values U_j, $1 \le j \le L$ are generated and $e'_{\mu+1}$ is obtained according to the following equations:

$$x'_{\mu+1,j} = \begin{cases} x_{a,j} & \text{if } U_j \le 0.5 \\ x_{b,j} & \text{if } U_j > 0.5 \end{cases}$$

and

$$\sigma'_{\mu+1,j} = \begin{cases} \sigma_{a,j} & \text{if } U_j \le 0.5 \\ \sigma_{b,j} & \text{if } U_j > 0.5 \end{cases}$$

where $1 \le j \le L$.

For the *intermediate recombination operator*, $e'_{\mu+1}$ is obtained according to the following equations:

$$x'_{\mu+1,j} = \frac{1}{2}\left(x_{a,j} + x_{b,j}\right)$$

and

$$\sigma'_{\mu+1,j} = \frac{1}{2}\left(\sigma_{a,j} + \sigma_{b,j}\right)$$

where $1 \le j \le L$.

In the *global recombination operators*, L pairs of elements (e_{a_j}, e_{b_j}), $1 \le j \le L$ are selected randomly using a uniform distribution. For the *global discrete recombination operator*, a number of uniform random value values U_j, $1 \le j \le L$ are created and $e'_{\mu+1}$ is obtained according to the following equations.

$$x'_{\mu+1,j} = \begin{cases} x_{a_j,j} & \text{if } U_j \le 0.5 \\ x_{b_j,j} & \text{if } U_j > 0.5 \end{cases}$$

and

$$\sigma'_{\mu+1,j} = \begin{cases} \sigma_{a_j,j} & \text{if } U_j \le 0.5 \\ \sigma_{b_j,j} & \text{if } U_j > 0.5 \end{cases}$$

where $1 \le j \le L$.

For the *global intermediate recombination,* $e'_{\mu+1}$ is obtained according to the following equations:

$$x'_{\mu+1,j} = \frac{1}{2}\left(x_{a_j,j} + x_{b_j,j}\right)$$

and

$$\sigma'_{\mu+1,j} = \frac{1}{2}\left(\sigma_{a_j,j} + \sigma_{b_j,j}\right)$$

where $1 \le j \le \mathrm{L}$.

The mating parents for the global recombination of component $x'_{\mu+1,j}$ and $\sigma'_{\mu+1,j}$ are chosen anew from the population. Thus, it causes a high mixing of the genetic materials of the whole population. Global recombination operators address the difficulty of pre-mature convergence in ES systems.

According to the biological observation that offspring are similar to their parents and that smaller modifications occur more often than larger ones. To achieve the similar effects in ES, the element $e''_{\mu+1}$ obtained by applying mutation operation on element $e'_{\mu+1}$ is specified as:

$$x''_{\mu+1,j} = x'_{\mu+1,j} + \mathrm{N}(0, \sigma'_{\mu+1,j}) \quad ,1 \le j \le \mathrm{L}$$

and

$$\sigma''_{\mu+1,j} = \begin{cases} c_d \sigma'_{\mu+1,j} & \text{if } r < \frac{1}{5} \\ c_i \sigma'_{\mu+1,j} & \text{if } r > \frac{1}{5} \\ \sigma'_{\mu+1,j} & \text{if } r < \frac{1}{5} \end{cases} \quad ,1 \le j \le \mathrm{L}$$

where N(0, σ) is a Gaussian random number with a mean of zero and a standard deviation σ, c_d and c_i are constants, and r is the ratio of successful mutations to all mutation. A mutation is successful if the mutated offspring performs better than its parent. The idea here is to change the strategy variables dynamically until r is 1/5.

Rechenberg (1973) calculated the convergence rate of an ES system for some model functions and found that the convergence rate is optimized if r is equal to 1/5. Thus, he suggested the 1/5 rule: The ratio of successful mutations to all mutation should be 1/5. If it is greater than 1/5 then increase σ by multiplying a constant c_i. If it is less than 1/5 then decrease σ by multiplying a constant c_d. When this rule decreases the standard deviation, the search becomes more focused, and the offspring are generally closer to their parents. When the standard deviation is increased, the search is broadened so that the offspring are further from their parents. Schewefel (1981) suggested that c_d and c_i should be 0.82 and 1/0.82, respectively.

The selection operator selects the best μ elements from μ+1 elements according to the objective function F. The termination function determines whether the optimization has been found or the computational resources are consumed. Different domain-dependent methods can be used to implement the termination function.

(1+1)-ES is the simplest and oldest ES model. The difference between it and (μ+1)-ES is that the population Pop(t) contains only one element and only recombination will be performed. It can be designated as a kind of probabilistic gradient search technique. There are two main drawbacks of (1+1)-ES: The convergence rate is slow because the standard deviations are equal in each dimension; the procedure is susceptible to stagnation at local minima because of the brittleness of the gradient search.

In the (μ+λ)-ES, the population size is still μ, but λ offspring are created at each generation from μ parents. All μ+λ elements compete for survival, with the best μ elements selected to survive in the next generation. Consequently, step 3 in table 3.4 is changed to:

3'. Create an intermediate population Pop(t') with μ+λ elements. The first μ elements are obtained from Pop(t).

In the (μ, λ)-ES, only the λ offspring compete for survival, and the μ parents are replaced in every generation. In other words, each element survives for only a generation. Thus, step 3 in table 3.4 is changed to:

3". Create an intermediate population Pop(t') with λ elements.

Because of the nature of this model, λ must be greater than or equal to μ. In the (μ+λ)-ES and (μ, λ)-ES, steps 4 through 6 in table 3.4 are repeated for λ times to create λ offspring. The mutation operator is also extended to allow for meta-control over the evolution process. Let $e'_{\mu+1} = (\mathbf{X}'_{\mu+1}, \sigma'_{\mu+1})$ be the offspring generated by the recombination operator. The mutation operator creates the offspring $e''_{\mu+1} = (\mathbf{X}''_{\mu+1}, \sigma''_{\mu+1})$ according to the following equations:

$$\sigma''_{\mu+1,j} = \sigma'_{\mu+1,j} \exp^{N(0,\Delta\sigma)} \qquad ,1 \le j \le L$$

and

$$x''_{\mu+1,j} = x'_{\mu+1,j} + N(0, \sigma''_{\mu+1,j}) \qquad ,1 \le j \le L$$

where $\Delta\sigma$ is a meta-control parameter. It allows the user to control the distribution of trials. It should be emphasized that in all models other than (1+1)-ES, more than one parent are participated in the recombination. Since the strategy variables $\sigma_{i,j}$, $1 \le j \le L$ are all stored in each element e_i, $1 \le i \le \mu$, these strategy variables are also involved in the recombination and evolution. These models allow strategy variables to adapt to the landscape of the objective function and thus trials can be distributed in an appropriate way.

3.5. Evolutionary Programming (EP)

Evolutionary Programming (EP) is a stochastic optimization strategy similar to GAs (Fogel et al. 1966, Fogel 1994; 1999). It emphasizes the behavioral linkage between parents and their offspring rather than emulating some genetic operators found in nature. Differing from GAs, EP does not require any specific genotype in the individual. EP employs a model of evolution at a higher abstraction. Mutation is the only operator used for evolution.

A typical process of EP is outlined in table 3.5. A set of individuals is randomly created to make up the initial population. Each individual is evaluated by the fitness function. Then each individual produces a child by mutation. There is a distribution of different types of mutation, ranging from minor to extreme. Minor modifications in the behavior of the offspring occur more frequently and substantial modifications occur less frequently. The offspring is evaluated by fitness function. Then, tournaments are performed to select the individuals for the next generation. For each individual, a number of rivals are selected among the parents and offspring. The tournament score of the individual is the number of rivals with lower fitness scores than itself. Individuals with higher tournament scores are selected as the population of next generation. There is no requirement that the population size is held constant. The process is iterated until the termination criterion is satisfied.

- `Initialize the generation, t, to be 0.`
- `Initialize a population of individual, Pop(t).`
- `Evaluate the fitness of all individual in Pop(t).`
- `While the termination criteria is not satisfied`
    - `Produce one or more offspring from each individual by mutation.`
    - `Evaluate the fitness of each offspring.`
    - `Perform a tournament for each individual.`
    - `Put the individuals with high tournament scores into Pop(t+1).`
    - `Increase the generation t by 1.`
- `Return the individual with the highest fitness value.`

Table 3.5: A high-level description of EP.

EP has two characteristics. First, there is no constraint on the representation. Mutation operator does not demand a particular genotype. The representation can follow from the problem. For example, a Bayesian network can be represented in the same manner as it is implemented (Wong et al. 1999).

Second, mutations in EP attempt to preserve behavioral similarity between offspring and their parents. An offspring is generally similar to its parent at the behavioral level with slight variations. EP assumes that the distribution of potential offspring is under a normal distribution around the parent. Thus, the severity of mutations follows a statistical distribution.

ES and EP both use a statistical distribution of mutations. However, ES typically uses deterministic selection that the worst individuals are eliminated, while EP typically uses a stochastic tournament selection. EP is an abstraction of evolution at the level of species and thus no recombination is used because recombination does not occur between species. In contrast, ES is an abstraction of evolution at the level of individual behavior and hence recombination is reasonable.

Chapter 4

INDUCTIVE LOGIC PROGRAMMING

In the previous chapter, we have presented an overview on evolutionary algorithms. Another approach of data mining is Inductive Logic Programming (ILP) that investigates the construction of logic programs from training examples and background knowledge. ILP is a new research field that combines the techniques and theories from inductive concept learning and logic programming. ILP systems are more powerful than traditional attribute-value based learning systems because the former systems use an expressive first-order logic framework to represent the concepts acquired and employ background knowledge to facilitate the learning. ILP has strong theoretical foundation from computational learning theory and logic programming. It has very impressive applications in scientific discovery, knowledge acquisition and, logic program synthesis (Muggletion 1994, Bratko and King 1994). In this chapter, we present a brief introduction to inductive concept learning first. Two approaches for ILP are discussed in section 4.2 followed by an introduction to the techniques and the methods of ILP.

4.1. Inductive Concept Learning

The goal of machine learning is to develop techniques and tools for building intelligent learning machines. In other words, learning machines can improve themselves to perform more efficiently and/or more accurately. They can also increase their abilities to process more problems. *Symbol-level learning* refers to the kind of learning that increases the efficiency of the system while *knowledge-level learning* improves the accuracy and/or coverage of the system (Dietterich 1986). Machine learning paradigms include inductive, deductive, genetic-based and connectionist learning (Michalski et al. 1983; 1986b, Kodratoff and Michalski 1990, Shavlik and Dietterich 1990, Carbonell 1990). Multistrategy learning integrates several learning paradigms (Michalski and Tecuci 1994). This chapter focuses on supervised, inductive learning of a single concept. If **U** is a universal set of observations, a concept **C** is formalized as a subset of observations in **U**. Inductive concept learning finds descriptions for various target concepts from positive and negative training instances of these concepts. In *single concept learning*, a target concept description is induced from training instances labeled positive or negative. In *multiple concept learning*, more than one target concept are being learned simultaneously, training examples are labeled by various concept names representing their categories.

In machine learning, formal languages for describing observations and concepts are called object and concept description languages, respectively. Typically, *object description languages* are attribute-value pair descriptions and first-order languages of Horn clauses. Concepts can be described extensionally or intensionally. A concept is described extensionally by listing the descriptions of all of its instances (observations). Thus *extensional concepts* are represented in the object description language. On the other hand, *intensional concepts* are expressed in a separate concept description language that permits compact and concise concept descriptions. Typical *concept description languages* are decision trees, decision lists, production rules, and first-order logic.

Inductive concept learning can be viewed as searching the space of hypotheses. A bias is a mechanism employed by a learning system to constrain the search for target hypotheses. A *search bias* determines how to conduct the search in the hypothesis space while a *language bias* determines the size and structure of the hypothesis space.

A *strong search bias*, such as the hill-climbing search strategy, employs existing knowledge about the size and the structure of the hypothesis space to exploit promising solutions so that it can find the target concept quickly. However, it may be trapped in a local maximum. A *weak search bias*, such as depth-first and breath-first search, explores the space completely; the learner is guaranteed to find the target concept that can be represented by the concept description language. Nevertheless, a weak bias is very inefficient. In other words, the search bias introduces the efficiency/completeness tradeoff into a learning system.

A *strong language bias* defines a less expressive description language such as the propositional logic. The hypothesis space created by the bias is comparatively smaller and the learning can be performed more efficiently. Nonetheless, the learner may fail to find the target concept that is not contained in the small hypothesis space. A *weak bias* defines a larger space and thus the target concept is more likely to be expressible in the space. The disadvantage is that the learner is less efficient. The language bias introduces the efficiency/expressiveness tradeoff into a learning system.

Background knowledge **B** is a prior knowledge that can be used by either the search bias to direct the search more efficient, or the languages bias to express the hypothesis space in a more natural and concise way. If a learning system is not provided with some a prior knowledge about the learning problem, it must learn exclusively from training examples. However, difficult learning problems typically require a lot of knowledge. The task of supervised inductive learning of a single concept **C** is formulated in table 4.1.

```
Given:
        -A set E of positive E+ and negative E- examples
         of a concept C.
        -Concept description language L.
        -Search and language bias.
        -Background knowledge B.
Find:
        A complete and consistent hypothesis H
        represented in the language L.

        A hypothesis H is complete if every positive
        example e ∈ E+ is covered by it with respect
        to B.

        A hypothesis H is consistent if no negative
        example e ∈ E- is covered by it with respect to
        B.
```

Table 4.1: Supervised inductive learning of a single concept.

4.2. Inductive Logic Programming (ILP)

Relational concept learning induces a new relation for the target concept (i.e., the target predicate) from training examples and known relations from the background knowledge. An ILP system is a relational concept learner. The training examples, the hypothesis space, and the background knowledge are represented in first-order Horn clause languages (Muggleton and Feng 1990). Tradeoffs between expressiveness and efficiency are introduced by some additional restrictions on these languages. This section describes two approaches of ILP, interactive and empirical ILP. Muggletion and De Raedt (1994) presented a comprehensive introduction of theory and methods of ILP. Before presenting these approaches, the terminology of logic programming is described first (Lloyd 1987).

The alphabet of a first-order language contains predicate symbols, function symbols, and variables. A *predicate symbol* is a lower case letter followed by a string of lower case letters and/or digits. A *function symbol* is a lower case letter followed by a string of lower case letters and/or digits. A *variable* is an upper case letter followed by a string of lower case letters and/or digits.

A *term* is a variable or a function. A *function* is a function symbol immediately followed by a sequence of terms enclosed in a pair of parentheses. The number of terms in the sequence is the *arity* of the function. For example, `f(g, h(X, Y), X)` is a function of arity 3 where `f`, `g`, and `h` are function symbols; and `X` and `Y` are variables. A constant is a function of arity 0. Thus `g` is a constant.

An *atomic formula*, or *atom*, is a predicate symbol immediately followed by a sequence of terms enclosed in a pair of parentheses. The number of terms in the sequence is the arity of the atomic formula. For example, `mother(X, Y)` is an atom of arity 2 where `mother` is a predicate symbol and `X` and `Y` are variables.

A *literal* can be classified as either a *positive literal* or a *negative literal*. A positive literal L is an atomic formula while a negative literal ¬L is the symbol ¬ followed by an atomic formula. A *clause* is a formula of the form $\forall X_1, X_2, \ldots, X_m (L_1 \vee L_2 \vee \ldots \vee L_n)$ where L_i, $1 \leq i \leq n$ are literals, and $X_1, X_2, \ldots, X_m$ are variables occurring in the clause. A clause $\forall X_1, X_2, \ldots, X_m (L_1 \vee L_2 \vee \ldots \vee L_i \vee \neg L_{i+1} \vee \neg L_{i+2} \vee \ldots \vee \neg L_n)$ can be represented as $L_1 \vee L_2 \vee \ldots \vee L_i \leftarrow L_{i+1} \wedge L_{i+2} \wedge \ldots \wedge L_n$. This clause can be written as $L_1, L_2, \ldots, L_i \leftarrow L_{i+1}, L_{i+2}, \ldots, L_n$ where commas on the left-hand side of ← denote disjunctions while commas on the right-hand side represent conjunctions.

A *definite program* is a set of definite program clause. A *definite program clause*, $\forall X_1, X_2, \ldots, X_m (T \vee \neg L_1 \vee \neg L_2 \vee \ldots \vee \neg L_n)$, is a clause that contains exactly one positive literal. It can be represented as the form

$T \leftarrow L_1, L_2, ..., L_n$ where T and L_i, $1 \le i \le n$ are atomic formulae. The positive literal T in a definite program clause is called the head or goal of the clause. The sequence of literals L_i, $1 \le i \le n$ is called the *body* of the clause. A *Horn clause* is a clause that contains at most one positive literal. Thus a Horn clause can be either a definite program clause or a *definite goal*: a clause with no positive literal. A definite goal can be represented as the form $\leftarrow L_1, L_2, ..., L_n$ where L_i, $1 \le i \le n$ are atomic formulae. A *positive unit clause* is a definite program clause with an empty body. It is called a *fact* in Prolog and is denoted simply as T.

A *normal program* is a set of program clauses. A program clause is a clause of the form $T \leftarrow L_1, L_2, ..., L_n$ where T is an atom and L_i, $1 \le i \le n$ are positive or negative literals. In the programming language Prolog, literals of the form `not L` are allowed in the body of a clause, where L is an atom and `not` is interpreted under the *negation-as-failure* rule (Clark 1978).

A *predicate definition* is a set of program clauses with the same predicate symbol (and arity) in their heads. A set of clauses is called a *theory* and represents the conjunction of the clauses. A *well-formed formula* is a literal, a clause, and a theory. A well-formed formula or term is *ground* if and only if there is no variable in the formula or term.

4.2.1. Interactive ILP

Interactive ILP is often used in incremental and interactive theory revision (De Raedt 1992). An interactive ILP system is provided with six inputs: 1) a set of correct examples **E** that has been examined before, 2) correct background knowledge **B**, 3) an incorrect theory **T**, 4) a concept description language **L**, 5) a new positive or negative training example e, and 6) a teacher that can answer questions generated by the system. The system modifies the definition of **T** and creates a new theory **T'** such that it is complete and consistent with respect to all examples seen (i.e. $\mathbf{E} \cup \{e\}$) and the background knowledge **B**.

Shapiro (1983) introduced the idea of *refinement operators* in the MIS system that is used to structure the search space of program clauses. The system searches the space in a breadth-first top-down manner. CLINT

(De Raedt 1992, De Raedt and Bruynooghe 1989; 1992) generates its own learning examples and asks questions about their classifications. It is featured with the applications of integrity constraints and its ability in changing concept description language dynamically.

Most interactive ILP systems are based on special forms of the general theory of *inverse resolution* introduced in CIGOL (Muggleton and Buntine 1988, Muggleton 1992). The three operators of CIGOL are absorption, intraconstruction and truncation. *Absorption* generalizes program clauses, *intraconstruction* learns definitions of new predicates and *truncation* generalizes unit clauses. The concept of absorption was first introduced by Sammut and Baneji (1986) in their MARVIN system. Wirth (1989) suggested two operators that are similar to absorption and intraconstruction. Rouveirol (1991; 1992) introduced *a saturation procedure* that overcomes some problems of absorption and truncation.

4.2.2. Empirical ILP

The task of *empirical ILP* is usually concerned with learning a single target concept from a given set of training examples and background knowledge. The task of empirical ILP is formulated in table 4.2.

The background knowledge **B** provides definitions of known predicates q_i that can be used in the definition of the target predicate p. It also provides additional information to ease the search of the definition of p. This information includes argument types, symmetry of predicates in pairs of arguments, input/output modes, rule models, predicate sets, parametrized languages, integrity constraints, determinations, and any knowledge that can modify the operations of the search and language biases (Lavrac and Dzeroski 1994).

In the definition, a training example is covered by **H** given background knowledge **B** if e is a logical consequence of **B** ∪ **H**. This notion of coverage is called *intensional coverage* (Lavrac and Dzeroski 1994). It allows the background knowledge **B** to include normal clauses and ground facts. For a particular concept description language **L**, an appropriate proof procedure must be used to check whether an example is entailed by **B** ∪ **H**. The *SLD-resolution proof procedure* with bounded or unbounded depth is usually employed to determine whether a training example is entailed (Lloyd 1987). In depth-bounded SLD-resolution, unresolved goals in the SLD-proof tree at depth h are not expanded and are treated as failed. MIS (Shapiro 1983) and CIGOL (Muggleton and Buntine 1988) use this proof procedure to prevent infinite loops.

```
Given:
      -A set E of positive E+ and negative E- training
       examples of the target predicate p. Training
       examples are represented as ground atoms
      -A concept description language L
      -Search and language bias.
      -Background knowledge B

Find:
      A definition H for the target predicate p
      expressible in L such that H is complete and
      consistent with respect to (w.r.t.) the training
      examples E and the background knowledge B

      H is complete if every positive example e+ in E+
      is covered by H w.r.t. the background knowledge
      B. i.e. B ∪ H |= e+

      H is consistent if no negative example e- in E-
      is covered by H w.r.t. the background knowledge
      B. i.e. B ∪ H |≠ e-
```

Table 4.2: *Definition of Empirical ILP.*

On the other hand, *extensional coverage* can also be used. In this case, extensional background knowledge **B** containing only ground facts must be employed to determine whether an example e is covered (Shapiro 1983). A hypothesis **H** extensionally covers an example e with respect to an extensional background knowledge **B** if there exists a clause $T \leftarrow L_1, L_2, ..., L_n$ in **H** and a substitution θ such that $T\theta$ = e and $\{L_1, L_2, ..., L_n\}\theta \subseteq \mathbf{B}$. If the background knowledge **B** provided by the users contains non-ground clauses, the empirical ILP systems have to transform it into a *ground model* of the background knowledge. The model contains all true ground facts that can be derived from the background knowledge by a SLD-proof tree of depth less than the depth-bound h (Shapiro 1983).

Empirical ILP systems include FOIL (Quinlan 1990; 1991), GOLEM (Muggleton and Feng 1990), LINUS (Lavrac and Dzeroski 1994), mFOIL (Lavrac and Dzeroski 1994), RX (Tangkitvanich and Shimura 1992), MOBAL (Morik et al. 1993), and ML-SMART (Bergadano et al. 1991). FOCL (Pazzani and Kibler 1992) is an extension of FOIL that combines ILP and explanation based learning. CHAM (Kijsirikul et al. 1992a) is an improvement of FOIL by applying a better search heuristics. CHAMP (Kijsirikul et al. 1992b) is an extension of CHAM that can invent useful predicates in learning relations. CHILLIN (Zelle et al. 1994) combines learning methods of GOLEM, FOIL, and CHAMP.

4.3. Techniques and Methods of ILP

An empirical ILP system can be classified into either a bottom-up or a top-down learner.

4.3.1. Bottom-up ILP Systems

Bottom-up systems search for program clauses by considering generalizations. They start from the most specific clause that covers a positive training example and then generalizes the clause until it cannot be further generalized without covering some negative examples. Two common generalization techniques are *relative least general generalization* (rlgg) introduced by Plotkin (1970) and *inverse resolution* proposed by Muggletion and Buntine (1988). Muggletion (1992) introduced a unifying framework covering both relative least general generalization and inverse resolution, based on the notion of a *most specific inverse resolvent*.

A successful representative of this class is GOLEM (Muggletion and Feng 1990). GOLEM is based on the construction of relative least-general generalizations that forces the background knowledge to be expressed extensionally as a set of ground facts. This ground model of background knowledge can be excessively large, and the clauses constructed from such models can grow explosively. To tackle this problem, Muggleton and Feng (1990) introduced the notion of *ij-determination* and employed the language bias of inducing only ij-determinate clauses. GOLEM is also sensitive to the distribution of training examples. If only a random sample of positive training examples is presented, the induced hypothesis of the target predicate is incomplete. Thus, GOLEM may fail to produce general and accurate hypotheses.

4.3.2. Top-down ILP Systems

Top-down methods apply specialization operators to learn program clauses by searching from general to specific. A *specialization operator* s produces a set of clauses **C'** permitted by the language bias from a clause c. It typically computes only the set of most general specialization of a clause c under θ-subsumption (Plotkin 1970). Most general specialization can be obtained by performing syntactic and/or semantic operations on the clause c (Shapiro 1983). Two basic syntactic operations on a clause are:

- applying a substitution θ to the clause, and
- adding a literal to the body of the clause.

4.3.2.1. FOIL

One of the most famous empirical top-down ILP system is FOIL (Quinlan 1990; 1991, Cameron-Jones and Quinlan 1993; 1994). It employs the techniques and methods applied in traditional attribute-value based learning systems. It also borrows the idea of specialization operators from MIS (Shapiro 1983) and the method of *determining coverage* of examples from ML-SMART (Bergadano et al. 1991).

FOIL is restricted to learning function-free program clauses. In other words, constants and functions cannot appear in the induced clauses. The body of a clause is a conjunction of positive or negative literals.

Literals in the body have either a predicate symbol q_i from the background knowledge **B**, or the target predicate symbol p. This implies that recursive clauses can be learned. When learning clauses with recursive literals, care must be taken to avoid infinite recursion. FOIL deals with this issue by attempting to establish an ordering on the arguments that may appear in a literal. Many sophisticated methods of finding an ordering on the arguments have been proposed (Cameron-Jones and Quinlan 1993; 1994). For each literal in the body of a clause, one or more of the variables in the arguments of the literal must appear in the head of the clause or in one of the literals to its left.

Training examples are function-free ground facts represented as a set of constant tuples. Background knowledge **B** consists of extensional predicate definitions. Each extensional predicate definition is a finite set of constant tuples representing the concept of the predicate. FOIL uses extensional background knowledge for efficiency reasons. Top-down algorithms can easily use intensionally defined background predicates to evaluate various competing hypotheses. An extension of FOIL, FOCL (Pazzani and Kibler 1992), allows background knowledge to be represented intensionally.

The FOIL algorithm is composed of three main phases. In the first phase, FOIL generates negative examples by applying the closed-world assumption if no negative example is provided. The second phase is the example covering loop. It implements the covering algorithm of AQ and INDUCE (Michalski 1983). The loop constructs a hypothesis by repeatedly performing the following operations:

- construct a clause,
- refine the clause by removing irrelevant literals from the clause,
- add the refined clause to the hypothesis **H**, and
- remove the positive examples covered by the clause from the set of positive training examples

until all the positive examples are covered or no more clause can be constructed. The last phase further refines the induced hypothesis **H** by eliminating irrelevant clauses from the hypothesis. The definitions of irrelevant literal and irrelevant clause are presented in Quinlan (1990).

The procedure that constructs a clause is the most important one in the FOIL algorithm. It starts from the most general clause and repeatedly specializes it by adding a literal to the body of the clause. The clause construction loop continues until a consistent clause covering at least one remaining positive example is found or no more specialization can be performed. During each iteration of the loop, a clause c can be refined by appending different literals to it. FOIL determines which one to be used by employing an information-based heuristics.

If the training examples are imperfect, FOIL may fail to find a consistent clause that covers some positive examples or it may find an overfitting clause that covers only a very few number of positive examples. Usually, these overfitting clauses cannot characterize the regularities in the training examples.

In FOIL, the noise handling mechanism is the *encoding length restriction*. The idea is that the number of bits required to encode the clause should never exceed the total number of bits needed to indicate explicitly the positive training examples covered by the clause. Thus, a clause covers r positive examples out of n examples in the training set. The number of bits available to encode the clause is $\log_2(n)+\log_2(\binom{n}{r})$. If there is no bit available for adding another literal, but the clause is more than 85% accurate, it is retained in the induced set of clauses, otherwise the clause is deleted. In the latter case, the clause construction procedure fails to produce a clause and it causes the termination of the FOIL algorithm. This heuristics avoids overfitting the training examples because insignificant literals are excluded from clauses of the inducing hypothesis. The obtained hypothesis is usually smaller, simpler, more accurate, and more comprehensible. Dzeroski and Lavrac (1993) argued that the encoding length restriction has two deficiencies. In exact domains, it sometimes prevents FOIL from learning complete description. In noisy domains, it allows very specific clauses.

FOIL has been extended to allow literals that bind a variable to a constant to appear in the body of a clause (Quinlan 1991, Cameron-Jones and Quinlan 1993; 1994). Other improvements include determinate literals, types and mode declarations of predicates, and advanced post-processing methods.

A fundamental weakness of FOIL is that recursive hypotheses are evaluated by employing the positive training examples as a model of the target predicate being learned. When the examples are incomplete over the domain of interest, they provide an incorrect model and FOIL has difficulty in learning even simple recursive concepts (Cohen 1993).

4.3.2.2. mFOIL

mFOIL (Lavrac and Dzeroski 1994) is largely based on the FOIL algorithm. The main difference is that mFOIL uses a different search heuristics and an improved noise-handling mechanism. Another major difference is the beam search strategy used in mFOIL as opposed to the hill-climbing search used in FOIL. To reduce its search space, mFOIL uses some additional information, such as the symmetry and different constraints on variables. Several parameters are used in mFOIL, which determine the search heuristics used, the width of the beam in the beam search, and the level of significance applied to the induced clauses.

mFOIL employs an accuracy estimate as its search heuristics. The accuracy estimate may be the *Laplace estimate* or the more sophisticated *m-estimate* (Cestnik 1990). Both estimates have been found to be useful in improving noise-handling abilities of attribute-value learning systems (Cestnik and Bratko 1991, Clark and Boswell 1991). If a clause c covers $n(\mathrm{c})$ training examples, out of which $n^{+}(\mathrm{c})$ are positive, its expected accuracy can be estimated by either the Laplace estimate

$$A(\mathrm{c}) = \frac{n^{+}(\mathrm{c})+1}{n(\mathrm{c})+2}$$

or the *m*-estimate

$$A(\mathrm{c}) = \frac{n^{+}(\mathrm{c}) + m \times \mathrm{a\text{-}prior\text{-}prob}^{+}}{n(\mathrm{c})+m}$$

where a-prior-prob^{+} is the a prior probability of the positive class and is estimated by the relative frequency of positive examples in the whole training set.

It uses a beam search method to find a significant clause. The clause construction procedure starts with a clause having an empty body. During the search, the best clause and a small set of promising clauses are stored in the beam. At each iteration of the clause construction loop, the significant refinements of each clause c in the beam are evaluated using their expected accuracy. The best of their significant improvements constitute the new beam. A significant improvement of a clause c is a refinement c' of the clause c such that $A(\mathrm{c}') > A(\mathrm{c})$ and c' passes the significance test. The search for a clause terminates when the new beam becomes empty. The best clause found so far is retained in the hypothesis if its expected accuracy is better than the default accuracy. The default accuracy, estimated from the entire training set by the relative frequency estimate, is the probability of the more frequent of the positive or negative classes.

The significance test used in mFOIL is based on the *likelihood ratio statistic* (Kalbfleish 1979). Assume that the training set has n^+ positive examples and n^- negative examples. If a clause c covers n(c) examples, n^+(c) of which are positive, the value of the statistic can be calculated as follows:

$$\text{Likelihood Ratio} = 2 \times n(\text{c}) \times \left\{ \text{prob}^+(\text{c}) * \log\left(\frac{\text{prob}^+(\text{c})}{\text{a}-\text{prior}-\text{prob}^+}\right) + \text{prob}^-(\text{c}) * \log\left(\frac{\text{prob}^-(\text{c})}{\text{a}-\text{prior}-\text{prob}^-}\right) \right\}$$

where

$$\text{prob}^+(\text{c}) = \frac{n^+(\text{c})}{n(\text{c})},$$

$$\text{prob}^-(\text{c}) = \frac{n^-(\text{c})}{n(\text{c})},$$

$$\text{a}-\text{prior}-\text{prob}^+ = \frac{n^+}{n^+ + n^-}, \text{ and}$$

$$\text{a}-\text{prior}-\text{prob}^- = \frac{n^-}{n^+ + n^-}$$

This statistic is distributed approximately as a χ^2 distribution with one degree of freedom. If its value is above a specified significance threshold, the clause is significant.

The covering algorithm of AQ and INDUCE (Michalski 1983) is used in mFOIL. Program clauses are constructed repetitively. The stopping criteria of the example covering loop terminate the search for clauses when too few positive examples are left for generating a significant clause or no significant clause can be found with expected accuracy greater than the default accuracy.

Chapter 5

THE LOGIC GRAMMARS BASED GENETIC PROGRAMMING SYSTEM (LOGENPRO)

As discussed in chapters 3 and 4, Inductive Logic Programming (ILP) and Genetic Programming (GP) are two of the approaches in data mining. It was demonstrated that ILP can be used to induce knowledge represented as logic programs (Dzeroski and Lavrac 1993, Dzeroski 1996, Dehaspe and Toivonen, 1999, Srinivasan and King 1999, Blockeel et al. 1999, Srinivasan 1999). GP (Koza 1992; 1994, Koza et al. 1999, Kinnear 1994) extends traditional Genetic Algorithms (Holland 1992, Goldberg 1989, Davis 1987; 1991) to induce automatically S-expressions in Lisp. It performs both exploitation of the most promising solutions and exploration of the search space. It is featured to tackle hard search problems and thus applicable to program induction and data mining.

In this chapter, we present a framework, called Generic Genetic Programming (GGP), that can combine GP and ILP to induce knowledge from databases. We can also specify the search space declaratively. This framework is based on a formalism of logic grammars and is implemented as a data mining system called LOGENPRO (The LOgic grammar based GENetic PROgramming system). The formalism is powerful enough to represent context-sensitive information and domain-dependent knowledge which can be used to accelerate the learning of knowledge. It is also very flexible and the knowledge acquired can be represented in different knowledge representations such as logic programs and production rules (Wong and Leung 1994a; 1994b; 1995a; 1995b; 1997, Wong 1998).

This chapter is organized as follows. The first section is an introduction to logic grammars. Section 5.2 presents a representation method of programs and a description of the mechanism used to generate the initial population of programs. One of the genetic operators, crossover, is detailed in section 5.3. Another genetic operator, mutation, is presented in the subsequent section. In section 5.5, we present a high-level description of LOGENPRO. The last section is a discussion.

5.1. Logic Grammars

The LOgic grammars based GENetic PROgramming system (LOGENPRO) can induce programs in various programming languages such as Lisp, C, and Prolog. Thus, LOGENPRO must be able to accept grammars of different languages and produce programs in them. Most modern programming languages are specified in the notation of BNF (Backus-Naur form) which is a kind of context-free grammars (CFGs). However, LOGENPRO is based on *logic grammars* because CFGs (Hopcroft and Ullman 1979, Lewis and Rapadimitrion 1981) are not expressive enough to represent context-sensitive information of some languages and domain-dependent knowledge of the target program being induced. The idea of using formal grammars to direct search for programs in the hypothesis space or to reduce the size of the space has also been independently studied by other researcher recently (Cohen 1992, Gruau 1996, Whigham 1996). This section introduces the formalism of logic grammars.

Logic grammars are the generalizations of CFGs. Their expressivenesses are much more powerful than those of CFGs, but equally amenable to efficient execution. In this book, logic grammars are described in a notation similar to that of definite clause grammars (Pereira and Warren 1980, Pereira and Shieber 1987, Sterling and Shapiro 1986). The logic grammar for some simple S-expressions in table 5.1 will be used throughout this chapter. Grammars for some logic programming languages can be found in the next chapter.

A logic grammar differs from a CFG in that the logic grammar symbols, whether terminal or non-terminal, may include arguments. The arguments can be any term in the grammar. A *term* is either a logic variable, a function, or a constant. A *variable* is represented by a question mark ? followed by a string of letters and/or digits. A *function* is a grammar symbol followed by a bracketed n-tuple of terms and a *constant* is simply a 0-arity function. Arguments can be used in a logic grammar to enforce context-dependency. Thus, the permissible forms for a constituent may depend on the context in which that constituent occurs in the program. Another application of arguments is to construct tree structures in the course of parsing, such tree structures can provide a representation of the semantics of the program.

The *terminal symbols*, which are enclosed in square brackets, correspond to the set of words of the language specified. For example, the terminal `[(- ?x ?y)]` creates the constituent `(- 1.0 2.0)` of a program if `?x` and `?y` are instantiated respectively to 1.0 and 2.0. *Non-terminal symbols* are similar to literals in Prolog, `exp-1(?x)` in table 5.1 is an example of non-terminal symbol. Commas denote concatenation and each grammar rule ends with a full stop.

1:	`start`	`->`	`[(*], exp(W), exp(W),` **`exp(W)`**`,` **`[)]`**`.`
2:	`start`	`->`	`{member(?x,[W, Z])}, [(*], exp-1(?x), exp-1(?x),` **`exp-1(?x)`**`,` **`[)]`**`.`
3:	`start`	`->`	`{member(?x,[W, Z])}, [(+], exp-1(?x), exp-1(?x),` **`exp-1(?x)`**`,` **`[)]`**`.`
4:	`exp(?x)`	`->`	`[(/ ?x 1.5)].`
5:	`exp-1(?x)`	`->`	`{random(1,2,?y)}, [(/ ?x ?y)].`
6:	`exp-1(?x)`	`->`	`{random(3,4,?y)}, [(- ?x ?y)].`
7:	`exp-1(W)`	`->`	`[(+ (- W 11) 12)].`

Table 5.1: A logic grammar.

The right-hand side of a grammar rule may contain *logic goals* and grammar symbols. The goals are pure logical predicates for which logical definitions have been given. They specify the conditions that must be satisfied before the rule can be applied. For example, the goal `member(?x, [W, Z])` in table 5.1 instantiates the variable `?x` to either `W` or `Z` if `?x` has not been instantiated, otherwise it checks whether the value of `?x` is either `W` or `Z`. If the variable `?y` has not been bound, the goal `random(1, 2, ?y)` instantiates `?y` to a random floating point number between 1 and 2. Otherwise, the goal checks whether the value of `?y` is between 1 and 2.

Domain-dependent knowledge can be represented in logic goals. For example, consider the following grammar rule:

```
a-useful-program ->   first-component(?X),
                      {is-useful(?X,    ?Y)},
                      second-component(?Y).
```

This rule states that a useful program is composed of two components. The first component is generated from the non-terminal `first-`

component(?X). The logic variable ?X is used to store semantic information about the first component produced. The logic goal then determines whether the first component is useful according to the semantic information stored in ?X. Domain-dependent knowledge about which program fragments are useful is represented in the logical definition of this predicate. If the first component is useful, the logic goal is-useful(?X, ?Y) is satisfied and some semantic information is stored into the logic variable ?Y. This information will be used in the non-terminal second-component(?Y) to guide the search for a good program fragment as the second component of a useful program.

The special non-terminal start corresponds to a program of the language. In table 5.1, some grammar symbols are shown in bold-face to identify the constituents that cannot be manipulated by genetic operators. For example, the last terminal symbol **[ )]** of the second rule is revealed in bold-face because every S-expression must be ended with a ')'. The number before each rule is a label for later discussions. It is not part of the grammar.

5.2. Representations of Programs

One of the fundamental contributions of our framework is in the representations of programs in different programming languages appropriately so that initial population can be generated easily and the genetic operators such as reproduction, mutation, and crossover can be performed effectively. A program can be represented as a *derivation tree* that shows how the program has been derived from the logic grammar. LOGENPRO applies deduction to randomly generate programs and their derivation trees in the language declared by the given grammar. These programs form the initial population. For example, the program (* (/ W 1.5) (/ W 1.5) (/ W 1.5)) can be generated by LOGENPRO given the logic grammar in table 5.1. It is derived from the following sequence of derivations:

```
start => [(*] exp(W) exp(W) exp(W) [)]
      => [(*] [(/ W 1.5)] exp(W) exp(W) [)]
```

```
=>    [(*] [(/ W 1.5)] [(/ W 1.5)] exp(W)
      [)]
=>    [(*] [(/ W 1.5)] [(/ W 1.5)]
      [(/ W 1.5)] [)]
=>    [(* (/ W 1.5) (/ W 1.5) (/ W 1.5))]
```

This sequence of derivations can be represented as the derivation tree depicted in figure 5.1.

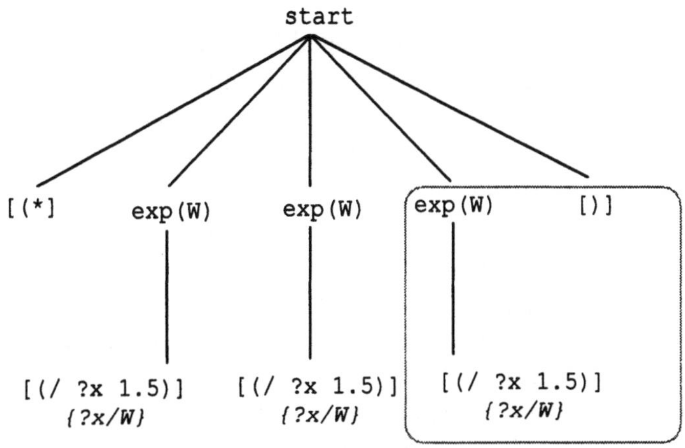

Figure 5.1: *A derivation tree of the S-expression in Lisp* `(* (/ W 1.5) (/ W 1.5) (/ W 1.5))`.

In literature, the terms of derivation trees and parse trees are usually used interchangeably. However, we will use the term derivation trees to refer to the tree structures in our framework and the term parse trees to refer to those in GP. The bindings of logic variables are shown in italic font and enclosed in a pair of braces. The sub-trees enclosed in a dashed rectangular are frozen. In other words, they are generated by bold-faced grammar symbols and they cannot be modified by genetic operators.

One advantage of logic grammars is that they specify what is a legal program without any explicit reference to the process of program generation and parsing. Furthermore, a logic grammar can be translated into an efficient logic program that can generate and parse the programs in the language declared by the logic grammar (Pereira and Warren 1980,

Pereira and Shieber 1987, Abramson and Dahl 1989). In other words, the process of program generation and parsing can be achieved by performing deduction using the produced logic program. Consequently, the program generation and analysis mechanisms of LOGENPRO can be implemented using a deduction mechanism based on the logic programs translated from the grammars. In the following paragraphs, we discuss the method of implementing LOGENPRO using a Prolog-like logic programming language.

The differences between the logic programming language used and Prolog are listed as follows:

- A variable is represented by a question mark ? followed by a string of letters and/or digits.
- The elements of a list can be separated by either commas or spaces. For example, `[a b c]` and `[a, b, c]` are equivalent.
- A pair of '`|`' is used to represent a frozen terminal symbol. For example, the symbol **[)]** in the second rule of the grammar in table 5.1 is translated into `|)|`.
- A pair of braces encloses a sequence of logic goals appearing in a logic grammar.
- If there are a number of clauses $C_1, C_2, ..., C_n$ that match a goal G, the ordering of evaluating these clauses is determined randomly.

Using the difference list approach (Sterling and Shapiro 1986), a grammar rule of the form:

$$A_0 \quad \texttt{->} \quad A_1, \ A_2, \ ..., \ A_n.$$

is translated into a logic program clause of the form:

$$A_0' \quad \texttt{->} \quad A_1', \ A_2', \ ..., \ A_n'.$$

in the logic programming language. Here, if A_i, for some `i` between 0 and n, is a non-terminal with M arguments, then A_i' is a literal with M+3 arguments. The predicate symbols of A_i and A_i' are the same. For example, A_i is translated into `exp(?X, ?Tree, `$?S_j$`, ? `S_{j+1}`)`, for some `j`, if A_i is `exp(?X)`. The literal `exp(?X, ?Tree, `$?S_j$`, `$?S_{j+1}$`)` states that the sequence of symbols between $?S_j$ and $?S_{j+1}$ is a sentence of the category represented by the non-terminal symbol `exp(?X)`. The derivation tree of the sentence is stored in the logic variable `?Tree`.

A terminal symbol such as `[a b c]` is translated to a literal with 3 arguments: `connect([a b c],` $?S_j$, $?S_{j+1}$`)`, for some `j`. The predicate `connect` is defined as:

```
connect(?A, ?S0, ?S1) :-
                    append(?A, ?S1, ?S0).
```

This predicate declares that the list of symbols stored in the logic variable `?A` can be found in the sequence of symbols between `?S0` and `?S1`.

If A_k, for some k between 1 and *n*, is a pair of braces enclosing a sequence of pure logic goals, i.e., A_k has the form of $\{G_0, G_1, \ldots, G_m\}$, then A_k' is obtained from A_k by removing the pair of braces.

This method of translating a logic grammar into a logic program is common in the field of natural language processing (Pereira and Warren 1980, Pereira and Shieber 1987, Abramson and Dahl 1989). The original idea of this approach is to rephrase the special purpose formalism of CFGs into a general purpose first-order predicate logic (Kowalski 1979, Colmerauer 1978, Pereira and Warren 1980). This approach is further refined and generalized to *Definite Clause Grammars* (DCGs) which can handle the properties of context-dependency of natural languages effectively.

Since DCGs, a kind of logic grammars, can be translated into efficient logic programs automatically, parsers and generators for the corresponding natural languages can be obtained easily. In other words, researchers in the field of natural language processing only declare the grammar for a particular natural language, and the translation process will produce the corresponding parser and generator for them. Moreover, for some cases, the same logic program can be used as both a parser and generator at the same time. For example, the grammar depicted in table 5.1 can be translated into the logic program presented in table 5.2.

```
1':   start(tree(start, [(*], ?E1, ?E2, frozen(?E3),
            |)|), ?S0, ?S5)
            :-              connect([(*], ?S0, ?S1),
                            exp(W, ?E1, ?S1, ?S2),
                            exp(W, ?E2, ?S2, ?S3),
                            exp(W, ?E3, ?S3, ?S4),
                            connect([)], ?S4, ?S5).
2':   start(tree(start, {member(?x, [W, Z])}, [(*],
            ?E1, ?E2, frozen(?E3), |)|),?S0, ?S5)
            :-              member(?x, [W, Z]),
                            connect([(*], ?S0, ?S1),
                            exp-1(?x, ?E1, ?S1, ?S2),
                            exp-1(?x, ?E2, ?S2, ?S3),
                            exp-1(?x, ?E3, ?S3, ?S4),
                            connect([)], ?S4, ?S5).
3':   start(tree(start, {member(?x, [W, Z])}, [(+],
            ?E1, ?E2, frozen(?E3), |)|),?S0, ?S5)
            :-              member(?x, [W, Z]),
                            connect([(+], ?S0, ?S1),
                            exp-1(?x, ?E1, ?S1, ?S2),
                            exp-1(?x, ?E2, ?S2, ?S3),
                            exp-1(?x, ?E3, ?S3, ?S4),
                            connect([)], ?S4, ?S5).
4':   exp(?x, tree(exp(?x), [(/ ?x 1.5)]),?S0, ?S1)
            :-              connect([(/ ?x 1.5)], ?S0,
                                  ?S1).
5':   exp-1(?x, tree(exp-1(?x), {random(1,2,?y)},
            [(/ ?x ?y)]),?S0, ?S1)
            :-              random(1, 2, ?y),
                            connect([(/ ?x ?y)], ?S0,
                                  ?S1).
6':   exp-1(?x, tree(exp-1(?x), {random(3,4,?y)},
            [(- ?x ?y)]),?S0, ?S1)
            :-              random(3, 4, ?y)
                            connect([(- ?x ?y)], ?S0,
                                  ?S1).
7':   exp-1(W, tree(exp-1(W), [(+ (- W 11) 12)]),?S0,
            ?S1)
            :-              connect([(+ (- W 11) 12)],
                                  ?S0, ?S1).
```

Table 5.2: A logic program obtained from translating the logic grammar presented in table 5.1.

In the clause 1' of the logic program shown in table 5.2, the compound term `tree(start, [(*], ?E1, ?E2, frozen(?E3), |)|)` indicates that it is a tree with a root labeled as `start`. The children of the root include the terminal symbol `[(*]`, a tree created from the non-terminal `exp(W)`, another tree created from the non-terminal `exp(W)`, a frozen tree generated from the non-terminal **exp(W)**, and the frozen terminal `|)|`.

Thus, a derivation tree can be generated randomly by issuing the following query:

```
?- start(?T, ?S, []).
```

This goal can be satisfied by deducing a sentence that is in the language specified by the grammar. One solution is:

```
?S = [(* (/ W 1.5) (/ W 1.5) (/ W 1.5))]
```

and the corresponding derivation tree is:

```
?T = tree(start, [(*],
            tree(exp(W), [(/ W 1.5)]),
            tree(exp(W), [(/ W 1.5)]),
            frozen(tree(exp(W),
                   [(/ W 1.5)])),
                  |)|)
```

This is exactly a representation of the derivation tree shown in figure 5.1. In fact, the bindings of all logic variables and other information are also maintained in the derivation trees to facilitate the genetic operations that will be performed on the derivation trees.

Alternatively, initial programs can be induced by other learning systems such as FOIL (Quinlan 1990; 1991) or given by the user. LOGENPRO analyzes each program and creates the corresponding derivation tree. If the language is ambiguous, multiple derivation trees can be generated. LOGENPRO produces only one tree randomly. For example, the program `(* (/ W 1.5) (/ W 1.5) (/ W 1.5))` can also be derived from the following sequence of derivations:

```
start =>    {member(?x, [W, Z])} [(*]
            exp-1(?x) exp-1(?x) exp-1(?x) [)]
      =>    [(*] exp-1(W) exp-1(W) exp-1(W)
            [)]
```

```
=>   [(*] {random(1, 2, ?y)}
     [(/ W ?y)] exp-1(W) exp-1(W) [)]
=>   [(*] [(/ W 1.5)] exp-1(W)
     exp-1(W) [)]
=>   [(*] [(/ W 1.5)]
     {random(1, 2, ?y)} [(/ W ?y)]
     exp-1(W) [)]
=>   [(*] [(/ W 1.5)] [(/ W 1.5)]
     exp-1(W) [)]
=>   [(*] [(/ W 1.5)] [(/ W 1.5)]
     {random(1, 2, ?y)} [(/ W ?y)] [)]
=>   [(*] [(/ W 1.5)] [(/ W 1.5)]
     [(/ W 1.5)] [)]
=>   [(* (/ W 1.5)(/ W 1.5)(/ W 1.5))]
```

The derivation tree of this sequence of derivations is depicted in figure 5.2. The ?y1, ?y2, and ?y3 in the figure are different instances of the logic variable ?y appearing in the same or different rules in the grammar.

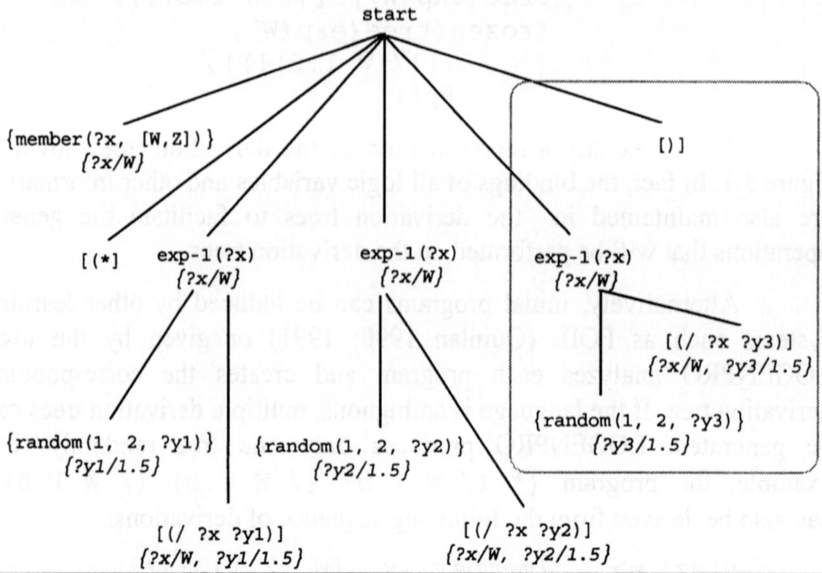

Figure 5.2: Another derivation tree of the S-expression ((/ W 1.5) (/ W 1.5) (/ W 1.5)).*

Using the logic program in table 5.2, a given program such as `(* (/ W 1.5) (/ W 1.5) (/ W 1.5))` can be analyzed using the following query:

```
?- start(?T,
      [(* (/ W 1.5)(/ W 1.5)(/ W 1.5))], []).
```

The given program is correct if the above goal can be satisfied and the corresponding derivation tree will be bound to the logic variable `?T`. As demonstrated previously, the logic grammar in table 5.1 is ambiguous and thus the corresponding logic program may produce multiple derivation trees for a given program. Since the search strategy of the underlying deduction mechanism selects randomly one clause to explore with backtracking from all unifiable clauses, the sequence of generating the derivation trees of a particular program is also random. Consequently, LOGENPRO takes the first tree returned from the query to represent the given program.

5.3. Crossover of Programs

The crossover is a sexual operation that starts with two parental programs and the corresponding derivation trees. One program is designated as the primary parent and the other one as the secondary parent. The derivation trees of the primary and secondary parents are called the primary and secondary derivation trees respectively. The algorithm in table 5.3 is used to produce an offspring program.

Consider two parental programs generated randomly from the grammar in table 5.1. The primary parent is `(+ (- Z 3.5) (- Z 3.8) (/ Z 1.5))` and the secondary parent is `(* (/ W 1.5) (+ (- W 11) 12) (- W 3.5))`. The corresponding derivation trees are depicted in figures 5.3 and 5.4 respectively. In the figures, the plain numbers identify sub-trees of these derivation trees, while the underlined numbers indicate the grammar rules used in deducing the corresponding sub-trees.

In step 1 of the crossover algorithm, the global variable PRIMARY-SUB-TREES contains the sub-trees **2**, **3**, **5**, **6**, and **8**. The primary derivation tree (i.e. the sub-tree **0**), the sub-trees **1**, **4**, **7**, and **10** that contain logic goals, and the frozen sub-trees **9**, **10**, **11**, and **12** are excluded. The whole primary derivation tree cannot be mated because it must be generated from the grammar symbol `start`. If the symbol `start` is not recursive (i.e. `start` does not appear on the right hand side of a rule), the whole secondary derivation tree must be chosen for crossover. Thus, the offspring program must be a copy of the secondary parental program. In fact, the same effect can be obtained by reproducing the secondary parental program.

The sub-trees containing logic goals are eliminated for two reasons. Firstly, the crossover algorithm can be greatly simplified if logic goals are prevented from performing crossover. Secondly, logic goals specify the conditions that must be satisfied before the rule can be applied and/or the computations that should be done. Hence, from the viewpoint of natural selection and reproduction, the interpretation of crossover between logic goals is unclear and unnatural. Thus this kind of operations is avoided.

Similarly, the sub-trees **13, 15, 16, 18, 19,** and **20** are assigned to the global variable SECONDARY-SUB-TREES in step 2. In the next step, a sub-tree in the variable PRIMARY-SUB-TREES is selected randomly using a uniform distribution because the variable is not empty. Assume that the sub-tree **2**, the SEL-PRIMARY-SUB-TREE, is selected. Thus, it is removed from the variable PRIMARY-SUB-TREES in step 4. A copy of the variable SECONDARY-SUB-TREES is made and stored into the global variable TEMP-SECONDARY-SUB-TREES in step 5.

Steps 6 to 8 form a loop that finds an appropriate sub-tree from the variable TEMP-SECONDARY-SUB-TREES. A sub-tree, SEL-SECONDARY-SUB-TREE, is appropriate if a valid offspring can be obtained by executing crossover between the SEL-PRIMARY-SUB-TREE and the SEL-SECONDARY-SUB-TREE. If no appropriate sub-tree can be found in this loop, the algorithm returns back to step 3 to find another SEL-PRIMARY-SUB-TREE. Assume that the sub-tree **15** is chosen as the SEL-SECONDARY-SUB-TREE. Step 8 determines whether a valid offspring can be obtained. It is the most complicate procedure in this algorithm and it is delineated in table 5.4 and explained in the following paragraphs.

In step 11 of the algorithm shown in table 5.4, the sub-trees **1, 3, 6, 9,** and **12** are found to be the siblings of the SEL-PRIMARY-SUB-TREE **2** and stored into the global variable SIBLINGS. The SIBLINGS can be thought as the context around the PRIMARY-CROSSOVER-POINT and the context's consistency has to be checked and computed.

The purpose of step 12 is to remove the bindings established solely by the SEL-PRIMARY-SUB-TREE which will be deleted by the crossover operation. To achieve this goal, the bindings of each sub-tree in the variable SIBLINGS is modified so that only the bindings established by itself is retained. The bindings instantiated by a sub-tree can be found easily using the techniques of explanation-based learning (DeJong 1993, Mitchell et al. 1986, DeJong and Mooney 1986). For example, the bindings `{?x/Z}` of the sub-tree **1** needs not be modified because the logic variable `?x` is instantiated to the value `Z` by the logic goal `member(?x, [W, Z])`. The bindings `{?x/Z}` of the sub-tree **3** is changed to an empty list because the logic variable `?x` is bound to the value `Z` by the sub-tree **1**. Similarly, the bindings `{?x/Z}` of the sub-trees **6** and **9** are changed to empty lists. The bindings of the sub-tree **12** is not changed because it is already empty.

In step 13, the bindings of the SEL-SECONDARY-SUB-TREE is modified so that only the bindings established by itself is retained. The purpose is to identify the effect of the sub-tree on the logic variables. In this example, since the grammar symbol of the SEL-SECONDARY-SUB-TREE **15** has no argument, its bindings is empty. In fact, the primary and secondary derivation trees are pre-processed by LOGENPRO using an algorithm based on the techniques of Explanation-Based Learning (EBL). The algorithm finds the bindings established solely by the corresponding sub-trees of the derivation trees. The results are stored in the sub-trees so that they can be retrieved in constant time C_r. Thus the time complexity of step 12 is $O(n)$ where n is the number of sub-trees in the global variable SIBLINGS. Similarly, the time complexity of step 13 is $O(1)$.

In step 14, the second grammar rule is satisfied by the sub-trees in SIBLINGS and the SEL-SECONDARY-SUB-TREE. Moreover, this rule reaches the conclusion `start` which is consistent with the requirement of the parent, the sub-tree **0**, of the SEL-PRIMARY-SUB-TREE. Thus, the offspring generated is valid. The procedure that checks whether a conclusion is consistent is presented in table 5.5.

```
Input:
    P:                   The primary derivation tree.
    S:                   The secondary derivation tree.

Output:
    Return a new derivation tree if a valid offspring can be obtained
    by performing crossover, otherwise return false.

Function crossover(P, S)
{
    1.    Find all sub-trees of the primary derivation tree P
          and store them into a global variable PRIMARY-SUB-
          TREES, excluding the primary derivation tree, all
          logic goals, and frozen sub-trees.
    2.    Find all sub-trees of the secondary derivation tree S
          and store them into a global variable SECONDARY-SUB-
          TREES, excluding all logic goals and frozen sub-
          trees.
    3.    If the variable PRIMARY-SUB-TREES is not empty,
          select randomly a sub-tree from it using a uniform
          distribution. Otherwise, terminate the algorithm
          without generating any offspring program.
    4.    Designate the sub-tree selected as the SEL-PRIMARY-
          SUB-TREE and the root of it as the PRIMARY-CROSSOVER-
          POINT. Remove the SEL-PRIMARY-SUB-TREE from the
          variable PRIMARY-SUB-TREES.
    5.    Copy the variable SECONDARY-SUB-TREES to the
          temporary variable TEMP-SECONDARY-SUB-TREES.
    6     If the variable TEMP-SECONDARY-SUB-TREES is not
          empty, select randomly a sub-tree from it using a
          uniform distribution. Otherwise, go to step 3.
    7.    Designate the sub-tree selected in step 6 as the SEL-
          SECONDARY-SUB-TREE. Remove it from the variable TEMP-
          SECONDARY-SUB-TREES.
    8.    If the offspring produced by performing crossover
          between the SEL-PRIMARY-SUB-TREE and the SEL-
          SECONDARY-SUB-TREE is invalid according to the
          grammar, go to step 6. The validity of the offspring
          generated can be checked by the procedure is-valid(P,
          SEL-PRIMARY-SUB-TREE, SEL-SECONDARY-SUB-TREE).
    9.    Copy the genetic materials of the primary parent P to
          the offspring, remove the SEL-PRIMARY-SUB-TREE from
          it and then impregnating a copy of the SEL-SECONDARY-
          SUB-TREE at the PRIMARY-CROSSOVER-POINT.
    10.   Perform some house-keeping tasks and return the
          offspring program.
}
```

Table 5.3: *The crossover algorithm of LOGENPRO.*

```
Input:
    P:                  The primary derivation tree
    P-sub-tree:         The sub-tree in the primary derivation tree
                        that is selected to be crossed over.
    S-sub-tree:         The sub-tree in the secondary derivation tree
                        that is selected to be crossed over.

Output:
    Return true if the offspring generated is valid, otherwise return
    false.

Function is-valid(P, P-sub-tree, S-sub-tree)
{
        11.   Find all siblings of the P-sub-tree in P and store
              them into the global variable SIBLINGS.
        12.   For each sub-tree in the variable SIBLINGS, perform
              the following sub-steps:
                •  Store the bindings of the sub-tree to the
                   global variable BINDINGS.
                •  For each logic variable in the variable
                   BINDINGS that is not instantiated by the sub-
                   tree, remove it from the variable BINDINGS.
                •  Modify the bindings of the sub-tree.
        13.   Modify the bindings of the S-sub-tree. A logic
              variable is retained only if it is instantiated in
              the S-sub-tree.
        14.   If there is a rule in the grammar such that:
                •  it is satisfied by the sub-trees in the
                   variable SIBLINGS and the S-sub-tree,
                •  the sub-trees in the variable SIBLINGS and the
                   S-sub-tree are used exactly once,
                •  the sub-trees are applied in the same order as
                   that in the original rule of the primary
                   derivation tree, and
                •  a consistent conclusion C is deduced from the
                   rule. The conclusion is consistent if the
                   function is-consistent(P, PARENT, C) returns
                   true where PARENT is the parent of the P-sub-
                   tree. The function is-consistent is presented
                   in table 5.5.
              then the offspring generated will be valid.
              Otherwise, the offspring will be invalid.
}
```

Table 5.4: *The algorithm that checks whether the offspring produced by LOGENPRO is valid.*

```
Input:
    P:          The primary derivation tree.
    PARENT:     The parent of the primary sub-tree.
    C:          The conclusion.
Output:
    Return true if the conclusion C is consistent, otherwise return
    false.
Comment:
    This operation can be viewed as performing a tentative crossover
    between PARENT and C and then determining whether the tentative
    offspring produced is valid. Here, PARENT is treated as the
    primary sub-tree while C is treated as the secondary sub-tree of
    the tentative crossover operation. The main difference between
    this algorithm and that in table 5.4 is that all rule
    applications in all ancestors of PARENT must be maintained.
Function is-consistent(P, PARENT, C)
{
     15.   If PARENT is the root of P then
                if C is labeled with the symbol start then
                          return true
                else false.
     16.   Find all siblings of PARENT in P and store them into
           the global variable SIBLINGS.
     17.   For each sub-tree in the variable SIBLINGS, perform
           the following sub-steps:
              • Store the bindings of the sub-tree to the
                global variable BINDINGS.
              • For each logic variable in the variable
                BINDINGS that is not instantiated by the sub-
                tree, remove it from the variable BINDINGS.
              • Modify the bindings of the sub-tree.
     18.   Let the grammar rule applied in the parent node of
           PARENT as RULE.
           If the following conditions are satisfied:
              • RULE is satisfied by the sub-trees in the
                variable SIBLINGS and C,
              • the sub-trees in SIBLINGS and C are used
                exactly once and the ordering of applications
                is maintained, and
              • a consistent conclusion C' is deduced from
                RULE. The conclusion is consistent if the
                function is-consistent(P, GRANDPARENT, C')
                returns true where GRANDPARENT is the parent
                node of PARENT.
           then
                return true
           else
                return false.
}
```

Table 5.5: The algorithm that checks whether a conclusion deduced from a rule is consistent with the direct parent of the primary sub-tree.

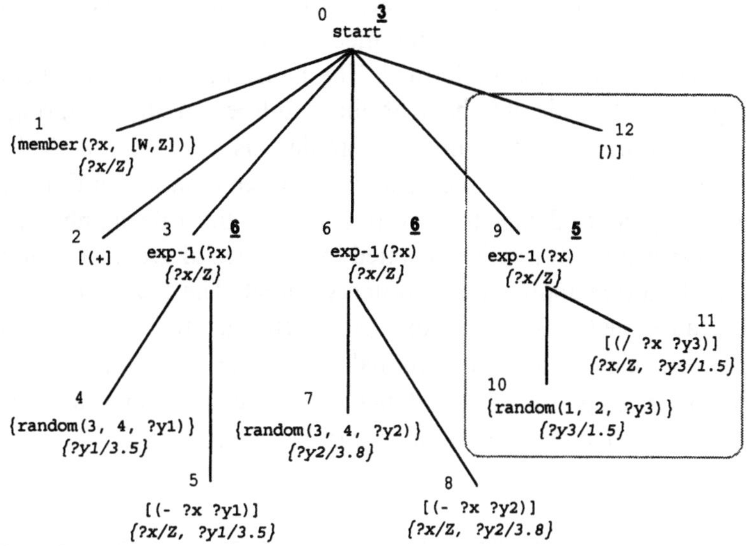

Figure 5.3: *The derivations tree of the primary parental program* *(+ (- Z 3.5) (- Z 3.8) (/ Z 1.5)).*

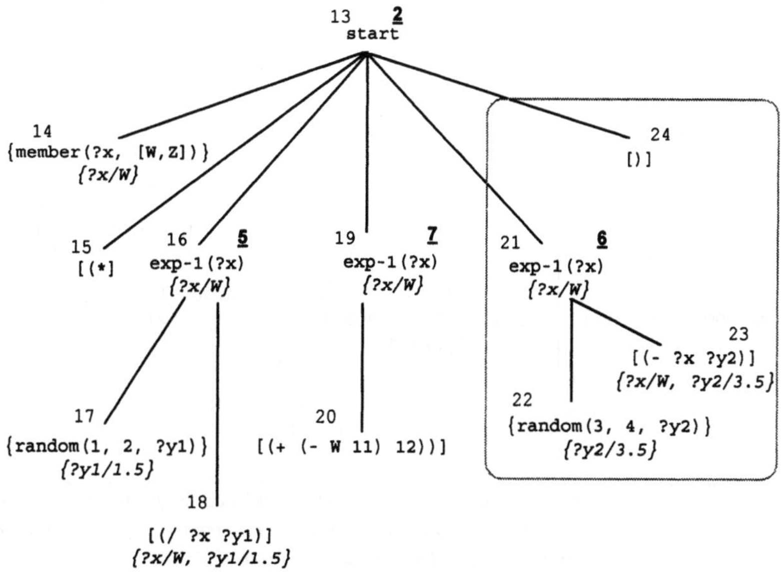

Figure 5.4: *The derivations tree of the secondary parental program* *(* (/ W 1.5) (+ (- W 11) 12) (- W 3.5)).*

In step 9 of the crossover algorithm in table 5.3, the offspring is generated. In the next step, it is returned as the solution after some house-keeping tasks have been performed. The house-keeping tasks update the bindings and the rule numbers of the sub-trees of the offspring. The offspring program of this example is `(* (- Z 3.5) (- Z 3.8) (/ Z 1.5))` and its derivation tree is shown in figure 5.5. It is interesting to find that the sub-tree **25** has the rule number 2. This indicates that the sub-tree is generated by the second grammar rule rather than the third rule applied to the primary parent. The second rule must be used because the terminal symbol `[(+]` is changed to `[(*]` and only the second rule can create the terminal `[(*]`. In fact, this situation is identified in step 14 of the function `is-valid` and a record is maintained so that the rule number can be changed to 2 by the house-keeping procedure.

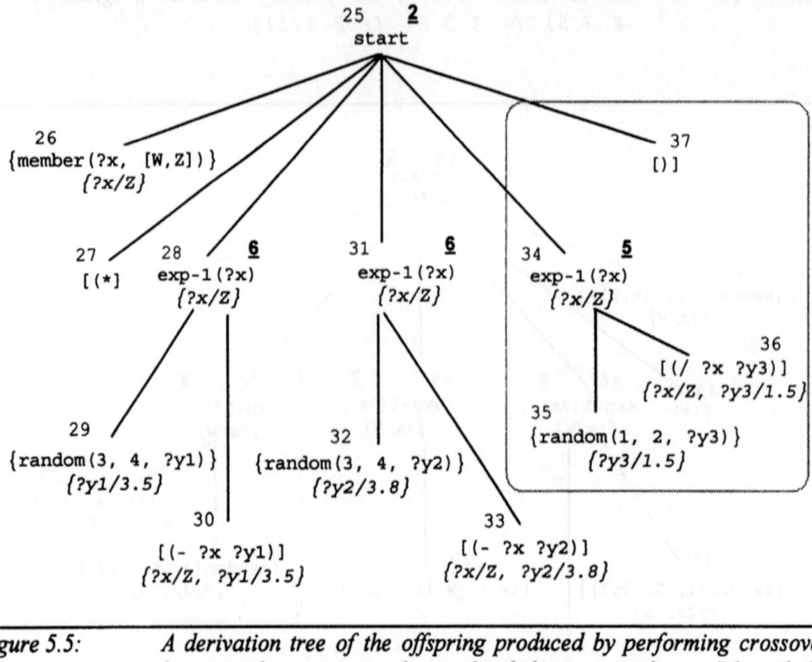

Figure 5.5: *A derivation tree of the offspring produced by performing crossover between the primary sub-tree **2** of the tree in figure 5.3 and the secondary sub-tree **15** of the tree in figure 5.4.*

In another example, the same primary and secondary parents are used. Assume that the SEL-PRIMARY-SUB-TREE **3** is selected in step 3 and the SEL-SECONDARY-SUB-TREE **16** is chosen in step 7 of the crossover algorithm. Now, the siblings of the SEL-PRIMARY-SUB-TREE **3** are the sub-trees **1**, **2**, **6**, **9**, and **12**. Although the SEL-PRIMARY-SUB-TREE has the bindings `{?x/Z}`, the instantiation of the logic variable `?x` to value `Z` is done by the sub-tree **1**. In other words, the SEL-PRIMARY-SUB-TREE has not established any binding. In step 12 of the function `is-valid`, the bindings `{?x/Z}` of the sub-tree **1** is not modified because the logic variable `?x` is instantiated to the value `Z` by the logic goal `member(?x, [W, Z])`. The bindings of the sub-trees **2** and **12** are not changed because they are already empty. The bindings `{?x/Z}` of the sub-trees **6** is changed to an empty list because the logic variable `?x` is bound to the value `Z` by the sub-tree **1**. Similarly, the bindings `{?x/Z}` of the sub-tree **9** is changed to an empty list.

The SEL-SECONDARY-SUB-TREE has the bindings `{?x/W}`, but the instantiation of `?x` is performed by the sub-tree **14**. Thus, the bindings of the SEL-SECONDARY-SUB-TREE is changed in step 13 to an empty list (i.e. the logic variable `?x` is not instantiated). In step 14, since the third rule satisfies all requirements, a valid offspring can be created.

The offspring program is `(+ (/ Z 1.5) (- Z 3.8) (/ Z 1.5))` and its derivation tree is depicted in figure 5.6. It should be emphasized that the constituent from the secondary parent is changed from `(/ W 1.5)` to `(/ Z 1.5)` in the offspring. This must be modified because the logic variable `?x` in the sub-tree **41** is instantiated to `Z` in the sub-tree **39**. The house-keeping procedure modifies the bindings of **41** in order to achieve this effect. This example demonstrates the use of logic grammars to enforce contextual-dependency between different constituents of a program.

As a further example, the same primary and secondary parents are used. Assume that the SEL-PRIMARY-SUB-TREE **6** is selected in step 3 of the crossover algorithm and the SEL-SECONDARY-SUB-TREE **19** is chosen in step 7. The variable SIBLINGS contains the sub-trees **1**, **2**, **3**, **9**, and **12**. In step 12 of the function `is-valid`, the bindings `{?x/Z}` of the sub-tree **1** is not modified. The bindings of the sub-trees **2** and **12** are not modified because they are already empty. The bindings `{?x/Z}` of the sub-trees **3** and **9** are changed to empty lists because the logic variable `?x` is bound to the value `Z` by the sub-tree **1**.

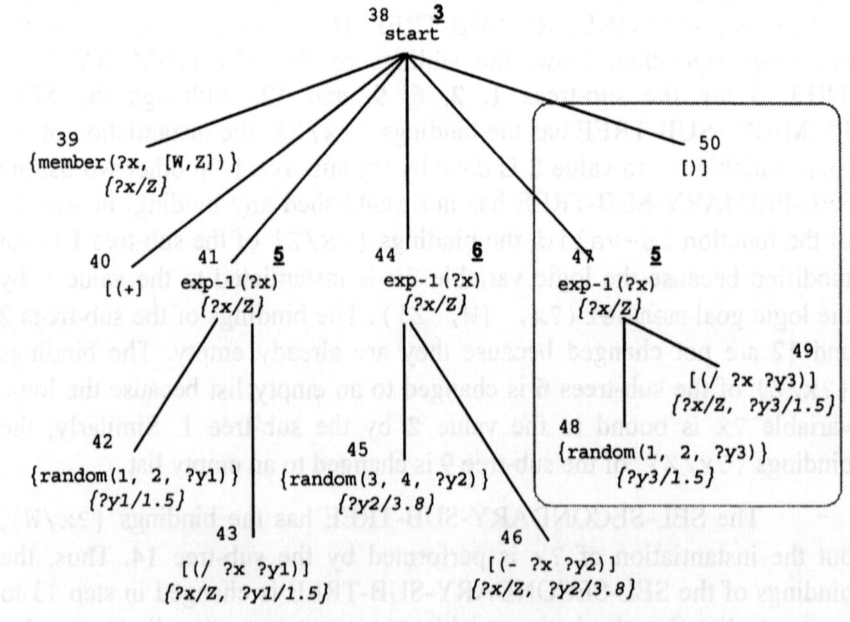

Figure 5.6: ***A derivation tree of the offspring produced by performing crossover between the primary sub-tree 3 of the tree in figure 5.3 and the secondary sub-tree 16 of the tree in figure 5.4.***

The SEL-SECONDARY-SUB-TREE **19** has the bindings {?x/W}. This sub-tree is generated from the rule 7 and the application of this rule will instantiate the logic variable ?x to the value W. In other words, the SEL-SECONDARY-SUB-TREE performs the instantiation of ?x to W. Thus, the bindings of the SEL-SECONDARY-SUB-TREE is not changed in step 13. It must be mentioned that the sub-tree **14** also instantiates ?x to W. Since the two sub-trees bind ?x to the same value W, this situation is valid. In step 14, no rule can be satisfied by the sub-trees in the variable SIBLINGS and the SEL-SECONDARY-SUB-TREE. Thus, the two sub-trees **6** and **19** cannot be mated. The reason is that the same logic variable ?x must be instantiated to different values Z and W: the sub-tree **19** requires the variable ?x to be instantiated to W while ?x must be instantiated to Z in the context of the primary parent. The function is-valid in table 5.4 can determine this situation and avoid the crossover algorithm from generating an offspring by exchanging the two sub-trees. Thus, only valid offspring can be produced and this operation can be achieved effectively.

In the following paragraphs, we estimate the time complexity of the crossover algorithm. Let the numbers of sub-trees in the primary and secondary derivation trees are respectively N_p and N_s. The numbers of sub-trees in the global variables PRIMARY-SUB-TREES and SECONDARY-SUB-TREES are respectively $N_p^{'}$ and $N_s^{'}$. Assume that the depth of the primary derivation tree is D_p (Depth starts from 0). Hence there are D_p rule applications along the longest path from the root to the leaf node. Let R be the grammar rule having the largest number of symbols on its right hand side. Then S is the number of symbols on the right hand side of R.

Since the most time-consuming operation of the crossover algorithm is step 8 which calls the function `is-valid`. We concentrate on the time complexity of this step first. In the worst case, this step will calls `is-valid` for $N_p^{'} * N_s^{'}$ times. In each execution of the function `is-valid`, the purpose of steps 11 to 13 is to find the bindings established solely by the SEL-SECONDARY-SUB-TREE and the siblings of the SEL-PRIMARY-SUB-TREE. Since the total number of sub-trees to be examined must be equal to or smaller than S, the steps can be completed in $S*C_r$ time, where C_r is the constant time to retrieve the bindings established solely by a particular sub-tree of the sub-trees being examined.

Step 14 is a loop that finds a grammar rule that can be satisfied. Suppose that the parent of the SEL-PRIMARY-SUB-TREE generates program fragments belonging to the category *CAT*. The loop examines all grammar rules for the category *CAT*. If there are N_r rules for *CAT*, step 14 repeats for N_r times.

In each iteration of step 14, the first three operations check whether the rule is satisfiable. These operations can be viewed as determining whether the SEL-SECONDARY-SUB-TREE and the sub-trees in the global variable SIBLINGS are unificable according to the rule (Mooney 1989). Since an efficient, linear time algorithm exists for unification (Paterson and Wegman 1978). These operations can be completed in $O(S)$ time (Mooney 1989).

The last operation of step 14 applies the function `is-consistent` whose time complexity depends on the depth D_c of the

PRIMARY-CROSSOVER-POINT, where $D_c \leq D_p$. There are three cases to be considered. Firstly, D_c cannot be equal to zero because the whole primary derivation tree cannot be crossed over with the SEL-SECONDARY-SUB-TREE. Secondly, if D_c is equal to 1, the function `is-consistent` can be completed in constant time C_1 because step 15 will be executed. Lastly, if D_c is greater than or equal to 2, the function `is-consistent` will recursively check the rules from the grandparent of the SEL-PRIMARY-SUB-TREE to the root of the primary derivation tree, to determine whether the rules are satisfied. As described previously, steps 16 and 17 can be completed in $S*C_r$ time and each rule can be checked in $O(S)$ time. In the worst case, the recursive process iterates for D_c times. Hence the function `is-consistent` can be completed in $[(D_c - 1) * (O(S) + S * C_r) + C_1]$ time.

In summary, each execution of the function `is-valid` requires $T_{\text{is-valid}}$ time which is presented in follows:

$$T_{\text{is-valid}} = S * C_r + N_r * [O(S) + ((D_c - 1) * (O(S) + S * C_r) + C_1)]$$

In the worst case, the depth D_c of the PRIMARY-CROSSOVER-POINT is equal to D_p. Then the worst case time complexity of the function `is-valid` is:

$$T_{\text{is-valid}} = S * C_r + N_r * [O(S) + ((D_p - 1) * (O(S) + S * C_r) + C_1)]$$

and the worst case time complexity of the crossover algorithm is:

$$T_{\text{crossover}} = N_p^{'} * N_s^{'} * T_{\text{is-valid}} + T_1 + T_2 + T_3 + T_4$$

where T_1 is the time used to perform steps 1 and 2, T_2 is the time employed to execute steps 3 and 4, T_3 is the execution time for steps 5 to 7, and T_4 is the time consumed by steps 9 and 10.

Obviously, T_1 depends on the sizes of the primary and secondary derivation trees, thus its complexity is $O(N_p + N_s)$. If the sub-trees in the variable PRIMARY-SUB-TREES are permuted randomly using an $O(N_p^{'})$ algorithm (Cormen et al. 1990) before executing steps 3 and 4, these steps can be completed in $T_2 = O(N_p^{'})$ time. Similarly, steps 5, 6, and 7 can be completed in $T_3 = O(N_p^{'} * N_s^{'})$ time. T_4 depends on the sizes of the primary and secondary derivation trees, thus its complexity is $O(N_p + N_s)$.

Assume that the first term of the above equation is much larger than the other terms, then the worst case time complexity is approximated by the following equation:

$$T_{crossover} \cong O(N_p' * N_s' * D_p * S * N_r).$$

If the primary derivation tree is a complete *m*-ary tree, then $\frac{m^{(D_p+1)}-1}{m-1} = N_p$. In other words, D_p is of the order of $\log_m(N_p)$. Furthermore, S and N_r are fixed for a given grammar. Thus, the worst case time complexity of the crossover algorithm is:

$$T_{crossover} \cong O(N_p' * N_s' * \log_m(N_p)).$$

Since the computation time consumed by performing crossover is insignificant when compare with the time used in evaluating the fitness of each program in the population. The issue of computational complexities of various crossover algorithms has not been addressed by other researchers in the field of Genetic Programming. In fact, it is easy to calculate that the worst case time complexity of the structure-preserving crossover algorithm of ADF (Koza 1994) is $O(N_{p_1} * N_{p_2})$, where N_{p_1} and N_{p_2} are respectively the sizes of the parental parse trees. Similarly, the crossover algorithm of STGP (Montana 1995) has the same complexity. Although the crossover algorithm of LOGENPRO is slightly slower than other algorithms by $O(\log_m(N_p))$, it is much more general and powerful than other algorithms.

5.4. Mutation of programs

The mutation operation in LOGENPRO introduces random modifications to programs in the population. Mutation is asexual and operates on only one program each time. A program in the population is selected as the parental program. The selection is based on various methods such as fitness proportionate and tournament selections. The algorithm in table 5.6 is used to produce an offspring program by mutation.

For example, assume that the program being mutated is `(+ (- Z 3.5) (- Z 3.8) (/ Z 1.5))` and the corresponding derivation tree is depicted in figure 5.3. In step 1 of the mutation algorithm, the global variable SUB-TREES contains the sub-trees **0**, **3**, and **6**. The frozen sub-trees **9**, **10**, **11**, and **12** are excluded. The sub-trees **1**, **4**, and **7** are also excluded because they contain logic goals of the grammar and thus should not be modified by genetic operations. The sub-trees **2**, **5**, and **8** containing terminal symbols are eliminated for two reasons. First, the mutation algorithm is significantly simplified if terminal symbol need not be modified. Second, the effect of mutating terminal symbols can be emulated by the crossover operation. Recalling the example described in the previous section, the primary sub-tree **2** are crossed with the secondary sub-tree **15** to generate the offspring `(* (- Z 3.5) (- Z 3.8) (/ Z 1.5))`. This offspring can be seen as the result of mutating the terminal symbol `[(+]` to the `[(*]`.

In step 2, a sub-tree in the variable SUB-TREES is selected randomly using a uniform distribution if the SUB-TREES is not empty. Otherwise, the mutation algorithm terminates without generating any modified program because no valid mutation can be found. In normal situation, this should not occur because it is almost always possible to select the whole derivation tree as the one to be mutated. The whole tree cannot be chosen only if it is frozen. The effect of mutating the whole tree, the sub-tree **0** in this example, is equivalent to generating a new program from scratch. A new program can be created successfully if the language specified by the grammar contains at least one program (this must be true for a grammar to be useful) and enough computational resources such as computer memory are available. Thus, the algorithm will fail to find a mutation only if the whole derivation tree is frozen or not enough computational resources are available.

```
Input:
   P:         The derivation tree of the parental program

Output:
   Return a new derivation tree if a valid offspring can be obtained
   by performing mutation, otherwise return false.

Function mutation(P)
{
      1.      Find all sub-trees of the derivation tree P of the
              parental program and store them into a global
              variable SUB-TREES, excluding all frozen sub-trees,
              logic goals, and terminal symbols
      2.      If SUB-TREES is not empty, select randomly a sub-tree
              from the SUB-TREES using a uniform distribution.
              Otherwise, terminate the algorithm without generating
              any offspring.
      3.      Designate the sub-tree selected as MUTATED-SUB-TREE.
              The root of the MUTATED-SUB-TREE is called the
              MUTATE-POINT. Remove the MUTATED-SUB-TREE from the
              variable SUB-TREES. The MUTATED-SUB-TREE must be
              generated from a non-terminal symbol of the grammar.
              Designate this non-terminal symbol as NON-TERMINAL.
              The NON-TERMINAL may have a list of arguments called
              ARGS.
      4.      For each argument in the ARGS, if it contains some
              logic variables, determine whether these variables
              are instantiated by other constituent of the
              derivation tree. If they are, bind the instantiated
              value to the variable. Otherwise, the variable is
              unbounded. Store the modified bindings to a global
              variable NEW-BINDINGS.
      5.      Create a new non-terminal symbol NEW-NON-TERMINAL
              from the NON-TERMINAL and the bindings in the
              variable NEW-BINDINGS.
      6.      Try to generate a new derivation tree NEW-SUB-TREE
              from the NEW-NON-TERMINAL using the deduction
              mechanism provided by LOGENPRO.
      7.      If a new derivation tree can be successfully created,
              the offspring is obtained by deleting the MUTATED-
              SUB-TREE from a copy of the parental derivation tree
              P and then impregnating the NEW-SUB-TREE at the
              MUTATE-POINT. Otherwise, go to step 3.
}
```

Table 5.6: *The mutation algorithm.*

Assume that the sub-tree **3** is selected as the MUTATED-SUB-TREE in step 2. In the next step, the sub-tree **3** is removed from the variable SUB-TREES. The NON-TERMINAL and the ARGS are exp-

1(?x) and {?x} respectively. Since the logic variable ?x is instantiated to Z in the sub-tree 1 by the logic goal member(?x, [W, Z]), the bindings {?x/Z} is stored into the variable NEW-BINDINGS in step 4.

In step 5, the new non-terminal NEW-NON-TERMINAL exp-1(Z) is created. Using this mechanism, contextual-dependent information can be transmitted between different parts of a program. In step 6, a new derivation tree for the S-expression (/ Z 1.9) can be obtained from the non-terminal symbol exp-1(Z) using the fifth rule of the grammar. This derivation tree is displayed in figure 5.7.

Since the NEW-SUB-TREE can be found, a new offspring is obtained by duplicating the genetic materials of its parental derivation tree, followed by deleting the MUTATED-SUB-TREE from the duplication, and then pasting the NEW-SUB-TREE at the MUTATE-POINT. The derivation tree of the offspring (+ (/ Z 1.9) (- Z 3.8) (/ Z 1.5)) can be found in figure 5.8.

LOGENPRO has an efficient implementation of the mutation algorithm. Moreover, an inference engine has been developed for deducing derivation trees (or programs) from a logic grammar given. Thus, only valid mutations can be performed and this operation can be achieved effectively and efficiently.

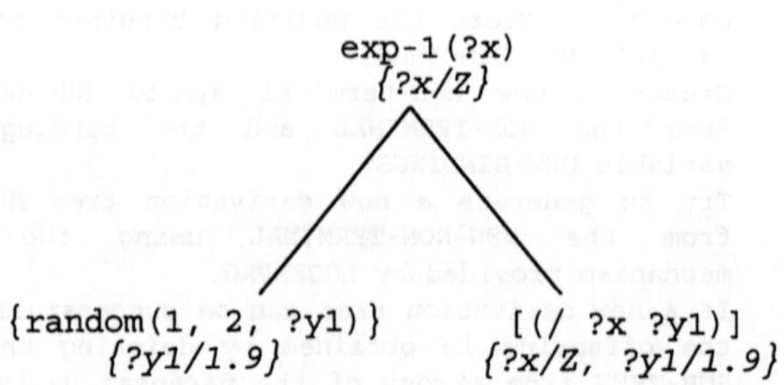

Figure 5.7: *A derivation tree generated from the non-terminal* exp-1(Z).

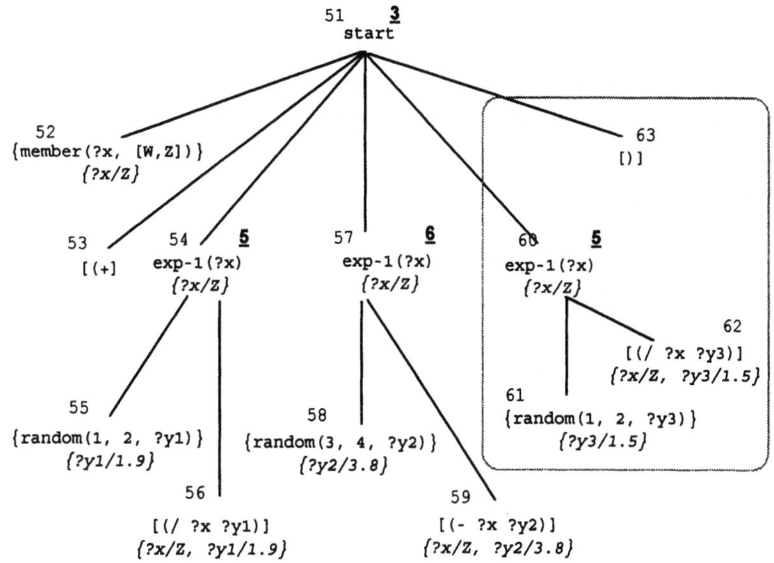

Figure 5.8: *A derivation tree of the offspring produced by performing mutation of the tree in figure 5.3 at the sub-tree 3.*

5.5. The Evolution Process of LOGENPRO

The problem of inducing S-expressions or logic programs can be formulated as a search for a highly fit program in the space of all possible programs (Mitchell 1982). In GP, this space is determined by the syntax of S-expressions in Lisp and the sets of terminals and functions. The search space of ILP is determined by the syntax of logic programs and the background knowledge. Thus, the search space is fixed once these elements are decided. On the other hand, the search space can be specified declaratively under the framework proposed because the space is determined by the logic grammar given.

LOGENPRO starts with an initial population of programs generated randomly, induced by other learning systems, or provided by the user. Logic grammars provide declarative descriptions of the valid programs that can appear in the initial population. A fitness function must be defined by the user to evaluate the fitness values of the programs.

Typically, each program is run over a set of fitness cases and the fitness function estimates its fitness by performing some statistical operations (e.g. average) to the values returned by this program.

Since each program generated in the evolution process must be executed. A compiler or an interpreter for the corresponding programming language must be available. This compiler or interpreter is called by the fitness function to compile or interpret the created programs. LOGENPRO can guarantee only that valid programs in the language specified by the logic grammar will be generated. However, it cannot ensure that the produced programs can be successfully compiled or interpreted if the appropriate compiler/interpreter is not provided by the user. Thus, the user must be very careful in designing the logic grammar and the fitness function. A high-level algorithm of LOGENPRO is presented in table 5.7.

The initial programs in generation 0 normally have poor performances. However, some programs in the population will be fitter than the others. Fitness of each program in the generation is estimated and the following process is iterated over many generations until the termination criterion is satisfied. The reproduction, sexual crossover, and asexual mutation are used to create new generation of programs from the current one. The reproduction involves selecting a program from the current generation and allowing it to survive by copying it into the next generation. Either fitness proportionate or tournament selection can be used.

The crossover is used to create a single offspring program from two parental programs selected. Mutation creates a modified offspring program from a parental program selected. Unlike crossover, the offspring program is usually similar to the parent program. Logic grammars are used to constraint the offspring programs that can be produced by these genetic operations.

This algorithm will produce populations of programs which tend to exhibit increasing average of fitness. LOGENPRO returns the best program found in any generation of a run as the result.

```
Input:
    Grammar:    It is a logic grammar that specifies the search space
                of programs.
    t           The termination function.
    f           The fitness function.

Output:
    A logic program induced by LOGENPRO.

Function LOGENPRO(Grammar, t, f)
{
    •   Translate the Grammar to a logic program.

    •   generation := 0.

    •   Initialize a population Pop(generation) of programs. They are
        generated by issuing the query ?-start(?Tree, ?S , []),
        provided from the user, or generated by other learning
        systems. If a program, Prog,  is provide by the user or
        generated by other learning systems, the program is
        translated to a derivation tree using the query
        ?-start(?Tree, ?P, []) where ?P contains the program Prog.

    •   Execute each program in the Pop(generation) and assign it a
        fitness value according to the fitness function f.

    •   While the termination function t is not satisfied do
            •   Create a new population Pop(generation+1) of programs
                by employing the reproduction, the crossover and the
                mutation. The operations are applied to programs
                chosen by either the fitness proportionate or
                tournament selections.
            •   Evaluate the fitness of each individual in the next
                population Pop(generation+1)
            •   generation := generation + 1.
    •   Return the best program found in any generation of the run.
}
```

Table 5.7: *A high-level algorithm of LOGENPRO.*

5.6. Discussion

We have proposed a framework for combining GP and ILP. This framework is based on a formalism of logic grammars. The formalism can represent context-sensitive information and domain-dependent knowledge. It is also very flexible and programs in various programming languages such as Lisp, Prolog, and C can be induced.

Since the framework is very flexible, different representations employed in other inductive learning systems can be specified easily. It facilitates the integration of LOGENPRO with other learning systems. One approach is to incorporate the learning techniques of other systems into LOGENPRO. These techniques include information guided hill-climbing (Quinlan 1990; 1991), explanation-based generalization (DeJong and Mooney 1986, Mitchell et al. 1986, Ellman 1989), explanation-based specialization (Minton 1989) and inverse resolution (Muggleton 1992). LOGENPRO can also invoke these systems as front-ends to generate the initial population. The advantage is that they can quickly find important and meaningful components (genetic materials) and embody these components into the initial population. The following chapters will illustrate some of these points clearly.

Chapter 6

DATA MINING APPLICATIONS USING LOGENPRO

The knowledge acquired by a data mining system can be expressed in different knowledge representations such as functional programs, decision trees, decision lists, production rules, and first-order logic programs. In the first section, we employ LOGENPRO to discover knowledge represented as functional programs. In the next section, LOGENPRO is used to induce knowledge represented in decision trees from a real-world database. Data mining systems induce knowledge from datasets which are frequently noisy (incorrect), incomplete, inconsistent, imprecise (fuzzy), and uncertain (Leung and Wong 1991a; 1991b; 1991c). In section 6.3, we employ LOGENPRO to combine evolutionary algorithms and a variation of FOIL (Quinlan 1990) to induce knowledge represented as logic programs from noisy datasets.

6.1. Learning Functional Programs

It seems that the framework proposed in the previous chapter is rather complicated but powerful. Consequently, the question of whether this framework can be applied easily arises. In the first sub-section, we show that this framework can emulate GP (Koza 1992; 1994, Koza et al. 1999) easily in learning S-expressions. A template is provided to facilitate the application of the framework. It must be emphasized that the example used in the first sub-section is deliberately constructed as simple as possible to illustrate the point. More realistic applications can be found in the following sub-sections.

6.1.1. Learning S-expressions Using LOGENPRO

A logic grammar template for learning S-expressions using the framework is depicted in table 6.1. To apply the template for a particular problem, various sets of terminals and primitive functions will substitute for the identifiers in italics.

Consider the problem of learning S-expressions such as `(- (* Z X) (+ Y Z))`. Using the terminology of GP, the set of primitive functions for this problem contains arithmetic operators +, –, and *. Each of them takes two arguments as inputs. The terminal set is `{X, Y, Z}`. The terminals can be treated as input arguments of the S-expression being learned.

It is observed that an S-expression is either a terminal or a function invocation. Thus an S-expression can be specified by the grammar rules 11 and 12 of the template in table 6.1. A function call consists of a list of elements enclosed by a pair of parentheses. The first element of the list is the name of the function and the other elements are arguments of the function. These arguments are also S-expressions. Since the primitives of a problem may have different numbers of arguments, there are a variety of function invocations. This fact can be specified by the grammar rules 13a, 13b, ..., 13n, and 14a, 14b, ..., 14n.

Since an S-expression containing only a terminal is usually excluded from consideration as a solution. This fact is declared by the grammar rule 10 which specifies that the target solution must be a function invocation. The non-terminal symbol `term` specifies the terminal set of the problem domain. For the problem studied in this sub-section, the terminal set is represented as:

```
term ->   { member(?w, [X, Y, Z]) }, [?w].
```

where the goal `member(?w, [X, Y, Z])` instantiates the logic variable `?x` to one of the values in the list `[X, Y, Z]`. This grammar rule is obtained from rule 15 in the template by replacing the identifier *`<TERMINAL SET>`* with `[X, Y, Z]`.

```
10:   start        ->   function.
11:   s-exp        ->   term.
12:   s-exp        ->   function.

13a:  function     ->   function-0.
13b:  function     ->   function-1.
13c:  function     ->   function-2.
  ...
  ...
13n:  function     ->   function-n.

14a:  function-0   ->   [(], op-0, [)].
14b:  function-1   ->   [(], op-1, s-exp, [)].
14c:  function-2   ->   [(], op-2, s-exp, s-exp, [)].
  ...
  ...
14n:  function-n   ->   [(], op-n, s-exp, ...,
                        s-exp, [)].

15:   term   ->   {member(?w, <TERMINAL SET>)}, [?w].

16a:  op-0   ->   {member(?w,<FUNCTION SET-0>)}, [?w].
16b:  op-1   ->   {member(?w,<FUNCTION SET-1>)}, [?w].
16c:  op-2   ->   {member(?w,<FUNCTION SET-2>)}, [?w].
  ...
  ...
16n:  op-n   ->   {member(?w,<FUNCTION SET-n>)}, [?w].
```

Table 6.1: A template for learning S-expressions using the LOGENPRO.

The non-terminal symbols `op-0`, `op-1`, ..., `op-n` in the template specify primitive functions with different numbers of arguments. They represent the primitive functions of the problem domain. For the above problem, all primitives have two arguments, thus only `op-2` will be used. It is represented by the following rule:

```
op-2 ->    { member(?w, [+, -, *]) }, [?w].
```

This rule is obtained from the grammar rule 16c in the template by replacing the identifier *<FUNCTION SET-2>* with `[+, -, *]`. Other non-terminal symbols such as `op-0`, `op-1`, `op-3`, ..., `op-n` will be used if the problem domain requires primitives with the corresponding numbers of arguments. In summary, the logic grammar for the example is:

```
start        ->   function.
s-exp        ->   term.
s-exp        ->   function.
function     ->   function-2.
function-2 ->     [(],op-2, s-exp, s-exp,[)].
term  ->      { member(?w, [X, Y, Z]) }, [?w].
op-2  ->      { member(?w, [+, -, *]) }, [?w].
```

6.1.2. The DOT PRODUCT Problem

In this sub-section, we describe how to use LOGENPRO to emulate traditional GP (Koza 1992). GP has the limitation that all the variables, constants, arguments for functions, and values returned from functions must be of the same data type. This limitation leads to the difficulty of inducing even some rather simple and straightforward functional programs. For example, one of these programs calculates the dot product of two given numeric vectors of the same size. Let `X` and `Y` be the two input vectors; then the dot product is obtained by the following S-expression:

```
(apply (function +)
       (mapcar (function *) X Y))
```

Let us use this example for illustrative comparisons below. To induce a functional program using LOGENPRO, we have to determine the logic grammar, fitness cases, fitness function, and termination criterion. The logic grammar for learning functional programs is given in table 6.2. In this grammar, we employ the argument of the grammar symbol `s-expr` to designate the data type of the result returned by the S-expression generated from the grammar symbol. For example,

```
(mapcar (function +) X
        (mapcar (function *) X Y))
```

is generated from the grammar symbol `s-expr([list, number, n])` because it returns a numeric vector of size *n*. Similarly, the symbol `s-expr(number)` can produce `(apply (function *) X)` that returns a number.

The terminal symbols `[+]`, `[-]`, and `[*]` represent functions that perform ordinary addition, subtraction, and multiplication, respectively. The symbol `[%]` represents a function that normally returns the quotient. However, if division by zero is attempted, the function returns 1.0. The symbol `[protected-log]` is a function that calculates the logarithm of the input argument x if x is larger than zero, otherwise it returns 1.0. The logic goal `random(-10, 10, ?a)` generates a random floating point number between -10 and 10 and instantiates ?a to the random number generated.

```
20:start      -> s-expr(number).
21:s-expr([list, number, ?n])
             -> [ (mapcar (function ], op2, [ ) ] ,
                s-expr([list, number, ?n]),
                s-expr([list, number, ?n]),[ ) ].
22:s-expr([list, number, ?n])
             -> [ (mapcar (function ], op1, [ ) ] ,
                s-expr([list, number, ?n]),[ ) ].
23:s-expr([list, number, ?n])
             -> term([list, number, ?n]).
24:s-expr(number) -> term(number).
25:s-expr(number) -> [ (apply (function ], op2,[ ) ] ,
                     s-expr([list, number, ?n]),[ ) ].
26:s-expr(number) -> [ ( ], op2, s-expr(number),
                     s-expr(number), [ ) ].
27:s-expr(number) -> [ ( ], op1, s-expr(number),
                     [ ) ].
28:op2            -> [ + ].
29:op2            -> [ - ].
30:op2            -> [ * ].
31:op2            -> [ % ].
32:op1            -> [ protected-log ].
33:term( [list, number, n] )  -> [ X ].
34:term( [list, number, n] )  -> [ Y ].
35:term( number ) -> { random(-10, 10, ?a) },   [ ?a ].
```

Table 6.2: The logic grammar for the DOT PRODUCT problem.

Ten random fitness cases are used for training. Each case is a 3-tuples ‹X_i, Y_i, Z_i›, where $1 \leq i \leq 10$, X_i and Y_i are vectors of size 3, and Z_i is the corresponding dot product. The fitness function calculates the sum, taken over the ten fitness cases, of the absolute values of the difference between Z_i and the value returned by the S-expression for $\boldsymbol{X}_i$ and $\boldsymbol{Y}_i$. Let S be an S-expression and $S(\boldsymbol{X}_i, \boldsymbol{Y}_i)$ be the value returned by the S-expression for $\boldsymbol{X}_i$ and $\boldsymbol{Y}_i$. The fitness function Val is defined as follows:

$$\mathrm{Val}(S) = \sum_{i=1}^{10} |S(\boldsymbol{X}_i, \boldsymbol{Y}_i) - Z_i|$$

A fitness case is said to be covered by an S-expression if the value returned by it is within 0.01 of the desired value. An S-expression that covers all training cases is further evaluated on a testing set containing 1000 random fitness cases. LOGENPRO will stop if the maximum number of generations of 100 is reached or an S-expression that covers all testing fitness cases is found.

For traditional GP, the terminal set $\boldsymbol{T}$ is `{X, Y, R}` where `R` is the ephemeral random floating point constant. `R` takes on a different random floating point value between -10.0 and 10.0 whenever it appears in an individual program in the initial population (Koza 1992). The function set $\boldsymbol{F}$ is `{protected+, protected-, protected*, protected%, protected-log, vector+, vector-, vector*, vector%, vector-log, apply+, apply-, apply*, apply%}`, taking 2, 2, 2, 2, 1, 2, 2, 2, 2, 1, 1, 1, 1, and 1 arguments, respectively.

The primitive functions `protected+`, `protected-`, and `protected*`, respectively, perform addition, subtraction, and multiplication if the two input arguments `X` and `Y` are both numbers. Otherwise, they return 0. The function `protected%` returns the quotient. However, if division by zero is attempted or the two arguments are not numbers, `protected%` returns 1.0. The function `protected-log` finds the logarithm of the argument `X` if `X` is a number larger than zero. Otherwise, `protected-log` returns 1.0.

The functions `vector+`, `vector-`, `vector*`, and `vector%`, respectively, perform vector addition, subtract, multiplication, and division if the two input arguments `X` and `Y` are numeric vectors with the same size; otherwise they return zero. The primitive function `vector-log` performs the following S-expression:

```
(mapcar (function protected-log) X),
```

if the input argument `X` is a numeric vector; otherwise, it returns zero. The functions `apply+`, `apply-`, `apply*`, and `apply%`, respectively, perform the following S-expressions if the input argument `X` is a numeric vector:

```
(apply (function protected+) X),
(apply (function protected-) X),
(apply (function protected*) X), and
(apply (function protected%) X),
```

otherwise they return zero.

It should be emphasized that the primitive functions `vector+`, `vector-`, `vector*`, and `vector%` can be emulated by using the grammar rules 21, 28, 29, 30, and 31. The primitive function `vector-log` can be emulated by using the grammar rules 22 and 32. The primitive functions `apply+`, `apply-`, `apply*`, and `apply%` can be emulated by using the grammar rules 25, 28, 29, 30, and 31. Thus, the set of effective functions represented by the grammar in table 6.2 is equivalent to the set used in traditional GP. The functions `mapcar` and `apply` cannot be used in traditional GP because the first argument of these functions must be a valid operators such as `+`, `-`, `*`, or `%`. But traditional GP cannot enforce this constraint; thus, we have to create some special functions such as `vector+` and `apply+`, to handle this problem.

The fitness cases, the fitness function, and the termination criterion are the same as those used by LOGENPRO. Three experiments have been performed. The first one evaluates the performance of LOGENPRO using a population of 100 programs. The other two experiments evaluate the performance of GP using, respectively, populations of 100 and 1000 programs. In each experiment, over sixty trials have been attempted and the results are summarized in figure 6.1. The figure delineates the best standardized fitness values for increasing generations for the three experiments. From the curves in figures 6.1, the lower values are better, thus, LOGENPRO has a performance superior to that of GP.

The curves in figure 6.2(a) show the experimentally observed cumulative probability of success $P(M, i)$ of solving the problem by generation i using a population of M programs (Koza 1992). The curves in figure 6.2(b) show the number of programs $I(M, i, z)$ that must be processed to produce a solution by generation i with a probability z (Koza 1992). Throughout this chapter, the probability z is set to 0.99. The curve for GP with a population of 100 programs is not depicted because the values are extremely large. For LOGENPRO curve, $I(M, i, z)$ reaches a minimum value of 8800 at generation 21. On the other hand, the minimum value of $I(M, i, z)$ for GP with population size of 1000 is 66000 at generation 1. LOGENPRO can find a solution much faster than GP, and the computation (i.e. $I(M, i, z)$) required by LOGENPRO is much smaller than that of GP.

The performance of LOGENPRO is better because knowledge of data type has been encoded in the grammar. Consequent, invalid programs such as

```
(+ (apply (function +) 9) 9)
```

cannot be produced. On the other hand, traditional GP may create the equivalent invalid program `(+ (apply+ 9) 9)`. In other words, the search space of traditional GP is larger than that of LOGENPRO. But, the former contains many invalid programs.

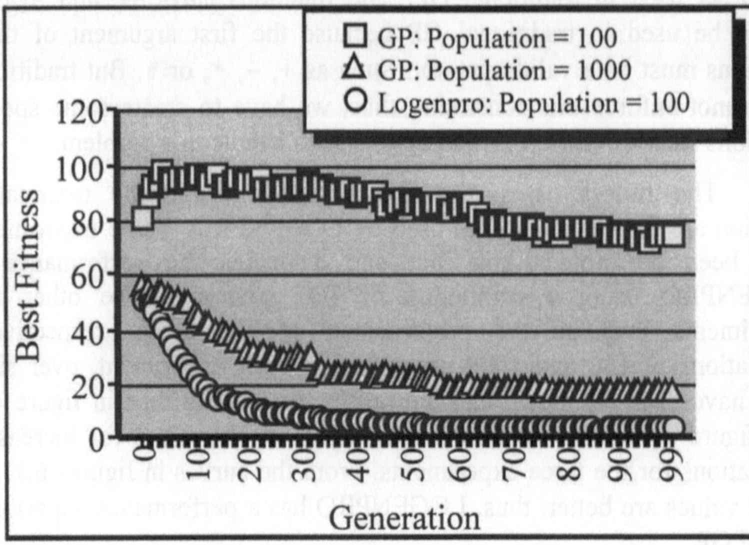

Figure 6.1: The fitness curves showing the best fitness values for the DOT PRODUCT problem.

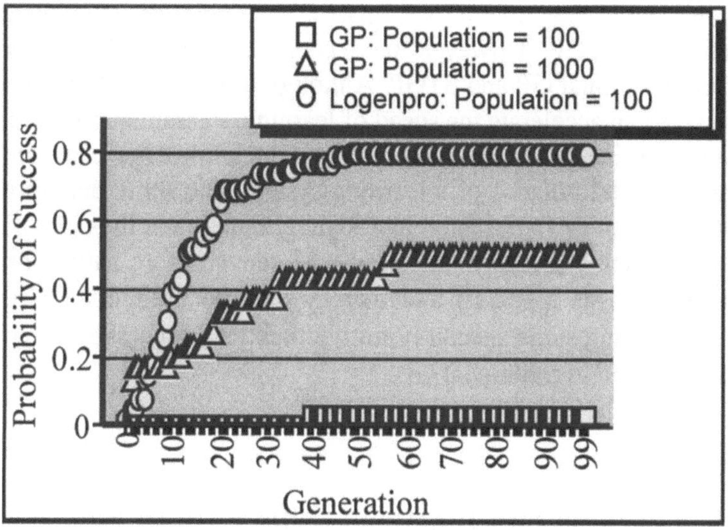

(a)

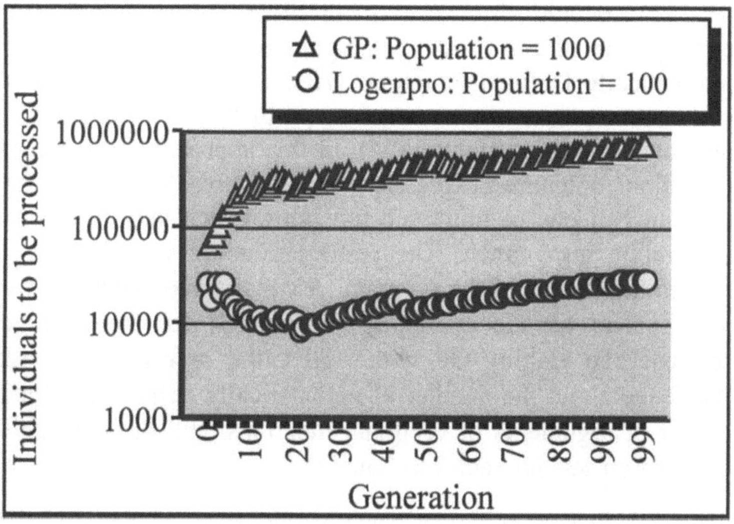

(b)

Figure 6.2: *The performance curves showing (a) cumulative probability of success P(M, i) and (b) I(M, i, z) for the DOT PRODUCT problem.*

The idea of applying knowledge of data type to accelerate learning has been investigated independently by Montana (1995) in his Strongly Typed Genetic Programming (STGP). He presents many examples involving vector and matrix manipulation to illustrate the operation of STGP. However, he has not compared the performance between traditional GP and STGP. Although it is commonly believed that knowledge can accelerate the speed of learning, Pazzani and Kibler (1992) showed that inappropriate and/or redundant knowledge can sometimes degrade the performance of a learning system. We show that knowledge of data type can be represented in a logic grammar and thus LOGENPRO can emulate the effect of STGP easily. Moreover, more natural primitive functions such as `mapcar` and `apply`, can be used in LOGENPRO, rather than using some special primitive functions such as `vector+` and `apply+`, found in traditional GP.

6.1.3. Learning Sub-functions Using Explicit Knowledge

Automatic discovery of problem representation primitives is certainly one of the most challenging research areas in GP. GP with Automatically Defined Functions (ADFs) is one of the approaches that have been proposed to acquire problem representation primitives automatically (Koza 1992; 1994). In this approach, each program in the population contains an expression, called the result-producing branch, and definitions of one or more sub-functions which may be invoked by the result-producing branch. The result-producing branch is evaluated to produce the fitness of the program. A constrained syntactic structure and some special genetic operators are required for the evolution of the programs. To employ GP with ADFs, the user must provide explicit knowledge about the number of automatically defined sub-functions, the number of arguments of each sub-functions, and the allowable terminal and function sets for each sub-function.

In this section, we demonstrate how to use LOGENPRO to emulate GP with ADFs. LOGENPRO is employed to learn a sub-function that calculates dot product and employ this sub-function in the main program. In other words, it is expected to induce the following S-expression:

```
(progn
  (defun ADF0 (arg0 arg1)
     (apply (function +)
        (mapcar (function *) arg0 arg1)))
  (+ (ADF0 X Y) (ADF0 Y Z)))
```

The logic grammar for this problem is depicted in table 6.3. In the grammar, we employ the argument of the grammar symbol `s-expr` to designate the data type of the result returned by the S-expression generated from the grammar symbol. The terminal symbols `[+]`, `[-]`, and `[*]` represent functions that perform ordinary addition, subtraction, and multiplication, respectively.

Ten random fitness cases are used for training. Each case is a 4-tuples $\langle \boldsymbol{X}_i, \boldsymbol{Y}_i, \boldsymbol{Z}_i, R_i \rangle$, where $1 \le i \le 10$, $\boldsymbol{X}_i$, $\boldsymbol{Y}_i$, and $\boldsymbol{Z}_i$ are vectors of size 3, and R_i is the corresponding desired result. The fitness function calculates the sum, taken over the ten fitness cases, of the absolute values of the difference between R_i and the value returned by the S-expression for $\boldsymbol{X}_i$, $\boldsymbol{Y}_i$, and $\boldsymbol{Z}_i$. Let S be an S-expression and $S(\boldsymbol{X}_i, \boldsymbol{Y}_i, \boldsymbol{Z}_i)$ be the value returned by the S-expression for $\boldsymbol{X}_i$, $\boldsymbol{Y}_i$, and $\boldsymbol{Z}_i$. The fitness function Val is defined as follows:

$$\mathrm{Val}(S) = \sum_{i=1}^{10} |S(\boldsymbol{X}_i, \boldsymbol{Y}_i, \boldsymbol{Z}_i) - R_i|$$

A fitness case is said to be covered by an S-expression if the value returned by it is within 0.01 of the desired value. An S-expression that covers all training cases is further evaluated on a testing set containing 1000 random fitness cases. LOGENPRO will stop if the maximum number of generations of 50 is reached or an S-expression that covers all testing fitness cases is found.

For GP with ADFs (with the modified genetic operator), the terminal set $\boldsymbol{T}_0$ for the automatically defined function (ADF0) is `{arg0, arg1}` and the function set $\boldsymbol{F}_0$ is `{protected+, protected-, protected*, vector+, vector-, vector*, apply+, apply-, apply*}`, taking 2, 2, 2, 2, 2, 2, 1, 1, and 1 arguments, respectively. The terminal set $\boldsymbol{T}_r$ for the result producing branch is `{X, Y, Z}` and the function set $\boldsymbol{F}_r$ is `{protected+, protected-, protected*, vector+, vector-, vector*, apply+, apply-, apply*, ADF0}`, taking 2, 2, 2, 2, 2, 2, 1, 1, 1, and 2 arguments, respectively. The primitive functions were defined in the previous sub-section. The fitness cases, the fitness function, and the termination criterion are the same as the ones used by LOGENPRO. We evaluate the performance of LOGENPRO and the ADFs using populations of 100 and 1000 programs, respectively.

```
start                          -> [(progn (defun ADF0 ],
                                  [(arg0 arg1)],
                                  s-expr2(number), [)],
                                  s-expr(number), [)].
s-expr([list, number, ?n])     -> [ (mapcar (function ], op2,
                                  [ ) ]
                                  s-expr([list, number, ?n]),
                                  s-expr([list, number, ?n]),[ ) ].
s-expr([list, number, ?n])     -> term([list, number, ?n]).
s-expr(number)                 -> [ (apply (function ], op2,
                                  [ ) ] ,
                                  s-expr([list, number, ?n]),[ ) ].
s-expr(number)                 -> [ ( ], op2, s-expr(number),
                                  s-expr(number), [ ) ].
s-expr(number)                 -> [ (ADF0 ],
                                  s-expr([list, number, ?n]),
                                  s-expr([list, number, ?n]), [ ) ].
term([list, number, n])        -> [ X ].
term([list, number, n])        -> [ Y ].
term([list, number, n])        -> [ Z ].
s-expr2([list, number, ?n])    -> [ (mapcar (function ], op2,
                                  [ ) ] ,
                                  s-expr2([list, number, ?n]),
                                  s-expr2([list, number, ?n]),[ ) ].
s-expr2([list, number, ?n])    -> term2([list, number, ?n]).
s-expr2(number)                -> [ (apply (function ], op2,
                                  [ ) ]
                                  s-expr2([list, number, ?n]),[ ) ].
s-expr2(number)                -> [ ( ], op2, s-expr2(number),
                                  s-expr2(number), [ ) ].
term2([list, number, n])       -> [ arg0 ].
term2([list, number, n])       -> [ arg1 ].
op2                            -> [ + ].
op2                            -> [ - ].
op2                            -> [ * ].
```

Table 6.3: ***The logic grammar for the sub-function problem.***

Thirty trials have been attempted and the results are summarized in figures 6.3 and 6.4. Figure 6.3 shows, by generation, the fitness (error) of the best program in a population. These curves are found by averaging the results obtained in thirty different runs using various random number seeds and fitness cases. From these curves, LOGENPRO has performance superior to that of GP with ADFs. The curves in figure 6.4(a) show the experimentally observed cumulative probability of success $P(M, i)$ of solving the problem by generation i using a population of M programs. The curves in figure 6.4(b) show the number of programs $I(M, i, z)$ that must be processed to produce a solution by generation i with a probability z of 0.99. The curve for LOGENPRO reaches a minimum value of 4900 at generation 6. On the other hand, the minimum value of $I(M, i, z)$ for GP with ADFs is 5712000 at generation 41. This experiment clearly shows the advantage of LOGENPRO. By employing various knowledge about the problem being solved, LOGENPRO can find a solution much faster than GP with ADFs and the computation (i.e. $I(M, i, z)$) required by LOGENPRO is much smaller than that of GP with ADFs.

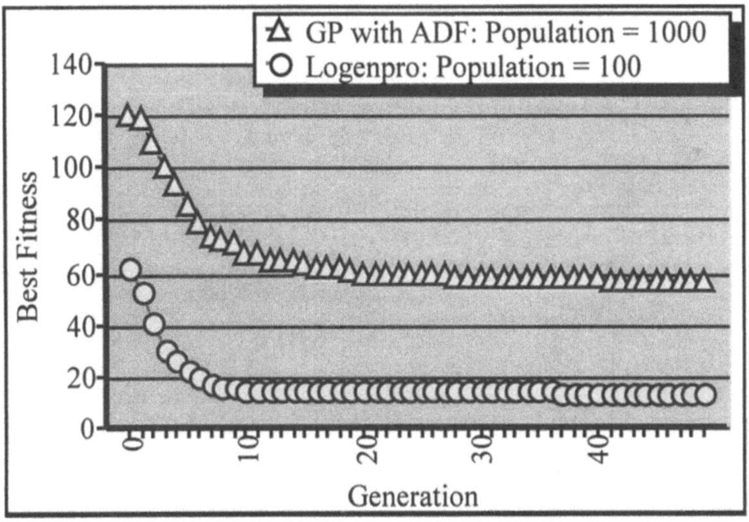

Figure 6.3: *The fitness curves showing the best fitness values for the sub-function problem.*

This experiment demonstrates that LOGENPRO can emulate GP with ADFs and represent easily the knowledge needed for using GP with ADFs. Moreover, LOGENPRO can employ other knowledge such as argument types in a unified framework. It has performance superior to that of GP with ADFs when more domain-dependent knowledge is available. One advantage of LOGENPRO is that it can emulate the effects of STGP and GP with ADFs simultaneously and easily.

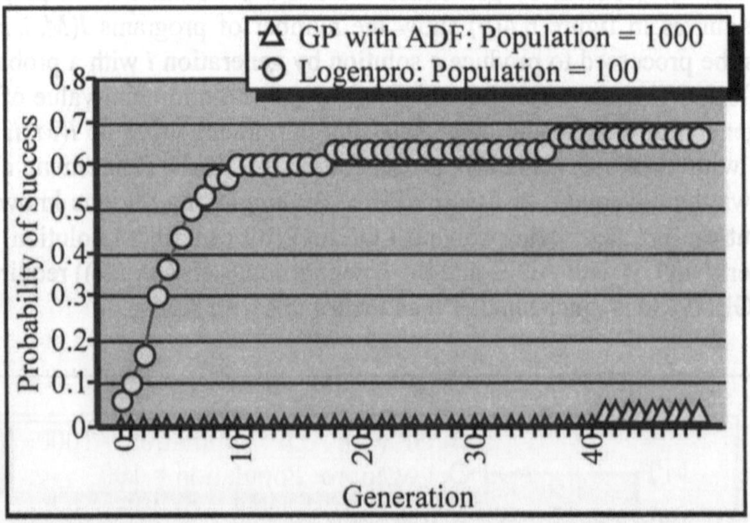

(a)

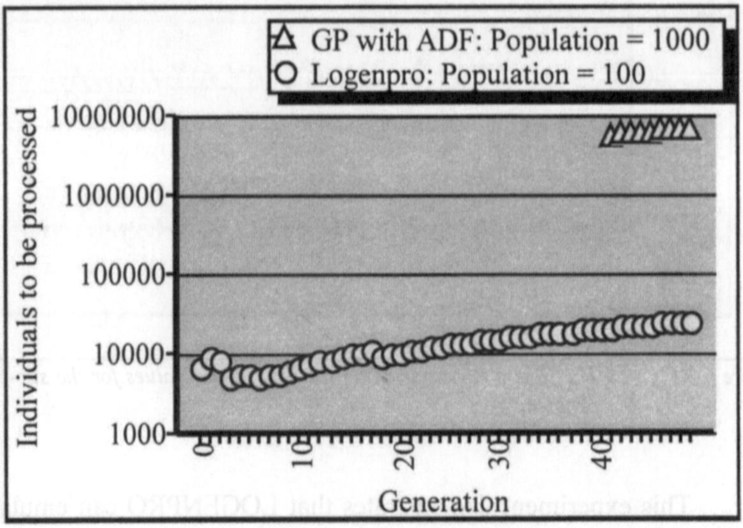

(b)

Figure 6.4: ***The performance curves showing (a) cumulative probability of success P(M, i) and (b) I(M, i, z) for the sub-function problem.***

6.2. Inducing Decision Trees Using LOGENPRO

In this section, we illustrate the application of LOGENPRO in inducing decision trees. We describe how to represent decision trees as S-expressions in sub-section 6.2.1. The credit screening problem used in the experiment is explained in the subsequent sub-section. We then present the results of the experiment in sub-section 6.2.3.

6.2.1. Representing Decision Trees as S-expressions

Koza (1992) presented a method to represent decision trees as S-expressions. For example, the decision tree in figure 2.1 is represented as the S-expression in table 6.4(a).

In the S-expression, the constants such as `positive` and `negative` representing the class names in this problem. These constants form the set of terminals in GP. On the other hand, the attribute-testing functions such as `outlook-test` and `windy-test` are obtained by transforming each of the attributes in the problem into a function. Thus, there are as many attribute-testing functions as there are attributes. These functions form the set of primitive functions in GP.

Consider the attribute outlook, it can assume one of three possible values. Therefore, the function `outlook-test` has three arguments and operates in the following way:

- if the value of the attribute outlook of the current example is sunny, the function returns its first argument as its return value;
- if the value of the attribute outlook of the current example is overcast, the function returns its second argument as its return value;
- if the value of the attribute outlook of the current example is rainy, the function returns its third argument as its return value;

The implementation of the function `outlook-test` is depicted in table 6.4(c). In this implementation, `X` is a global variable that stores the current example being evaluated. Since an example belongs to the class `EXAMPLES` depicted in table 6.4(b), the S-expression `(outlook X)` returns the value of the attribute outlook of the example stored in `X`. The constants `sunny` and `overcast` represent the attribute values of the attribute outlook.

```
(outlook-test
  (humidity-test 'negative 'positive)
  'positive
  (windy-test 'negative 'positive))
```

(a)

```
(defclass EXAMPLES ()
  ((temperature :accessor temperature)
   ;; The value of the attribute temperature can be
   ;; either hot, mild, or cool.
   (humidity  :accessor humidity)
   ;; The value of the attribute humidity can be
   ;; either high, or normal.
   (outlook   :accessor outlook)
   ;; The value of the attribute outlook can be either
   ;; sunny, overcast, or rain.
   (windy     :accessor windy)))
   ;; The value of the attribute windy can be either
   ;; true, or false.
```

(b)

```
(defun outlook-test (arg1 arg2 arg3)
 (cond ((equal (outlook X) 'sunny) arg1)
       (equal (outlook X) 'overcast) arg2)
       (t arg3)))
```

(c)

Table 6.4: ***(a) An S-expression that represents the decision tree in figure 2.1. (b) The class definition of the training and testing examples. (c) A definition of the primitive function outlook-test.***

To classify a new example, it is first stored into the global variable `X`. It is then presented to an S-expression representing a decision tree. The outermost function tests the designated attribute of the example and then executes the particular argument designated by the outcome of the test. If the designated argument is a constant, the function returns the corresponding class names (i.e. `positive` or `negative`). If the designated argument is another function, the above process is repeated until a constant is returned. In summary, the S-expression is a representation of a decision tree that classifies an example into one of the classes.

6.2.2. The Credit Screening Problem

The aim of this problem is to induce decision trees or rules for assessing applications for credit cards. This problem was studied by Quinlan in his ID3 and C4.5 systems (Quinlan 1987; 1992). The original dataset of this problem was provided by Quinlan and stored in the UCI Repository of Machine Learning Databases and Domain Theories. The dataset was modified in the Statlog project (Michie et al. 1994) so that one of the 15 attributes was removed. The modified dataset has a good mix of attributes of different types. There are 690 instances, 14 attributes and two class names. There are 307 positive instances (44.5%) and 383 negative instances (55.5%).

All attribute names, class names, and attribute values were changed to meaningless symbols to protect confidentiality of the data. Thus, interpretations of the induced decision trees or rules are relatively difficult. This dataset is interesting because there is a good mix of attribute types: linear, nominal with small numbers of values, and nominal with larger numbers of values. The attribute names, types, and values are depicted in table 6.5.

Attribute name	Attribute type	Attribute values
A1	nominal	{a, b}
A2	linear	13.75 - 80.25
A3	linear	0 - 28
A4	nominal	{g, p, gg}
A5	nominal	{c, d, cc, i, j, k, m, r, q, w, x, e, aa, ff}
A6	nominal	{v, h, bb, j, n, z, dd, ff, o}
A7	linear	0 - 28.5
A8	nominal	{t, f}
A9	nominal	{t, f}
A10	linear	0 - 67
A11	nominal	{t, f}
A12	nominal	{g, p, s}
A13	linear	0 - 2000
A14	linear	0 - 100001
class	nominal	{positive, negative}

Table 6.5: The attribute names, types, and values attributes of the credit screening problem.

There are 37 instances (5%) having one or more missing attribute values. The frequencies of missing values from different attributes are summarized as follows:

Attribute name	Frequency
A1	12
A2	12
A4	6
A5	9
A6	9
A13	13

For our purposes, we replaced the missing values by the overall medians or means.

6.2.3. The Experiment

In this sub-section, we describe how to use LOGENPRO to induce decision trees for the credit screening problem. The representation scheme described in sub-section 6.2.1 is not used directly because it can only express decisions on nominal attributes. To handle linear attributes using the representation, we must first transform these attributes into nominal attributes by assigning disjoint intervals of values to various symbols. Thus, the sizes and the number of intervals must be determined before applying the representation scheme to the credit screening problem.

For example, the range of the values of the attribute A2 is between 13.75 and 80.25. By examining the distribution of the attribute values, the range may be divided into two mutual exclusive intervals: from inclusive 13.75 to exclusive 40; from inclusive 40 to inclusive 80.25. The transformed attribute can be represented as the following attribute-testing function `A2-test`:

```
(defun A2-test (arg1 arg2)
  (if (>= (A2 X) 40)
   arg2
   arg1))
```

In this function, `X` is a global variable that stores the current example being evaluated. Since an example belongs to the class `EXAMPLES` depicted in table 6.6, the S-expression `(A2 X)` returns the value of the attribute A2 of the example stored in `X`. The function `A2-test` has two arguments and operates in the following way:

- if the value of the attribute A2 is greater than or equal to 40, the function returns its second argument as its return value;
- Otherwise, the function returns its first argument as its return value;

The major problem of this representation is that one or more intervals must be determined before performing induction. If the sizes and the number of intervals are inappropriate, they will greatly reduce the performance of the learning system. In order to tackle this problem, we decide that the number of intervals of all linear attributes is fixed to two, and allow the sizes of these intervals to adjust dynamically during the evolution process.

```
(defclass EXAMPLES ()
  ((A1  :accessor A1)
   (A2  :accessor A2)
   (A3  :accessor A3)
   (A4  :accessor A4)
   (A5  :accessor A5)
   (A6  :accessor A6)
   (A7  :accessor A7)
   (A8  :accessor A8)
   (A9  :accessor A9)
   (A10 :accessor A10)
   (A11 :accessor A11)
   (A12 :accessor A12)
   (A13 :accessor A13)
   (A14 :accessor A14)))
```

Table 6.6: The class definition of the training and testing examples.

Thus, the following attribute-testing function `A2-test` is used in our representation:

```
(defun A2-test (exp arg1 arg2)
  (if (>= (A2 X) exp)
  arg2
  arg1))
```

This function has three arguments and operates in the following way:

- if the value of the attribute A2 is greater than or equal to the value of the first argument, the function returns its third argument as its return value;
- Otherwise, the function returns its second argument as its return value;

From this function, we can observe that the first argument `exp` must return a numerical value while the other two arguments, `arg1` and `arg2`, must return a class name. In other words, data types must be used to guarantee only appropriate S-expressions can appear as a particular argument of a particular primitive function.

To induce a functional program using LOGENPRO, We have to determine the logic grammar, fitness cases, fitness functions, and termination criterion. The logic grammar for the credit screening problem is given in table 6.7. In this grammar, we employ the grammar symbol exp to designate the S-expression that returns a numerical value and the grammar symbol node to designate the S-expression that returns a class name.

```
start    ->    node.
node     ->    [ (A1 ], node, node, [ ) ].
node     ->    [ (A2 ], exp, node, node, [ ) ].
node     ->    [ (A3 ], exp, node, node, [ ) ].
node     ->    [ (A4 ], node, node, node [ ) ].
node     ->    [ (A5 ], node, node, node, node,
               node, node, node, node, node,
               node, node, node, node, node, [ ) ].
node     ->    [ (A6 ], node, node, node, node,
               node, node, node, node, node, [ ) ].
node     ->    [ (A7 ], exp, node, node, [ ) ].
node     ->    [ (A8 ], node, node, [ ) ].
node     ->    [ (A9 ], node, node, [ ) ].
node     ->    [ (A10 ], exp, node, node, [ ) ].
node     ->    [ (A11 ], node, node, [ ) ].
node     ->    [ (A12 ], node, node, node, [ ) ].
node     ->    [ (A13 ], exp, node, node, [ ) ].
node     ->    [ (A14 ], exp, node, node, [ ) ].
node     ->    [ positive ].
node     ->    [ negative ]
exp      ->    [ ( ], op, exp, exp, [ ) ].
op       ->    [ + ].
op       ->    [ - ].
op       ->    [ * ].
op       ->    [ % ].
exp      ->    { random(-10, 10, ?a) },  [ ?a ].
```

Table 6.7: Logic grammar for the credit screening problem.

The terminal symbols [+], [-], and [*] represent functions that perform ordinary addition, subtraction, and multiplication, respectively. The symbol [%] represents function that normally returns the quotient. However, if division by zero is attempted, the function returns 1.0. The logic goal random(-10, 10, ?a) generates a random floating point number between -10 and 10 and instantiates `?a` to the random number generated.

A 10-fold *cross-validation procedure* is employed in this problem. In a general *n*-fold cross-validation procedure, the examples are randomly divided into *n* mutually exclusive test partitions of approximately equal size. The examples not found in a particular test partition are used for training, and the resulting decision tree is tested on the corresponding test partition. The above train and test procedure is repeated *n* times until all test partitions are examined. The average classification accuracy over all *n* test partitions is the cross-validated classification accuracy. Breiman et al. (1984) evaluated their CART system extensively with vary numbers of partitions, and 10-fold cross-validation seemed to be adequate and accurate.

Since there are 690 examples in the credit screening dataset, each test partition contains 69 examples and the other 621 examples form the training set. In other words, 10 independent experiments have been attempted. In each experiment, LOGENPRO induces a decision tree using 621 examples as the fitness cases and we estimate the classification accuracy of the induced decision tree using the remaining testing examples.

The fitness function measures how well a genetically evolved decision tree classifies the fitness cases. When an evolved decision tree in the population is tested against a particular fitness case, the outcome can be either a *true positive*, a *true negative*, a *false positive*, or a *false negative*.

The *correlation coefficient* (Matthews 1975) indicates the classification performance of a decision tree. A correlation coefficient C of 1.0 indicates perfect agreement between the decision tree and the fitness cases; a coefficient of -1.0 indicates total disagreement; a coefficient of 0.0 indicates that the decision tree is not better than a random classifier. For a two-classes classification problem, the correlation coefficient can be computed as:

$$C = \frac{N_{tp}N_{tn} - N_{fp}N_{fn}}{\sqrt{(N_{tn} + N_{fn})(N_{fp} + N_{tn})(N_{tp} + N_{fn})(N_{tp} + N_{fp})}}$$

where N_{tp} is the number of true positives, N_{tn} is the number of true negatives, N_{fp} is the number of false positives, and N_{fn} is the number of false negatives. The coefficient is set to 0 if the denominator is 0.

Since C ranges between -1.0 and 1.0, standardized fitness is defined as $\frac{1-C}{2}$. Thus, a standardized fitness value ranges between 0.0 and 1.0. A standardized fitness value of 0 indicates perfect agreement between the decision tree and the training examples. On the other hand, a value of 1.0 indicates total disagreement. A value of 0.5 shows that the decision tree is not better than a random classifier (Koza 1992).

In each of the ten experiments, LOGENPRO induces a decision tree using a population size of 300. LOGENPRO will terminate if the maximum number of generations of 50 is reached or a decision tree that has a standardized fitness below 0.01 is found. The decision tree evolved in any generation that has the smallest standardized fitness value is returned as the result of the run. The best decision tree induced by LOGENPRO is further evaluated on the training examples and the testing examples to obtain the corresponding classification accuracy. The results of the ten experiments are summarized in table 6.8.

Generation	Accuracy (train)	Accuracy (test)
0	0.857	0.870
14	0.850	0.928
26	0.873	0.754
32	0.862	0.884
45	0.860	0.870
2	0.849	0.928
25	0.868	0.797
4	0.858	0.826
28	0.852	0.913
22	0.863	0.812
Average	0.859	0.858

Table 6.8: *Results of the decision trees induced by LOGENPRO for the credit screening problem. The first column shows the generation in which the best decision tree is found. The second column contains the classification accuracy of the best decision tree on the training examples. The third column shows the accuracy on the testing examples.*

Michie et al. (1994) performed a series of experiments in the Statlog project. In these experiments, they compared the performances of different learning systems for the credit screening problem. The results are summarized in table 6.9.

Algorithm	**Accuracy (train)**	**Accuracy (test)**
Cal5	0.868	0.869
ITrule	0.838	0.863
Discrim	0.861	0.859
Logdisc	0.875	0.859
DIPOL92	0.861	0.859
LOGENPRO	**0.859**	**0.858**
CART	0.855	0.855
RBF	0.893	0.855
CASTLE	0.856	0.852
NaiveBay	0.864	0.849
IndCART	0.919	0.848
Back-propagation	0.913	0.846
C4.5	0.901	0.845
SMART	0.910	0.842
Baytree	1.000	0.829
k-NN	1.000	0.819
NewID	1.000	0.819
AC2	1.000	0.819
LVQ	0.935	0.803
ALLOC80	0.806	0.799
CN2	0.999	0.796
Quadisc	0.815	0.793

Table 6.9: ***Results of various learning algorithms for the credit screening problem.***

By comparing the results in table 6.8 and those in table 6.9, we find that Cal5, ITrule, Discrim, Logdisc, and DIPOL92 perform better than LOGENPRO. Cal5 and ITrule learns decision trees/rules and their classification accuracy is over 86%. The classification accuracy of Discrim, Logdisc, and DIPOL92 is all 85.9%, The differences in accuracy between them and LOGENPRO are only 0.1%. Since the detailed information of the accuracy of these systems is not available, it cannot be concluded that whether the differences in accuracy are significant.

On the other hand, LOGENPRO performs better than CART, RBF, CASTLE, NaiveBay, IndCART, Back-propagation, C4.5, SMART, Baytree, k-NN, NewID, AC2, LVQ, ALLOC80, CN2, and Quadisc for the credit screening problem. Interestingly, LOGENPRO is better than C4.5 and CN2, two systems that were reported in the literature (Quinlan 1992, Clark and Niblett 1989) about their outstanding performances in inducing decision trees/rules. The difference is 1.3% for C4.5 and is 6.2% for CN2.

6.3. Learning Logic Program From Imperfect Data

The problem of learning knowledge from huge, incomplete, and imperfect datasets is very important in data mining (Fayyad et al. 1996, Frawley et al. 1991, Piatetsky-Shapiro and Frawley 1991). The various kinds of imperfections in data are listed as follows:

- random noise in training examples and background knowledge;
- the number of training examples is too small;
- the distribution of training examples fails to reflect the underlying distribution of instances of the concept being learned;
- an inappropriate example description language is used: some important characteristics of examples are not represented, and/or irrelevant properties of examples are provided;
- an inappropriate concept description language is used: it does not contain an exact description of the target concept; and
- there are missing values in the training examples.

Existing inductive learning systems employ noise-handling mechanisms to cope with the first five kinds of data imperfections. Missing values are usually handled by a separate mechanism. These noise-handling mechanisms are designed to prevent the induced concept from overfitting the imperfect training examples by excluding insignificant patterns (Lavrac and Dzeroski 1994). They include tree pruning in CART (Breiman et al. 1984), rule truncation in AQ15 (Michalski et al. 1986a) and significant test in CN2 (Clark and Niblett 1989). However, these mechanisms may ignore some important patterns because they are statistically insignificant.

Moreover, these learning systems use a limiting attribute-value language for representing the training examples and induced knowledge. This representation limits them to learn only propositional descriptions in which concepts are described in terms of values of a fixed number of attributes. Currently, only a few relation learning systems such as FOIL and mFOIL address the issue of learning knowledge represented as logic programs from imperfect data.

In this section, we describe the application of LOGENPRO to learn logic programs from noisy and imperfect training examples. Empirical comparisons of LOGENPRO with FOIL (the publicly available version of FOIL, version 6.0 , is used in this experiment) and with mFOIL (Lavrac and Dzeroski 1994) in the domain of learning illegal chess endgame positions from noisy examples are presented.

As described in sub-section 4.3.2.2, mFOIL is based on FOIL that has adapted several features from CN2 (Clark and Niblett 1989), such as the use of the Laplace and *m*-estimate as its search heuristics and the use of significance testing as its stopping criterion. Moreover, mFOIL uses beam search and can apply mode and type information to reduce the search space. The parameters that can be set by a user are: 1) the beam width, 2) the search heuristics, 3) the value of *m* if *m*-estimate is used as the search heuristics, and 4) the significance threshold used in the significance test. A number of different instances of mFOIL have been tested on the chess endgame problem. Their parameter values are summarized in table 6.10.

In this section, LOGENPRO employs a variation of FOIL to find the initial population of logic programs. Thus, it uses the same noise-handling mechanism of FOIL. The variation is called BEAM-FOIL because it uses a beam search method rather than the greedy search strategy of FOIL. BEAM-FOIL produces a number of different logic programs when it terminates and the best program among them is the solution of the problem. The logic programs created by BEAM-FOIL are used by LOGENPRO to initialize the first generation. In order to study the effects of the genetic operations performed by LOGENPRO on the initial programs provided by BEAM-FOIL, a comparison between them is also discussed.

	beam width	heuristics	m	significance threshold
mFOIL1	5	m-estimate	0.01	0
mFOIL2	10	m-estimate	0.01	0
mFOIL3	5	m-estimate	0.01	6.35
mFOIL4	10	m-estimate	32	0

Table 6.10: The parameter values of different instances of mFOIL examined in this section.

The chess endgame problem is presented in the following sub-section. The experimental setup is detailed in sub-section 6.3.2. We compare LOGENPRO with other learning systems in the subsequent sub-sections.

6.3.1. The Chess Endgame Problem

The chess endgame problem is a benchmark problem in the field of data mining for evaluating performance of data mining systems (Dzeroski and Lavrac 1993). In the problem, the setup is white king and rook versus black king (Quinlan 1990). The target concept illegal(WKf, WKr, WRf, WRr, BKf, BKr) states whether the positions where the white king at (WKf, WKr), the white rook at (WRf, WRf), and the black king at (BKf, BKr) are not a legal white-to-move position.

The background knowledge is represented by two predicates, adjacent(X, Y) and less_than(W, Z), indicating that rank/file X is adjacent to rank/file Y and rank/file W is less than rank/file Z, respectively.

There are 11000 examples in the dataset (3576 positive and 7424 negative examples). Muggleton et al. (1989) used smaller datasets to evaluate the performances of CIGOL and DUCE for the chess endgame problem. There were five small sets of 100 examples each and five large sets of 1000 examples each. In other words, there were 5500 examples in total. Each of the sets was used as a training set. The induced programs obtained from a small training set was tested on the 5000 examples from the large sets, the programs obtained from each large training set was tested on the remaining 4500 examples.

6.3.2. The Setup of Experiments

In each experiment of the ten experiments performed, the training set contains 1000 examples (336 positive and 664 negative examples) and the disjoint testing set has 10000 examples (3240 positive and 6760 negative examples). These training and testing sets are selected from the dataset using different seeds for the random number generator.

Different amounts of noise are introduced into the training examples in order to study the performances of different systems in learning logic programs from noisy environment. To introduce *n*% of noise into argument X of the training examples, the value of argument X is replaced by a random value of the same type from a uniform distribution, independent to noise in other arguments. For the class variable, *n*% positive examples are labeled as negative ones while *n*% negatives examples are labeled as positive ones. Noise in an argument is not necessarily incorrect because it is chosen randomly, it is possible that the correct argument value is selected. In contrast, noise in classification implies that this example is incorrect. Thus, the probability for an example to be incorrect is $1-\{[(1-n\%)+n\%*\frac{1}{8}]^6*(1-n\%)\}$. For each experiment, the percentages of introduced noise are 5%, 10%, 15%, 20%, 30%, and 40%. Thus, the probabilities for an example to be noisy are respectively 27.36%, 48.04%, 63.46%, 74.78%, 88.74% and 95.47%. Background knowledge and testing examples are not corrupted with noise.

A chosen level of noise is first introduced in the training set. Logic programs are then induced from the training set using LOGENPRO, FOIL, different instances of mFOIL, and BEAM-FOIL. Finally, the classification accuracy of the learned logic programs is estimated on the testing set. For BEAM-FOIL, the size of beam is ten and thus ten logic programs are returned. The best one among the programs returned is designated as the solution of BEAM-FOIL.

LOGENPRO uses the logic grammar in table 6.11 to solve the problem. In the grammar, [adjacent(?x, ?y)] and [less_than(?x, ?y)] are terminal symbols. The logic goal member(?x, [WKf, WKr, WRf, WRr, BKf, BKr]) will instantiate logic variable ?x of the grammar to either WKf, WKr, WRf, WRr, BKf, or BKr, the logic variables of the target logic program.

```
start          ->   clauses.
clauses        ->   clauses, clauses.
clauses        ->   clause.
clause         ->   consq, [:-], antes, [.].
consq          ->   [illegal(WKf,WKr,WRf,WRf,BKf,BKr)].
antes          ->   antes, [,], antes.
antes          ->   ante.
ante           ->   {member(?x,
                       [WKf, WKr, WRf, WRf, BKf, BKr])},
                    {member(?y,
                       [WKf, WKr, WRf, WRf, BKf, BKr])},
                    literal(?x, ?y).
literal(?x, ?y)     ->    [?x = ?y].
literal(?x, ?y)     ->    [ not ?x = ?y].
literal(?x, ?y)     ->    [ adjacent(?x, ?y) ].
literal(?x, ?y)     ->    [ not adjacent(?x, ?y) ].
literal(?x, ?y)     ->    [ less_than(?x, ?y) ].
literal(?x, ?y)     ->    [ not less_than(?x, ?y) ].
```

Table 6.11: The logic grammar for the chess endgame problem.

The population size for LOGENPRO is 10 and the maximum number of generations is 50. In fact, different population sizes have been tried and the results are still satisfactory even for a very small population. This observation is interesting and it demonstrates the advantage of combining inductive logic programming and evolutionary algorithms using the proposed framework.

For concept learning (DeJong et al. 1993, Janikow 1993, Greene and Smith 1993), each individual logic program in the population can be evaluated in terms of how well it covers positive examples and excludes negative examples. Thus, the fitness functions for concept learning problems calculate this measurement. Typically, each logic program is run over a number of training examples so that its fitness is measured as the total number of misclassified positive and negative examples. Sometimes, if the distribution of positive and negative examples is extremely uneven, this method of estimating fitness is not good enough to focus the search. For example, assume that there are 2 positive and 10000 negative examples, if the number of misclassified examples is used as the fitness value, a logic program that deduces everything are negative will have very good fitness. Thus, in this case, the fitness function should find a weighted sum of the total numbers of misclassified positive and negative examples.

In this problem, the fitness function of LOGENPRO evaluates the number of training examples misclassified by each individual in the population. Since LOGENPRO is a probabilistic system, five runs of each experiment have been performed and the average of the classification accuracy of these five runs is returned as the classification accuracy of LOGENPRO for the particular experiment. In other words, fifty runs of LOGENPRO have been performed in total. The average execution time of LOGENPRO is 1 hour 43 minutes on a Sun Sparc Workstation. The results of these systems are summarized in table 6.12. The performances of these systems are compared using the one-tailed paired *t*-test with 0.05% level of significance. The sizes of logic programs induced by these learning systems are summarized in table 6.13.

	Noise Level						
	0.00	0.05	0.10	0.15	0.20	0.30	0.40
LOGENPRO (Average)	0.996	0.983	0.960	0.938	0.855	0.733	0.670
Variance	0.00E+00	7.74E-06	2.96E-04	7.85E-04	2.57E-03	2.47E-03	1.44E-04
FOIL (Average)	0.996	0.898	0.819	0.761	0.693	0.596	0.529
Variance	0.00E+00	5.07E-04	6.56E-04	5.15E-04	5.30E-04	3.35E-04	3.11E-04
BEAM-FOIL (Average)	0.996	0.802	0.757	0.744	0.724	0.685	0.674
Variance	0.00E+00	7.07E-04	1.62E-04	1.88E-04	2.00E-04	1.40E-04	1.04E-04
mFOIL1 (Average)	0.985	0.883	0.845	0.815	0.785	0.719	0.685
Variance	0.00E+00	5.15E-05	7.29E-05	3.12E-04	2.15E-04	1.39E-04	1.30E-04
mFOIL2 (Average)	0.985	0.932	0.888	0.842	0.798	0.713	0.680
Variance	0.00E+00	7.47E-05	9.16E-05	9.26E-04	3.09E-04	1.41E-04	3.05E-04
mFOIL3 (Average)	0.896	0.836	0.805	0.771	0.723	0.677	0.676
Variance	1.97E-16	7.83E-04	1.05E-04	1.89E-04	9.81E-04	7.74E-06	0.00E+00
mFOIL4 (Average)	0.985	0.985	0.880	0.806	0.740	0.692	0.668
Variance	0.00E+00	4.05E-06	7.85E-03	5.14E-03	2.14E-03	3.72E-04	2.86E-04

Table 6.12: The averages and variances of accuracy of LOGENPRO, FOIL, BEAM-FOIL, and different instances of mFOIL at different noise levels.

	Noise Level						
	0.00	0.05	0.10	0.15	0.20	0.30	0.40
LOGENPRO (#clauses)	4.000	9.540	8.960	8.620	6.680	4.220	2.540
#literals/clause	1.50	2.59	2.94	3.20	3.40	4.39	4.98
FOIL (#clauses)	4.000	35.100	48.000	48.700	56.200	59.800	71.300
#literals/clause	1.50	3.65	4.44	4.73	5.06	5.23	5.40
BEAM-FOIL (#clauses)	4.000	5.000	4.400	4.200	4.000	3.500	2.800
#literals/clause	1.50	3.75	3.93	4.17	4.63	5.25	6.07
mFOIL1 (#clauses)	3.000	31.900	35.700	31.100	28.300	18.100	15.700
#literals/clause	2.00	3.07	3.20	3.18	3.42	3.34	3.57
mFOIL2 (#clauses)	3.000	48.800	50.600	48.200	44.500	41.400	34.900
#literals/clause	1.67	3.18	3.33	3.44	3.57	3.62	3.70
mFOIL3 (#clauses)	2.000	12.400	10.400	7.300	3.300	0.100	0.000
#literals/clause	1.50	2.68	3.10	3.02	3.46	4.00	0.00
mFOIL4 (#clauses)	3.000	3.000	2.400	1.800	1.200	1.200	11.200
#literals/clause	1.67	1.73	1.80	2.15	2.00	1.46	3.55

Table 6.13: The sizes of logic programs induced by LOGENPRO, FOIL, BEAM-FOIL, and different instances of mFOIL at different noise levels.

6.3.3. Comparison of LOGENPRO With FOIL

The classification accuracy of both systems degrades seriously as the noise level increases (figure 6.5). The classification accuracy of LOGENPRO decreases smoothly when the noise level is on or below 0.15. It reduces from 0.996 to 0.938, a 5.8% decrement. There are sudden drops of accuracy when the noise level is between 0.15 and 0.40. It falls from 0.938 to 0.670, a 28.5% reduction. The accuracy of FOIL decreases rapidly when the noise level is on or below 0.20. It drops from 0.996 to 0.693, a 30.4% reduction. The decrease slightly slows down between the noise levels of 0.20 and 0.40. It drops from 0.693 to 0.529, a 23.7% reduction.

The results are statistically evaluated using the one-tailed paired *t*-test. For each noise level, the classification accuracy is compared to test the null hypothesis against the alternative hypothesis. The null hypothesis states that the difference in accuracy is zero at the 0.05% level of significance. On the other hand, the alternative hypothesis declares that the difference is greater than zero at the 0.05% level of significance. The t-statistics are listed as follows:

Noise Level	0.00	0.05	0.10	0.15	0.20	0.30	0.40
t-statistics	NA	12.59	17.78	19.33	14.17	8.07	26.82

The *t*-statistics at the 0.00 noise level is not available because the variances are very small (near zero). The t-statistics at the 0.05 noise level is 12.59 which is greater than the critical value of 4.78. Thus, we can reject the null hypothesis and assert that the classification accuracy of LOGENPRO is higher than that of FOIL. Similarly, the classification accuracy of LOGENPRO at the noise levels between 0.05 and 0.40 is significantly higher than that of FOIL. The largest difference reaches 0.177 at the 0.15 noise level. The average number of induced clauses and the average number of literals per clause show that LOGENPRO generates compact and comprehensive logic programs even at the high noise levels. On the other hand, the complexity of the logic programs learned by FOIL increases when the noise level increase. In other words, FOIL overfits noise in the dataset.

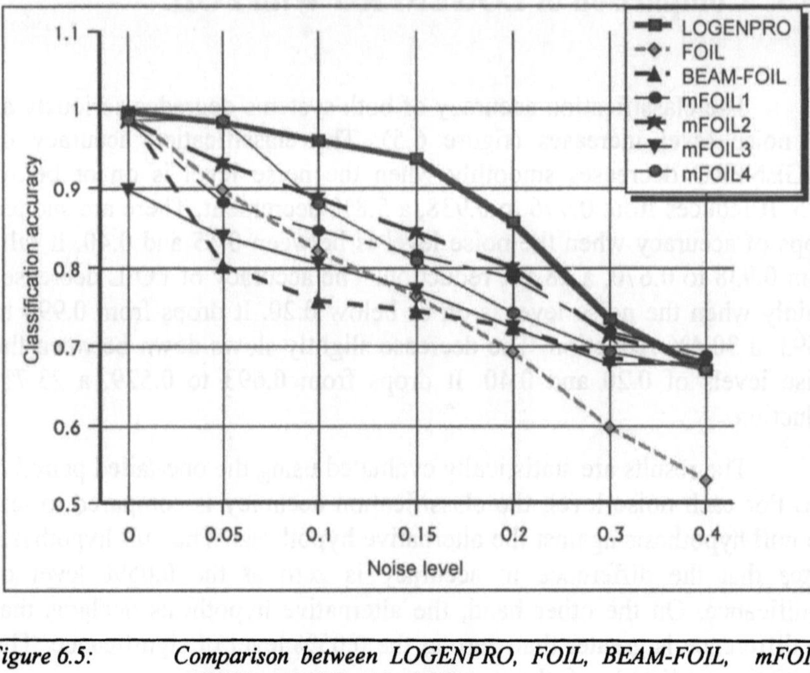

Figure 6.5: *Comparison between LOGENPRO, FOIL, BEAM-FOIL, mFOIL1, mFOIL2, mFOIL3 and mFOIL4.*

6.3.4. Comparison of LOGENPRO With BEAM-FOIL

The classification accuracy of BEAM-FOIL degrades seriously as the noise level increases (figure 6.5). There is a significant fall in accuracy of BEAM-FOIL when the noise level is increased from 0.0 to 0.05. It reduces from 0.996 to 0.802, a more than 19.4% of decrement. It falls from 0.802 to 0.757 between the noise levels of 0.05 and 0.10, a smaller reduction (5.6%) is encountered in this interval. The decrease slows down between the noise levels of 0.10 and 0.40. The accuracy drops from 0.757 to 0.674 in this interval. The reduction is about 11%. The results of the one-tailed paired *t*-test are listed as follows:

Noise Level	0.00	0.05	0.10	0.15	0.20	0.30	0.40
t-statistics	NA	22.20	33.82	21.91	9.19	3.26	-0.81

The *t*-statistics at the 0.00 noise level is not available because the variances are very small (near zero). The classification accuracy of LOGENPRO at the noise levels between 0.05 and 0.20 is significantly higher than that of BEAM-FOIL. At the noise level of 0.30, the accuracy of LOGENPRO is higher than that of BEAM-FOIL, but the difference is not significant. On the other hand, the accuracy of BEAM-FOIL at the noise level of 0.40 is higher than that of LOGENPRO, but the difference is insignificant. This comparison indicates that the genetic operations of LOGENPRO can actually improve the logic programs generated by other learning systems such as BEAM-FOIL. The sizes of logic programs induced by BEAM-FOIL show that BEAM-FOIL over-generalizes at the high noise levels.

6.3.5. Comparison of LOGENPRO With mFOIL1

We compare LOGENPRO with mFOIL1 to mFOIL4 one by one in this and the following sub-sections. The parameters of this instance are presented in table 6.10. Lavrac and Dzeroski (1994) compare the performances of mFOIL1 with FOIL2.0, a version of FOIL, for the chess endgame problem using the smaller dataset described in sub-section 6.3.1.

They find that mFOIL1 outperforms FOIL2.0 at all noise levels. Our results depicted in figure 6.5 are inconsistent with those obtained by Lavrac and Dzeroski. We find that FOIL outperforms mFOIL1 at the noise levels of 0.0 and 0.05. On the other hand, mFOIL1 has better performance when the noise level is on or over 0.1. The inconsistency may be explained because we employ an improved version of FOIL, FOIL6.0, and larger sets of training and testing examples. The results of the one-tailed paired *t*-test between LOGENPRO and mFOIL1 are listed as follows:

Noise Level	0.00	0.05	0.10	0.15	0.20	0.30	0.40
t-statistics	3.03E+08	35.38	17.29	14.98	5.15	1.11	-3.37

The classification accuracy of LOGENPRO at the noise levels between 0.0 and 0.20 is significantly higher than that of mFOIL1. At the noise level of 0.30, the accuracy of LOGENPRO is higher than that of mFOIL1 by about 0.014, but the difference is not significant. On the other hand, the accuracy of mFOIL1 at the noise level of 0.40 is higher than that of LOGENPRO, the difference is insignificant.

6.3.6. Comparison of LOGENPRO With mFOIL2

The results of the one-tailed paired *t*-test between LOGENPRO and mFOIL2 are listed as follows:

Noise Level	0.00	0.05	0.10	0.15	0.20	0.30	0.40
t-statistics	3.03E+08	21.59	13.05	9.95	4.37	1.23	-1.65

The classification accuracy of LOGENPRO at the noise levels between 0.0 and 0.15 is significantly higher than that of mFOIL2. At the noise levels of 0.20 and 0.30, the accuracy of LOGENPRO is higher than that of mFOIL2, but the differences are not significant. On the other hand, the accuracy of mFOIL2 at the noise level of 0.40 is higher than that of LOGENPRO, but the difference is insignificant.

6.3.7. Comparison of LOGENPRO With mFOIL3

The accuracy of mFOIL3 at the noise levels of 0.00, 0.30, and 0.40 is not acceptable. By comparing mFOIL3 with mFOIL1 (figure 6.5), we can conclude that the significance threshold for noise-handling affects the performance of mFOIL severely (see table 6.10). The results of the one-tailed paired *t*-test between LOGENPRO and mFOIL3 are listed as follows:

Noise Level	0.00	0.05	0.10	0.15	0.20	0.30	0.40
t-statistics	NA	16.99	22.29	16.44	8.12	3.65	-1.66

The *t*-statistics at the 0.00 noise level is not available because the variances are very small (near zero). The classification accuracy of LOGENPRO at the noise levels between 0.05 and 0.40 is significantly higher than that of mFOIL3.

6.3.8. Comparison of LOGENPRO With mFOIL4

The results of the one-tailed paired *t*-test between LOGENPRO and mFOIL4 are listed as follows:

Noise Level	0.00	0.05	0.10	0.15	0.20	0.30	0.40
t-statistics	2.22E+08	-1.45	2.77	6.37	8.00	2.20	0.24

The classification accuracy of LOGENPRO at the noise levels 0.00, 0.15 and 0.20 is significantly higher than that of mFOIL4. The sizes of the logic programs learned by mFOIL4 illustrate that mFOIL4 over-generalizes at the noise levels between 0.10 and 0.30. On the other hand, mFOIL4 overfits the noise in the dataset at the 0.40 noise level.

6.3.9. Discussion

In this section, we employ LOGENPRO to combine evolutionary algorithms and BEAM-FOIL, to discover knowledge represented as logic programs. The performance of LOGENPRO in a noisy domain has been evaluated by using the chess endgame problem. Detailed comparisons between LOGENPRO and other ILP systems have been conducted. It is found that LOGENPRO outperforms these ILP systems significantly at most noise levels. These results are surprising because the LOGENPRO uses the same noise-handling mechanism of FOIL by initializing the population with programs created by BEAM-FOIL.

One possible explanation of the better performance of LOGENPRO is that the Darwinian principle of survival and reproduction of the fittest is a good noise handling method. It avoids overfitting noisy examples, but at the same time, it finds interesting and useful patterns from these noisy examples.

Chapter 7

APPLYING LOGENPRO FOR RULE LEARNING

A rule is a statement in the format of "if *antecedents* then *consequent*", which is commonly used by human to represent knowledge. Rule learning tries to learn rules from a set of data. It can be modeled as a search problem of finding the best rules. Because the search space can be very large, a robust search algorithm is required. Thus, LOGENPRO is used as a possible approach. This chapter introduces how the problem of rule learning is modeled such that LOGENPRO can be applied.

To apply LOGENPRO, firstly a suitable representation has to be designed to encode a rule in an individual. In LOGENPRO, a derivation tree is used to represent an individual, so a grammar for rules has to be designed to create the appropriate derivation tree. Secondly, a set of suitable genetic operators has to be used to evolve new individuals. Thirdly, we have to design a suitable fitness function to evaluate the fitness value of an individual. These three issues are discussed in the first three sections. The detailed techniques for learning a set of rules are discussed in the last section.

7.1. Grammar

The grammar of LOGENPRO governs the structures to be evolved. Rule learning can be achieved in LOGENPRO by using a suitable grammar to compose rules. The grammar should specify the structure of a rule, which is of the form "if *antecedents* then *consequent*". The format of rules in each problem can be different. Thus for each problem, a specific grammar is written so that the format of the rules can best fit the domain. However, in general, the antecedent part is a conjunction of attribute descriptors. The consequent part is also an attribute descriptor. An attribute descriptor characterizes an attribute, which can be described in many ways, thus there are many different formats of descriptors. A descriptor can assign a value to a nominal attribute, a range of values to a continuous attribute, or can be used to compare attribute values.

LOGENPRO provides a powerful knowledge representation and allows a great flexibility on the rule format. The representation of rules is not fixed but depends on the grammar. Most of the rule learning methods can only learn a particular format of rules, for example, rules with descriptors that compare the attributes with values. However, LOGENPRO allows a large variation in the attribute description. Rules with different formats or the user desired structure can be learned, provided that the suitable grammar is supplied.

An example is used to illustrate the use of grammar to represent the suitable rule format. Consider a database with 4 attributes. We want to learn rules about `attr4`, which is Boolean. The attribute `attr1` is nominal and coded with 0, 1, or 2. The attribute `attr2` is continuous between 0-200 and can be categorized into high, medium, or low. The domain of `attr3` is identical to `attr2` and thus it is possible for the rule to compare them.

An example of the grammar for this database is given in table 7.1. The symbols `erc1`, `erc2`, `erc3`, `boolean_erc`, and `category_erc` in this grammar are ephemeral random constants (ERCs). Each ERC has its own range for instantiation: `erc1` is one of the set {0, 1, 2}, `erc2` and `erc3` is between 0-200, `boolean_erc` can only be `T` or `F`, `category_erc` can be either `high`, `medium`, or `low`. The symbol '`any`' serves as a 'don't care' in the rule. An attribute will not be considered in the rule if its attribute descriptor is '`any`'. In this grammar, each attribute can be described by a descriptor in the rule, or by '`any`' such that it is ignored by the rule. The attribute `attr1` has only one form of descriptor. The attribute `att2` can have two forms of descriptors: it can be described by a range or by the category it belongs to. The attribute `attr3` can be specified by a comparator. Its descriptor can be a comparison with `attr2` or a comparison with a constant. This grammar allows rules like:

```
if attr1 = 0 and attr2 between 50 180
   and any, then attr4 = T.
if attr1 = 2 and attr2 is high and
   attr3 ≠ 50, then attr4 = T.
```

```
if attr1 = 1 and any and attr3 >= attr2,
   then attr4 = F.
```

```
1:    start              ->    [if], antes, [, then], consq, [.].
2:    antes              ->    attr1, [and], attr2, [and], attr3.
3:    attr1              ->    [any].
4:    attr1              ->    attr1_descriptor.
5:    attr2              ->    [any].
6:    attr2              ->    attr2_descriptor.
7:    attr3              ->    [any].
8:    attr3              ->    attr3_descriptor.
9:    attr1_descriptor   ->      [attr1 =], erc1.
10:   attr2_descriptor   ->      [attr2 is], category_erc.
11:   attr2_descriptor   ->      [attr2 between],erc2, erc3.
12:   attr3_descriptor   ->      [attr3], comparator,
                                 attr3_term.
13:   comparator         ->      [=].
14:   comparator         ->      [≠].
15:   comparator         ->      [<=].
16:   comparator         ->      [>=].
17:   comparator         ->      [<].
18:   comparator         ->      [>].
19:   attr3_term         ->      attr2.
20:   attr3_term         ->      erc3.
21:   consq              ->      attr4_descriptor.
22:   attr4_descriptor   ->      [attr4 =], boolean_erc.
23:   erc1               ->      {member(?a,[0,1,2])}, [?a].
24:   erc2               ->      {random(0, 200, ?a)}, [?a].
25:   erc3               ->      {random(0, 200, ?a)}, [?a].
26:   category_erc ->    {member(?a, [high, medium, low])},
                                 [?a].
27:   boolean_erc  ->    {member(?a, [T, F])}, [?a].
```

Table 7.1: An example grammar for rule learning.

The grammars for other problems are similar to the grammar in table 7.1. According to the type of attribute, a descriptor similar to `attr1_descriptor`, `attr2_descriptor` or `attr3_descriptor` can be used. The following list illustrates how the grammar is written for each situation.

- The attribute is nominal.

  The attribute can be described by its value. The descriptor similar to `attr1_descriptor` or `attr4_descriptor` can be used.

- The attribute is continuous.

  The attribute can be described by a range. The descriptor similar to `attr2_descriptor` can be used.

- The attribute can be compared with other attributes in the rule.

  In many cases, describing an attribute by a value is not powerful enough to represent the knowledge. If a comparison between variables is needed, the descriptor similar to `attr3_descriptor` can be used.

- The attribute has more than one kind of descriptions.

  In some cases, an attribute can be described by more than one way. An example is `attr2` in the previous example. Using a grammar, we do not need to restrict the rule to use either one descriptor. Another example is that an address is described by the city, the state, and the country. This can be achieved by writing the grammar as follows:

```
address_descriptor  ->   [address between],
                         city_erc, city_erc.
address_descriptor  ->   [address between],
                         state_erc,
                         state_erc.
address_descriptor  ->   [address between],
                         country_erc,
                         country_erc.
```

- The antecedent part has more than one format.

  The use of grammar allows the antecedents to have more than one format. For example, the user may want that if `attr1` is included in the antecedent, then `attr3` and `attr4` should also be included. Otherwise, if `attr2` is used instead of `attr1`, then `attr5` and `attr6` should be included in the rule. This can be done by replacing the grammar rule 2 of table 7.1 with the following grammar rules:

```
antes ->    attr1, [and], attr3, [and], attr4.
antes ->    attr2, [and], attr5, [and], attr6.
```

- There are more than one target variable and thus more than one kind of rules.

  Usually data mining is not restricted to one target variable. The user may want to find knowledge describing all the dependent variables. Thus this leads to more than one kind of rules. Different kinds of rules can be searched by replacing the grammar rule 1 of table 7.1 with the following grammar rules:

```
start ->    [if], antes1, [, then], consq1.
start ->    [if], antes2, [, then], consq2.
```

7.2. Genetic Operators

In rule learning using LOGENPRO, the search space is explored by generating new rules using three genetic operators: crossover, mutation and dropping condition. A rule is composed of attribute descriptors. The genetic operators try to change the descriptors in order to search for better rules.

As described in section 5.3, crossover is a sexual operation that produces one child from two parents. One parent is designated as the primary parent and the other one as the secondary parent. A part of the primary parent is selected and replaced by another part from the secondary parent. Suppose that the following primary and secondary parents are selected:

```
if attr1=0 and attr2 between 100 150 and attr3 ≠ 50,
   then attr4=T.
if attr1=1 and any and attr3 >= attr2, then attr4=F.
```

The underlined parts are selected for crossover. The offspring will be

```
if attr1=0 and attr2 between 100 150 and
   attr3 >= attr2, then attr4=T.
```

In LOGENPRO, each individual is represented by a derivation tree. The replaced part is actually a subtree selected randomly from the derivation tree of the primary parent (see section 5.3). The subtree may represent different structures in the rule, hence the genetic change may occur on the whole rule, several descriptors, or just one descriptor. The replacing part is also selected randomly from the derivation tree of the secondary parent, but under the constraint that the offspring produced must be valid according to the grammar. If a conjunction of descriptors is selected in the primary parent, it will be replaced by another conjunction of descriptors, but never by a single descriptor. If a descriptor is selected in the primary parent, then it can only be replaced by another descriptor of the same attribute. This can maintain the validity of the rule.

Mutation is an asexual operation. A part in the parental rule is selected and replaced by a randomly generated part (see section 5.4). Similar to crossover, the selected part is a subtree of the derivation tree. The genetic change may occur on the whole rule, several descriptors, one descriptor, or the constants in the rule. The new part is generated by the same derivation mechanism as in the population creation. Because the offspring have to be valid according to the grammar, a selected part can only mutate to another part with a compatible structure. For example, the parent

```
if attr1=0 and attr2 between 100 150 and attr3 ≠ 50,
   then attr4=T.
```

may mutate to

```
if attr1=0 and attr2 between 100 150 and
   attr3 >= attr2, then attr4=T.
```

Dropping condition is an genetic operator tailor-made for rule learning using LOGENPRO. Due to the probabilistic nature of GP, redundant constraints may be generated in the rule. For example, suppose that the actual knowledge is 'if *A*<20 then *X*=T'. We may learn rules like 'if *A*<20 and *B*<10 then *X*=T'. This rule is, of course, correct; but it does not concisely represent the actual knowledge. It is just a subsumed rule of the actual rule. Dropping condition (Michalski 1983) is incorporated in LOGENPRO to generalize rules. A rule is generalized if one descriptor in the antecedent part is dropped. Dropping condition selects randomly one attribute descriptor, and then turns it into `any`. That particular attribute is no longer considered in the rule, hence the rule can be generalized. For example, the rule

```
if attr1=0 and attr2 between 100 150 and attr3 ≠ 50,
   then attr4=T.
```

can be changed to

```
if attr1=0 and attr2 between 100 150 and any,
   then attr4=T.
```

7.3. Evaluation of Rules

An evaluation (fitness) function is needed to evaluate rules. There are a lot of rule evaluation functions. Piatetsky-Shapiro (1991) stated that for a rule 'if A then B', the function measuring the interest of the rule should be a function of $p(A)$ (probability of A), $p(B)$, $p(A$ and $B)$, rule complexity, and possibly other parameters. Let N be the total number of training examples. Let $|A|$ denotes the number of cases that satisfy condition A, and $|A$ and $B|$ denotes the number of cases that satisfy condition 'A and B'. It is suggested that the rule-interest function RI should satisfy the following principles:

1. $RI = 0$ if $|A$ and $B| = (|A| * |B|) / N$. If A and B are statistically independent, the rule is not interesting.
2. RI monotonically increases with $|A$ and $B|$ when other parameters remain the same.
3. RI monotonically decreases with $|A|$ or $|B|$ when other parameters remain the same.

For a rule 'if A then B', the probability $p(B|A)=p(A$ and $B)/p(A)$ is the accuracy of the rule. According to the accuracy, a rule can be categorized as an *exact*, *strong*, or *weak* rule. An exact rule is the rule that always correct, that is, $p(B|A)=1$. A strong rule is a rule that almost always correct, that is, $p(B|A)=$is high. A weak rule is a rule that the conditional probability of the consequent under the antecedents is much higher than the probability of consequent, that is $p(B|A) >> p(B)$. In the real-life situation, an exact or strong rule may not exist. Thus a useful data mining system should not just search for exact or strong rules. It should be able to discover weak rules because the difference from the average may already provide interesting knowledge. Consequently, accuracy cannot be the sole metric for rule-interest. Another measurement of rule-interest is the applicability of the rule to future cases. If the rule can match a larger number of training cases, it is less likely that the rule is obtained by chance, and thus the rule should be more applicable to future cases.

An evaluation function based on the support-confidence framework (Agrawal et al. 1993) is developed as the fitness function in our rule learning approach. *Support* measures the coverage of a rule. It is a ratio of the number of records covered by the rule to the total number of records. *Confidence factor* (*cf*) is the confidence of the consequent to be true under the antecedents, and is just the same as the rule accuracy. It is the ratio of the number of records matching both the consequent and the antecedents to the number of records matching only the antecedents. For a rule 'if *A* then *B*' and with a training set of *N* cases, support is $|A \text{ and } B|/N$ and confidence factor is $|A \text{ and } B|/|A|$.

In the evaluation process, each rule is checked with every record in the training set. Three statistics are counted. *antes_hit* is the number of records matching the antecedents (the 'if' part), *consq_hit* is the number of records that match the consequent (the 'then' part), and *both_hit* is the number of records that match the whole rule (both the 'if' and the 'then' parts).

The confidence factor *cf* is the fraction *both_hit*/*antes_hit*. But a rule with a high confidence factor does not mean that it behaves significantly different from the average. Therefore we need to consider the average probability of consequent (*prob*). The value *prob* is equal to *consq_hit*/*total*, where *total* is the total number of records in the training set. This value measures the confidence for the consequent under no particular antecedent.

A formula similar to the likelihood ratio used in CN2 (equation 2.9) is used to define the normalized confidence factor *normalized_cf*:

$$normalized\_cf = cf \times \log(\frac{cf}{prob}) \tag{7.1}$$

The log function measures the order of magnitude of the ratio *cf*/*prob*. The normalized value is a product of two factors: *cf* and log(*cf*/*prob*). A high value of *normalized_cf* requires simultaneously a high value on the rule confidence factor (*cf*) and a high value on the rule confidence factor over the average probability (*cf*/*prob*). The definition of the value in 7.1 matches with the three previously stated principles proposed by Piatetsky-Shapiro (1991). Using his notation, *cf* is actually $|A \text{ and } B|/|A|$, and *prob* is $|B|/N$. If $|A \text{ and } B|/|A|=|B|/N$, $cf/prob=1$ and $normalized\_cf=0$. The value *cf* (and so does *normalized_cf*) monotonically increases with $|A \text{ and } B|$ and monotonically decreases with $|A|$. The value *prob* monotonically increases with $|B|$ and thus *normalized_cf* monotonically decreases with $|B|$.

Support is another measure that we need to consider. A rule can have a high accuracy but the rule may be formed by chance and based on a few training examples. This kind of rules does not have enough support.

The value *support* is defined as *both_hit/total*. If *support* is below a user-defined minimum threshold (*min_support*), the confidence factor of the rule should not be considered. This can avoid the waste of effort to evolve those rules with a high confidence but cannot be generalized.

Finally, We define our fitness function to be:

$$raw\_fitness = \begin{cases} support, & \text{if } support < min\_support \\ w_1 \times support + w_2 \times normalized\_cf, & \text{otherwise} \end{cases} \quad (7.2)$$

where the weights w_1 and w_2 are user-defined to control the balance between the confidence and the support in searching. We have set the values to 1 and 8 respectively so that the confidence of the rule plays a more important role in the evaluation function.

7.4. Learning Multiple Rules From Data

The knowledge of a data set is unlikely to be sufficiently described by a single rule. Thus, multiple rules are required to represent the knowledge. To perform rule learning using evolutionary computation, a suitable model for an individual must be designed such that a set of rules can be learned. There are two different approaches. In the Pittsburgh approach (Smith 1980; 1983), each individual in the population encodes a whole solution, that is, a set of rules. In the Michigan approach (Holland and Reitman 1978, Booker et al. 1989), each individual encodes only one rule. The individuals in the population can be combined together to provide a rule set. However this approach requires special techniques such that multiple good individuals can coexist in the population. Our approach follows the Michigan approach. The structure of an individual can be simpler because it only represents one rule. Thus the evolution for good individuals are easier.

This section begins with an review of previous approaches for maintaining groups of individuals evolving different solutions. Then our approach, token competition, is presented in section 7.4.2. Section 7.4.3 summarizes the complete approach for rule learning. Experimental results of rule learning from two machine learning databases are presented in section 7.4.4.

7.4.1. Previous Approaches

Genetic algorithms and genetic programming are weak search algorithms to search for a solution that optimize the fitness function. These algorithms aim to search for a single solution only. Those individuals with higher fitness scores can survive while those with lower fitness scores will be extinct. If a part of the search space gives a higher fitness scores, eventually all the individuals will converge into this part.

However there are many situations that multiple solutions are required. For example, we may need to search for all the peaks in a multimodal function. In this case, it is desirable to maintain groups of individuals, with different groups evolving different solutions. Each group of individuals is referred to as a sub-population or a species, and the part of the search space being explored by a species is referred to as a niche. Maintaining diversity of the population is important for the formulation of niches. The individuals are not allowed to converge to a single niche and hence forced to explore different parts of the search space. Several approaches have been designed in GAs to accomplish this task and they are reviewed as follows:

7.4.1.1. Pre-selection

Pre-selection (Cavicchio 1970) maintains the diversity by trying to reduce the existences of similar individuals. It uses the idea that parents should be among the most similar individuals to the offspring. A new individual is evolved by using a genetic operator. The offspring can replace one of the parents if it has a better fitness. Otherwise the parents survives but not the child.

7.4.1.2. Crowding

In crowding (DeJong 1975), a certain percentage of the population is selected to produce offspring. The percentage is denoted as the generation gap (*G*). Offspring are evolved by crossover and mutation to replace the original individuals in the population. To determine which individual is replaced, for each offspring several individuals are selected randomly from the population. The number of individuals selected is denoted as the crowding factor (*CF*). The similarities of the selected individuals with respect to the offspring are computed. Similarity is defined in turn of bit-wise (i.e. genotypic) matching. The most similar individual is replaced by the offspring.

7.4.1.3. Deterministic Crowding

Deterministic crowding (Mahfoud 1992) improves pre-selection and crowding. In each generation, the individuals in the population are randomly paired without replacement. Each pair evolves two offspring by crossover. Deterministic crowding uses the idea of pre-selection that the offspring should be similar to its parent, and uses the idea of crowding that a similarity measure should used to determine the replacement. Deterministic crowding uses the phenotypic similarity. The bit strings of the individuals are decoded and the similarity measure is defined in the decoded parameters. The offspring is compared only with the two parents for similarity. There are two possible replacements of two parents by their two offspring: offspring 1 replaces parent 1 and offspring 2 replaces parent 2, or offspring 1 replaces parent 2 and offspring 2 replaces parent 1. The pair of replacements that yields the greater sum of phenotypic similarities between the offspring and the replaced parents is used. The parent is replaced by the offspring only if the corresponding offspring has a better fitness score.

7.4.1.4. Fitness Sharing

Fitness sharing (Goldberg and Richardson 1987) is apparently a time consuming algorithm which maintains a diversity of individuals by discouraging individuals to converge into one niche. The fitness of one individual gained from one niche must be shared by similar individuals. A distance function $d(x_i, x_j)$ measures the distance (i.e. dissimilarity) between two individuals x_i and x_j. For each individual, the distances with all other individuals are calculated. A sharing function s defines the degree of fitness sharing by the similar individuals. The shared fitness f_s of one individual is the un-shared fitness f divided by the accumulated number of shares:

$$f_s(x_i) = \frac{f(x_i)}{\sum_j s(d(x_i, x_j))}$$

Thus when more individuals converge to one niche, the fitness is shared by more individuals. The fitness will decrease to a level such that it is no longer better than the fitness on other niches. Eventually a distribution of individuals on different niches can be achieved.

7.4.2. Token Competition

The token competition (Leung et al. 1992) technique is employed in our rule learning approach to increase the diversity, so that good individuals in different niches are maintained in the population. The concept is as follows: In the natural environment, once an individual has found a good place for living, it will try to exploit this niche and prevent other newcomers to share the resources, unless the newcomer is stronger than it is. The other individuals are hence forced to explore and find their own niches. In this way, the diversity of the population is increased.

Based on this mechanism, we assume each record in the training set can provide a resource called a token. If a rule can match a record, it set a flag to indicate the token is seized. Other weaker rules then cannot get the token. The priority of receiving tokens is determined by the strength of the rules. A rule with a high score on *raw_fitness* (equation 7.2) can exploit the niche by seizing as many tokens as it can. The other rules entering the same niche will have their strength decreased because they cannot compete with the stronger rule. The fitness score of each individual is modified based on the token it can seize. The modified fitness is defined as :

$$modified\_fitness = raw\_fitness \times count \,/\, ideal \qquad (7.3)$$

where *raw_fitness* is the fitness score obtained from the evaluation function, *count* is the number of tokens that the rule actually seized, *ideal* is the total number of tokens that it can seize, which is equal to the number of records that the rule matches. Token competition is a greedy operation. It favors strong rules as their chance of survival is maintained, while their close competitors are weakened as they cannot get the tokens in the niche.

From another point of view, each rule contributes to the system by covering several records of the database. If a record has already been covered by one rule, then another rule covering the same record will make no contribution to the system. Thus the fitness of the latter rule should be discounted.

Token competition is a simple method to force the increase of the diversity of the population. It has an advantage that it does not require a distance function. In crowding or fitness sharing, it is required to define a similarity or a distance function, so as to measure the similarity or dissimilarity between two individuals. However, it may be difficult to define how one individual is similar to another individual, especially in Genetic Programming. Genetic Algorithms use a fixed length binary string as the chromosome. Thus the genotypic difference (i.e. difference in the bits) can be used as a general similarity measurement. However this is not valid in the tree structure of Genetic Programming. Moreover, the similarity in genotype may not truly reflect the similarity of the individuals. Token competition simplifies the problem by simply regarding two individuals to be similar if they cover similar sets of records.

The execution of token competition is faster than that of fitness sharing. To calculate the fitness score of one individual in fitness sharing, the similarity scores of *all* other individuals with respect to this individual have to be calculated. If a similarity score can be computed in time $O(t)$, and the population size is p, each individual needs a time $O(pt)$ to calculate the similarity score, and the time needed to complete fitness sharing in each generation is $O(p^2t)$. On the other hand, calculations of similarity are not needed in token competition. The required information of token counting is the list of records that each individual covered. This information is already stored during the evaluation process. If an individual covers m records, a time of $O(m)$ is needed to seize the tokens, and token competition in each generation can be completed in $O(\overline{m}p)$, where $\overline{m}$ is average value of m. This computation is straight forward and can be faster than fitness sharing if $O(\overline{m}) < O(pt)$.

As a result of token competition, there are rules that cannot seize any token. These rules are redundant as all of its records are already covered by the stronger rules. They can be replaced by new individuals. Introducing these new individuals can inject a larger degree of diversity into the population, and provide extra chances for generating good rules. To create the new individuals, we can use seeds to generate better rules. Those records with their tokens not taken are the possible seeds. These records are not yet covered by any existing rules, and thus introducing rules covering them can improve the system. To create a new rule, a seed is selected, and then the rule is generated to cover the seed.

7.4.3. The Complete Rule Learning Approach

Figure 7.1 is the flowchart of the complete process for learning multiple rules from a set of data using LOGENPRO. A grammar is provided by the user as a template for rules. A set of rules is derived by using this grammar and forms the initial population. Then, the main loop of LOGENPRO is entered. In each generation, individuals are selected stochastically to evolve offspring by the three genetic operators: crossover, mutation, and dropping condition. In each generation, the number of new individuals evolved equals to the population size. Thus at this stage, the number of individuals in the population is doubled. All individuals participate in the token competition and the replacement step, so as to eliminate similar rules and increase the diversity. One half of the individuals with the higher fitness scores after token competition are retained and passed to the next generation. The whole process iterated until the maximum number of generations is reached.

Parents for the genetic operators are selected by the rank selection method. The probabilities of using crossover, mutation, and dropping condition in our approach are 0.5, 0.4, and 0.1, respectively. These setting is chosen because they gave the best results in preliminary executions of the system.

The data set for learning can be partitioned into a training and a testing sets. Only the training set is available for the learning process. After the maximum number of generations is reached, the discovered rules are further evaluated with the unseen testing set, so as to verify their accuracy and reject the rules that over-fit the training set.

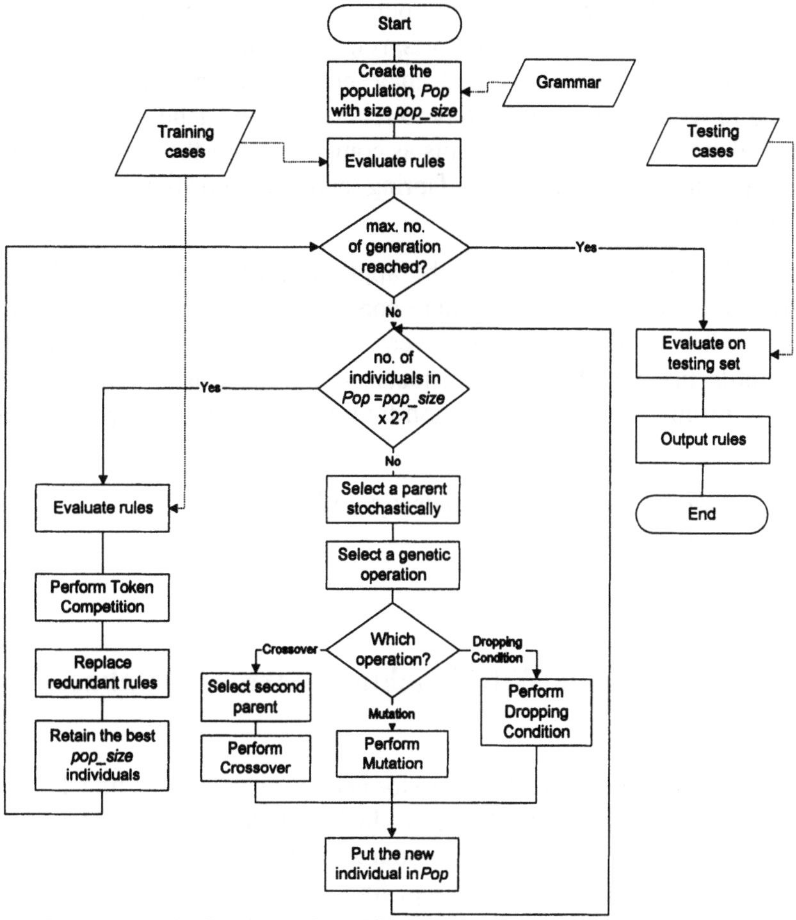

Figure 7.1: *The flowchart of the Rule Learning process.*

Our system differs from conventional GP in that reproduction operator is not used, and the parents compete with the offspring for places in the new generation. In conventional GP, the next generation of population only consists of the offspring. An individual will be passed to the next generation of population through the use of the reproduction operator. Good individuals can export their genes to the new generation by reproducing more children, and gradually dominate the population. Thus many individuals contain the good genes, and a good gene has a high probability of being passed to the offspring. However, in our rule learning approach, we do not want a good rule to replicate itself and dominate the population. Rather, we need to find several good rules and diversify the population. Token competition only allows one copy of each good individual to be kept in the population. Consequently, the chance of a good gene being passed to the offspring is much less than conventional GP, because a good individual may not be selected as the parent. Therefore we need an explicit way to retain the good genes of the parents. This is done by keeping the parents as competitors for the new generation. Good parents can win poor offspring and gain positions in the new generation.

The execution time can be approximated by assuming that the evaluation of rules is the most time consuming step. In each generation, each rule has to be checked with every training case to count the number of records that match the antecedents or the consequent. Thus we can roughly estimated that the execution time should be directly proportional to:

number of database records × *population size* ×
number of generations

7.4.4. Experiments With Machine Learning Databases

Experiments have been performed to evaluate the rule learning system. Two databases from the UCI Machine Learning Repository (Merz and Murphy 1998) are used as the source of data. Using these databases, our target is to search for knowledge for classification. A useful measure of the accuracy of the learned knowledge is to apply it to an unseen testing set. Thus the database is divided into a training and a testing sets. To measure the accuracy in the testing set, the rules are applied to see whether each testing case is classified correctly. Since the discovered rules can overlap, the testing case may match more than one rule. Starting from the rule with the highest fitness value, the testing case is checked by the rule. If the antecedent part does not match with the testing case, the next rule is applied until there is a match or no rule can apply. If no rule can be applied or the testing case matches the antecedents but not the consequent part, then the testing case is considered as a miss.

We should note that the aim of our rule learning approach is to discover knowledge instead of classifying unseen cases. No special technique is designed to make the rules cover all the cases. Thus the classification accuracy is only an indirect measurement of our approach.

7.4.4.1. Experimental Results on the Iris Plant Database

The first experiment uses the iris plants database as the data set. This database is one of the most frequently used database in machine learning. It consists of 150 records with 5 attributes (table 7.2). The task is to discover knowledge about the three classes. Each class has 50 records in the database. 100 records are randomly selected as the training set and the remaining 50 records are used as the testing set.

Attribute	Type	Possible Value
Sepal length (in cm)	continuous	4.3-7.9
Sepal width (in cm)	continuous	2.0-4.4
Petal length	continuous	1.0-6.9
Petal width	continuous	0.1-2.5
class	nominal	Iris setosa, Iris Vericolor, Iris Virginica

Table 7.2: The iris plants database.

The grammar in table 7.3 is used for learning rules from this database. This grammar is very simple. Each of the four continuous attributes is described by a range in the rule, and the nominal attribute is described by a value. The population size is 50 and the maximum number of generations is 50.

Preliminary experiments have been performed to investigate the effects of different parameter settings. We found that by lowering the value of w_2 in the fitness function (equation 7.2), a higher accuracy on the testing set can be achieved, as shown in table 7.4. In this database it is quite easy to find a rule with a high confidence, but the rule may not be general enough. Since the rule set needs to cover all testing cases, the goal of the evolution process is not just to evolve rules with high confidence, but also to evolve rules with high support. A lower value of w_2 in the fitness function can favor more general rules with a better support. We also found that the classification accuracy on using a lower value of minimum support is somewhat better, and the result is less sensitive to the rates of the genetic operators. The results are shown in tables 7.5 and 7.6.

```
1:    start                -> [if], antes, [, then], consq, [.].
2:    antes                -> slength, [and], swidth, [and],
                              plength, [and], pwidth.
3:    slength              -> [any].
4:    slength              -> slength_descriptor.
5:    swidth               -> [any].
6:    swidth               -> swidth_descriptor.
7:    plength              -> [any].
8:    plength              -> plength_descriptor.
9:    pwidth               -> [any].
10:   pwidth               -> pwidth_descriptor.
11:   slength_descriptor   -> [sepal length is between],
                              slength_const,
                              slength_const.
12:   swidth_descriptor    -> [sepal width is between],
                              swidth_const, swidth_const.
13:   plength_descriptor   -> [petal length is between],
                              plength_const,
                              plength_const.
14:   pwidth_descriptor    -> [petal width is between],
                              pwidth_const, pwidth_const.
15:   consq                -> [class is], class_const.
16:   slength_const        -> {random(4.3, 7.9, ?a)}, ?a.
17:   swidth_const         -> {random(2.0, 4.4, ?a)}, ?a.
16:   plength_const        -> {random(1.0, 6.9, ?a)}, ?a.
17:   pwidth_const         -> {random(0.1, 2.5, ?a)}, ?a.
18:   class_const          -> {member(?a, [Iris setosa,
                              Iris Vericolor,Iris Virginica])},
                              ?a.
```

Table 7.3: The grammar for the iris plants database.

w_1	w_2	Accuracy
1	8	87.6%
1	1	91.6%

Table 7.4: Results of different value of w_2.

Minimum support	Accuracy
0.03	91.6%
0.01	94.8%

Table 7.5: Results of different value of minimum support.

Rate of			
Crossover	Mutation	Dropping condition	Accuracy
0.50	0.40	0.1	94.8%
0.35	0.55	0.1	92.4%
0.60	0.30	0.1	91.6%
0.45	0.35	0.2	94.8%

Table 7.6: Results of different probabilities for the genetic operators.

A more complete result was obtained by executing 25 runs using the best setting that we have tried. The best setting uses a rate of 0.5 for crossover, 0.4 for mutation, and 0.1 for dropping condition, 0.01 for minimum support, 1 and 1 respectively for the values of w_1 and w_2 for the fitness function. The execution time for each run was about 70 seconds in a Sun Ultra 1/140. Our system achieved an average classification accuracy of 91.04%. The results of these runs are shown in table 7.7. The best run gives an accuracy of 100% and is listed in Appendix A.1

Accuracy				
Mean	Standard Derivation	Maximum	Minimum	Time
0.9104	0.0548	1.00	0.76	70 seconds

Table 7.7: Experimental result on the iris plants database.

The results of other approaches are quoted from Holte (1993) as references (table 7.8). It should be notice that these results were obtained using different number of runs and different setting in the training and testing sets. The average accuracy of our approach is not as good as the other approaches. However, the perfect result can be obtained in the best run. A characteristic of evolutionary algorithms is that they are stochastic. Thus our approach has larger fluctuations in different runs. In order to get a better result, the user may execute several trials of the algorithm to get the result with the best fitness score.

Approach	Accuracy
Our approach	91.04%
C4.5	93.8%
ID3	94.2%
Nearest Neighbor	96.0%
Neural Net	96.7%

Table 7.8: ***The classification accuracy of different approaches on the iris plants database.***

7.4.4.2. Experimental Results on the Monk Database

The second experiment has been performed on the Monk database (Thrun et al. 1991). This database contains attributes for artificial robots, as shown in table 7.9. There are three data sets. Each data set has a hidden knowledge on the robots that belong to the class (i.e. class = 1). The training set contains randomly selected robots while the testing set contains all the 432 possible robots. The task is to discover the knowledge on classification.

1. The monk1 data set has 124 examples in the training set, which contains 62 positive examples (i.e. `class`=1) and 62 negative examples (i.e. `class`=2). The testing set contains 216 positive and 216 negative examples. The hidden knowledge for classification is "(`head_shape` = `body_shape`) or (`jacket_color` = 1)". There are no mis-classifications.

2. The monk2 data set has 169 examples in the training set, which contains 105 positive and 64 negative examples. The testing set contains 190 positive and 142 negative examples.

The knowledge hidden is "exactly two of the six attributes have the values 1". For example, a robot with `head_shape=1`, `body_shape=3`, `is_smiling=1`, `holding=3`, `holding=2` and `jacket_color=2` is positive. There are no mis-classifications.

3. The monk3 data set has 122 examples in the training set, which contains 62 positive and 60 negative examples. The testing set contains 204 positive and 228 negative examples. The knowledge hidden is "(`holding` = 1 and `jacket_color` = 3) or (`body_shape` ≠ 3 and `jacket_color` ≠ 4)". There are 5% mis-classifications in the training set.

Attribute	Possible Value
head_shape	1 (round), 2 (square), 3 (octagon)
body_shape	1 (round), 2 (square), 3 (octagon)
is_smiling	1 (yes), 2 (no)
holding	1 (sword), 2 (ballon), 3 (flag)
jacket_color	1 (red), 2 (yellow), 3 (green), 4 (blue)
has_tie	1 (yes), 2 (no)
class	1 (positive), 2 (negative)

Table 7.9: The monk database.

The knowledge in monk1 is in the standard disjunctive normal form (DNF). The knowledge in monk2 is similar to a parity problem, and is difficult to be described in DNF using the given attributes only. The knowledge in monk3 is again in DNF but under the presence of noise.

The grammar for learning rules from this database is listed in table 7.10. In this problem, there should be only rules describing knowledge about positive robots. Thus these rules can only have one consequent: "`positive`". A default rule "if `any` then `negative`" is used to classify a case as negative and the fitness of this default rule is calculated. A discovered rule will not be used if its fitness is less than that of the default rule. In this grammar, the attributes `head_shape` and body_shape can be described by their values, or a comparison between them. The other attributes are described by their values. The symbols erc2, erc3, and erc4 have ranges 1 to 2, 1 to 3, and 1 to 4, respectively.

```
1:     start              ->   [if], antes, [, then], consq, [.].
2:     antes              ->   shape, [and], smile, [and], hold,
                               [and], jacket, [and], tie.
3:     shape              ->   shape_comparison.
4:     shape              ->   head, [and], body.
5:     shape_comparison   ->     [head_shape], comparator,
                                 [body_shape].
6:     head               ->   [any].
7:     head               ->   head_descriptor.
8:     body               ->   [any].
9:     body               ->   body_descriptor.
10:    smile              ->   [any].
11:    smile              ->   smile_descriptor.
12:    hold               ->   [any].
13:    hold               ->   hold_descriptor.
14:    jacket             ->   [any].
15:    jacket             ->   jacket_descriptor.
16:    tie                ->   [any].
17:    tie                ->   tie_descriptor.
18:    head_descriptor    ->     [head_shape], comparator,
                                 erc3.
19:    body_descriptor    ->     [body_shape], comparator,
                                 erc3.
20:    smile_descriptor   ->     [is_smiling], comparator,
                                 erc2.
21:    hold_descriptor    ->     [holding], comparator,
                                 erc3.
22:    jacket_descriptor  ->     [jacket_color], comparator,
                                 erc4.
23:    tie_descriptor     ->     [has_tie], comparator,
                                 erc2.
24:    tie_descriptor     ->     [=]
25:    tie_descriptor     ->     [≠].
26:    erc2               ->     {member(?x, [1, 2])}, ?x.
27:    erc3               ->     {member(?x, [1, 2, 3])},
?x.
28:    erc4               ->     {member(?x, [1,2,3,4])},?x.
29:    consq              ->     [positive].
```

Table 7.10: ***The grammar for the monk database.***

For each data set, rule learning has been executed for 25 runs using the following settings:

- the population size is 50,
- the maximum number of generations is 50,
- the minimum support is 0.01,
- w_1 is 1,
- w_2 is 8,
- the rates for crossover, mutation, and dropping condition are 0.5, 0.4, and 0.1, respectively.

The execution time for each run was around 120 seconds. The result is shown in table 7.11. The results of other approaches are quoted from Thrun et al. (1991) in table 7.12 as references.

	Accuracy			
	Mean	Standard Derivation	Maximum	Minimum
Monk1	1.000	0.000	1.00	1.00
Monk2	0.600	0.091	0.69	0.31
Monk3	0.954	0.029	1.00	0.89

Table 7.11: Experimental result on the Monk database.

Approach	Monk1	Monk2	Monk3
ID3	98.6%	67.9%	94.4%
AQR	95.9%	79.7%	87.0%
CN2	**100%**	69.0%	89.1%
AQ17-DCI	**100%**	**100%**	94.2%
AQ15-GA	**100%**	86.8%	**100%**
Assistant Professional	**100%**	81.3%	**100%**
Backpropagation	**100%**	**100%**	93.1%
Our apporach	**100%**	60%	95.4%

Table 7.12: The classification accuracy of different approaches on the monk database.

- Monk1 database

  For the monk1 database, the hidden knowledge can be easily reconstructed by the above grammar. Thus we can obtain classification accuracy of 100% on each run. The rule set is shown in Appendix A.2.1. If the grammar does not include a comparison between `head_shape` and `body_shape`, the perfect rule set can still be found but at a later generation, and three rules are needed to represented the concept (`head_shape = body_shape`) using the three possible values.

- Monk2 database

  The hidden knowledge is difficult to be represented using rules. The simple hidden rule must be represented by a large number of rules. Thus, our system cannot evolve all of these rules and results in poor classification accuracy. The best rule set is shown in Appendix A.2.2.

- Monk3 database

  Our system can discover knowledge with high classification accuracy under this noisy environment. The accuracy is the third best among different approaches. The best rule set, which is given in Appendix A.2.3, can classify all testing cases correctly.

From these experiments, we can see that our rule learning approach can successfully learn rules with high accuracy from the data, although the perfect rule set may not be discovered in every run.

Chapter 8

MEDICAL DATA MINING

LOGENPRO has been applied to real-life medical databases (Ngan et al. 1999). The following two sections are two case studies of knowledge discovery from a fracture and a scoliosis databases.

8.1. A Case Study on the Fracture Database

The fracture database consists of records of children with limb fractures, admitted to the Prince of Wales Hospital of Hong Kong in the period 1984-1996. These data can provide information for the analysis of children fracture patterns. The database has 6500 records and 8 attributes, which are listed in table 8.1.

From the database, we expect to learn knowledge about these attributes. The medical expert provides extra knowledge on how the rules should be formulated. He suggests that the attributes can be divided into three time stages: a diagnosis is first given to the patient, then an operation is performed, and after that the patient stays in the hospital. This knowledge leads to three kinds of rules. Firstly, sex, age, and admission date are the possible causes of diagnoses. Secondly, these three attributes and diagnosis are the possible causes of operations and surgeons. Thirdly, length of stay has all the other attributes as the possible causes. A grammar (see Appendix B.1) is written to specify these three kinds of rules. In this experiment, we have used a population size of 300 to run for 50 generations. The minimum support is 0.01, w_1 is 1, w_2 is 8, the rates for crossover, mutation, and dropping condition are 0.5, 0.4, and 0.1, respectively. The execution time was about 3 hours on a Sun Ultra 1/140 for the 6500 records. The results are summarized in table 8.2. The rules are listed in Appendix A.3.

Attribute Name	Type	Description	Possible Value
`Sex`	Nominal	Sex	'M' or 'F'
`Age`	Numeric	Age	Between 0 to 16 years old
`Admday`	Date	Admission date	Between year 1984 to 1996; Divided into four parts:Day, Month, Year and Weekday
`Stay`	Numeric	Length of staying in hospital	Between 0 to 1000 days Discretized into 18 non-uniform ranges.
`Diagnosis`	Nominal	Diagnosis of fracture	10 different values, based on the location of fracture
`Operation`	Nominal	Operation	'CR' (Simple Closed Reduction), 'CR+K-wire' (Closed Reduction with K-wire), 'CR+POP' (Closed Reduction with POP), 'OR' (Open Reduction), or Null (no operation)
`Surgeon`	Nominal	Surgeon	One of 61 surgeons or Null if no operation
`Side`	Nominal	Side of fracture	'Left', 'Right', 'Both' or 'Missing'

Table 8.1: Attributes in the fracture database.

About	No. of	*cf*			*cf/prob*			*support*		
	Rules	Mean	Max	Min	Mean	Max	Min	Mean	Max	Min
Diagnosis	2	45.6%	51.4%	39.8%	1.6	1.7	1.4	9.2%	10.0%	8.4%
Operation	9	42.6%	74.0%	28.0%	2.0	2.9	1.1	5.4%	16.2%	3.2%
Stay	13	71.1%	81.1%	47.0%	2.5	7.0	1.4	4.5%	8.7%	3.1%

Table 8.2: Summary of the rules for the fracture database.

Two interesting rules about diagnosis have been found. The one with the highest confidence factor is:

```
If age is between 2 and 5,
then diagnosis is Humerus.                    (cf=51.43%)
```

The confidence factors of the rules about diagnosis are just around 40%-50%. It is partly because there are actually no strong rules affecting the value of diagnosis. However the ratio *cf/prob* shows that the patterns discovered deviate significantly from the average. LOGENPRO found that humerus fracture is the most common fracture for children between 2 and

5 years old, while radius fracture is the most common fracture for boys between 11 and 13.

Nine interesting rules about operation have been found. The one with the highest confidence factor is presented as follows:

```
If age is between 0 and 7 and
   admission year is between 1988 and 1993
   and diagnosis is Radius,
then operation is CR+POP.                        (cf=74.05%)
```

These rules suggest that radius and ulna fractures are usually treated with CR+POP (i.e. plaster). Usually, it is not necessary to perform operation for tibia fracture. For children older than 11 years old, open reductions are performed commonly. Usually, it is not necessary to perform operation for children younger than 7 years old. LOGENPRO did not find any interesting rules about surgeons, as the surgeons for operation are more or less randomly distributed in the database.

Thirteen interesting rules about length of stay have been found. The one with the highest confidence factor is:

```
If admission year is between 1985 and 1996
   and diagnosis is Femur ,
then stay is more than 8 days.                   (cf=81.11%)
```

Because Femur and Tibia fractures are serious injuries, these kinds of patients have to stay longer in hospital. If open reduction is performed, the patient requires longer time to recover because the wound has been cut open for operation. If no operation is needed, it is likely that the patient can return home within one day. Relatively, radius fracture requires a shorter time for recovery.

The results have been evaluated by the medical expert. The rules provide interesting patterns that were not recognized before. The analysis gives an overview of the important epidemiological and demographic data of the fractures in children. It has clearly demonstrated the treatment pattern and rules of decision making. It can provide a good monitor of the change of pattern of management and the epidemiology if the data mining process is continued longitudinally over the years. It also helps to provide the information for setting up a knowledge-based instruction system to help young doctors in training to learn the rules in diagnosis and treatment.

8.2. A Case Study on the Scoliosis Database

We have also employed LOGENPRO to learn rules from the database of scoliosis patients. Scoliosis refers to the spinal deformation. A scoliosis patient has one or more curves in his/her spine. Among them, the curves with severe deformations are identified as major curves. The database stores measurements on the patients, such as the number of curves, the curve locations, degrees, and directions. It also records the maturity of the patient, the class of scoliosis, and the treatment. The database has 500 records. According to the domain expert, 20 attributes are useful and extracted from the database. They are listed in table 8.3.

Attribute Name	Description	Possible Value
Sex	Sex	'M' or 'F'
Age	Age	positive integer
Lax	Joint Laxity	integer between 0 and 3
1stCurveT1	Whether 1st curve started at vertebra T1	Y or N
1stMCGreater	Whether the degree of 1st Major Curve is greater than the 2nd Major Curve	Y or N
L4Tilt	Whether vertebra L4 is tilted	Y or N
1stMCDeg	Degree of 1st Major Curve	positive integer
2ndMCDeg	Degree of 2nd Major Curve	positive integer
1stMCApex	Apex of 1st Major Curve	any vertebra
2ndMCApex	Apex of 2nd Major Curve	any vertebra
Deg1	Degree of 1st Curve	positive integer
Deg2	Degree of 2nd Curve	positive integer
Deg3	Degree of 3rd Curve	positive integer
Deg4	Degree of 4th Curve	positive integer
Class	Scoliosis Classification	K-I, K-II, K-III, K-V, TL, L
Mens	Period of Menstruation	positive integer
TSI	Trunk Shift (in cm)	positive integer
TSIDir	Trunk Shift Direction	null, left or right
RI	Risser Sign	integer between 0 and 5
Treatment	Treatment	Observation, surgery or bracing

(Vertebras are coded with T1-T12 or L1-L5)
(Trunk Shift measures the displacement of the curve)
(Risser Sign measures the maturity of the patient)

Table 8.3: Attributes in the scoliosis database.

The medical expert is interested in discovering knowledge about classification of scoliosis and treatment. Scoliosis can be classified as Kings, Thoracolumbar(TL), or Lumbar(L), while Kings can be further subdivided into K-I, II, III, IV, and V. Treatment can be classified as observation, surgery, or bracing. The domain expert is more interested in finding relationships among classification of scoliosis and the attributes `1stCurveT1`, `1stMCGreater`, `L4Tilt`, `1stMCDeg`, `2ndMCDeg`, `1stMCApex`, and `2ndMCApex`, and relationships among treatment and age, laxity, degrees of the curves, maturity of the patient, displacement of the vertebra, and the class of scoliosis. This domain knowledge can be easily incorporated into the logic grammar. There are two types of rules, one for classification of scoliosis and the other for suggesting treatments. The grammar is outlined in Appendix B.2. The population size is 100 and the maximum number of generations is 50. The minimum support is 0.01, w_1 is 1, w_2 is 8, the rates for crossover, mutation, and dropping condition are 0.5, 0.4, and 0.1, respectively. The execution time was about one hour on a Sun Ultra 1/140. The results of rule learning from this database are listed below.

8.2.1. Rules for Scoliosis Classification

For each class of scoliosis, a number of rules are mined. The results are summarized in table 8.4. The rules are listed in Appendix A.4.1. A typical rule of this kind is:

```
If 1stMCGreater = N and 1stMCApex between T1 and T8
   and 2ndMCApex between L3 and L4 ,
then diagnosis is K-I.                        (cf=100%)
```

For King-I and II, the rules have high confidence and generally match with the knowledge of medical experts. However the fourth rules of King-II is an unexpected rule for the classification of King-II. Under the conditions specified in the antecedents, our system found a rule with a confidence factor of 52% that the classification is King-II. However, the domain expert suggests the class should be King-V! After an analysis on the database, we revealed that serious data errors existed in the current database and that some records contained an incorrect scoliosis classification.

For King-III and IV, the confidence factors of the rules discovered are just around 20%. According to the domain expert, one common characteristic for these two classes is that there is only one major curve or the second major curve is insignificant. However there is no rigid definition for a 'major curve' and the concept of 'insignificant' is fuzzy. It depends on the interpretation of the doctors. Because of the inadequacy of information from the training data, the system cannot find accurate rules for these two classes. Another problem is that only a small number of patients in the database were classified as King-III or IV (see the values of *prob* in table 8.4). The database cannot provide a large number of cases for training.

Similar problems also exist for King-V, TL, and L. For the classes, the system found rules with confidence factors around 40% to 60%. Nevertheless, the rules for TL and L show something different in comparison with the rules suggested by the clinicians. According to our rules, the classification always depends on the location of the *first major curve*, while according to the domain expert, the classification always depends on the *larger major curve*. After discussion with the domain expert, it is agreed that the existing rules are not defined clearly enough, and our rules are more accurate than theirs. Our rules provide hints to the clinicians to re-formulate their concepts.

Class	No. of Rules	*cf*			*support*			*prob*
		mean	max	min	mean	max	min	
King-I	3	94.84%	100%	90.48%	5.67%	10.73%	0.86%	28.33%
King-II	4	80.93%	100%	52.17%	6.61%	14.38%	1.07%	35.41%
King-III	2	23.58%	25.87%	16.90%	1.56%	2.58%	0.86%	7.94%
King-IV	2	24.38%	29.41%	19.35%	1.18%	1.29%	1.07%	2.79%
King-V	3	54.13%	62.50%	45.45%	0.97%	1.07%	0.86%	6.44%
TL	1	41.18%	41.18%	41.18%	1.50%	1.50%	1.50%	2.15%
L	3	54.04%	62.50%	45.45%	2.00%	2.79%	1.07%	4.51%

Table 8.4: ***Results of the rules for scoliosis classification.***

8.2.2. Rules About Treatment

The results of rules about treatment are summarized in table 8.5. The rules are listed in Appendix A.4.2. A typical rule of this kind is:

```
If age between 2 and 12 and Deg1 between 20 and 26 and
   Deg2 between 24 and 47 and
   Deg3 between 27 and 52 and
   Deg4 is 0 ,
then treatment is Bracing.                      (cf=100%)
```

The rules for observation and bracing have very high confidence factors. However, the support is not high, showing that the rules only cover fragments of the cases. Our system prefers accurate rules to general rules. If the user prefers more general rules, the weights in the fitness function can be tuned. For surgery, no interesting rule was found because only 3.65% of the patients were treated with surgery.

The biggest impact on clinicians from the data mining analysis of the scoliosis database is the fact that many rules set out in the clinical practice are not clearly defined. The usual clinical interpretation depends on the subjective experience. Data mining revealed quite a number of mismatches in the classification on the types of Kings curves. After a careful review by the senior surgeon it appears that the database entries by junior surgeons may not be accurate and that the rules discovered are in fact more accurate! The classification rules must therefore be quantified. The rules discovered can therefore help in the training of younger doctors and act as an intelligent means to validate and evaluate the accuracy of the clinical database. An accurate and validated clinical database is very important for helping clinicians to make decisions, to assess and evaluate treatment strategies, to conduct clinical and related basic research, and to enhance teaching and professional training.

Type	No. of Rules	*cf*			*support*			*prob*
		mean	max	min	mean	max	min	
Observation	3	98.89%	100%	95.55%	3.49%	6.01%	1.07%	62.45%
Bracing	3	79.57%	100%	71.43%	1.03%	1.29%	0.86%	24.46%
Surgery	0	-	-	-	-	-	-	3.65%

Table 8.5: Results of the rules about treatment.

Chapter 9

CONCLUSION AND FUTURE WORK

9.1. Conclusion

Data mining is defined as the non-trivial process of identifying valid, novel, potentially useful, and ultimately understandable patterns in data stored in databases (Fayyad et al. 1996, Frawley et al. 1991, Piatetsky-Shapiro and Frawley 1991). The knowledge discovered can be expressed in different knowledge representations such as logic programs, decision trees, decision lists, and production rules.

Two of the approaches in data mining are Inductive Logic Programming (ILP) and Genetic Programming (GP). It was demonstrated that ILP can be used to induce knowledge represented as logic programs (Dzeroski and Lavrac 1993, Dzeroski 1996, Dehaspe and Toivonen, 1999, Srinivasan and King 1999, Blockeel et al. 1999, Srinivasan 1999). GP (Koza 1992; 1994, Koza et al. 1999 Kinnear 1994) extends traditional Genetic Algorithms (Holland 1992, Goldberg 1989, Davis 1987; 1991) to induce automatically S-expressions in Lisp. It performs both exploitation of the most promising solutions and exploration of the search space. It is featured to tackle hard search problems and thus applicable to program induction and data mining.

We have proposed a framework for data mining in chapter 5, called Generic Genetic Programming (GGP), that combines Genetic Programming and Inductive Logic Programming. This framework is based on a formalism of logic grammars. To implement the framework, a data mining system called LOGENPRO (The LOgic grammar based GENetic PROgramming system) has been developed. The formalism can represent context-sensitive information and domain-dependent knowledge. The formalism is also very flexible and the knowledge learned can be represented in various knowledge representations such as functional programs, logic programs, and production rules. LOGENPRO has been tested on some learning tasks.

An experiment that employs LOGENPRO to induce an S-expression for calculating dot product has been described in chapter 6.

This experiment illustrated that LOGENPRO, when used with domain knowledge, accelerates the learning of programs.

Automatic discovery of sub-functions is one of the most important research areas in genetic programming. In GP with ADFs, the user must provide explicit knowledge about the number of available sub-functions, the number of arguments of each sub-function, and the allowable terminal and function sets for each sub-function. An experiment has been performed to demonstrate that LOGENPRO can emulate GP with ADFs and represent the knowledge easily. Moreover, LOGENPRO can employ other knowledge such as argument types in a unified framework. This experiment shows that LOGENPRO has superior performance to that of GP with ADFs when more domain-dependent knowledge is available.

In chapter 6, we have also presented two applications of LOGENPRO in acquiring knowledge from databases. These applications have demonstrated the advantages of LOGENPRO over other learning systems. In the first application, we have employed LOGENPRO to induce knowledge represented in decision trees from a real-world database and compared the results obtained by Michie et al. (1994) for the same problem. We have found that Cal5, ITrule, Discrim, Logdisc and DIPOL92 perform better than LOGENPRO marginally. Since the detailed information about the accuracy of the former systems is not available, it cannot be concluded that whether the differences in accuracy are significant. On the other hand, LOGENPRO performs better than CART, RBF, CASTLE, NaiveBay, IndCART, Back-propagation, C4.5, SMART, Baytree, k-NN, NewID, AC2, LVQ, ALLOC80, CN2, and Quadisc for the problem. Interestingly, LOGENPRO is better than C4.5 and CN2, two systems that have been reported in the literature (Quinlan 1992, Clark and Niblett 1989) about their outstanding performances in inducing decision trees or rules.

In the second application, we have described how to combine LOGENPRO and a variation of FOIL, BEAM-FOIL, in learning logic programs. The initial population of logic programs is provided by BEAM-FOIL. The performance of LOGENPRO in inducing logic programs from imperfect training examples is evaluated using the chess endgame problem. A detailed comparison to FOIL, BEAM-FOIL, and mFOIL has been conducted. It is found that LOGENPRO outperforms the other systems significantly in this domain.

In chapters 7 and 8, we have employed LOGENPRO for learning rules from databases. Rules capture the specific relationships between particular values of the variables.

The grammar used in LOGENPRO can provide a powerful knowledge representation. It can specify the format of the rules to be discovered. The format can be changed according to different domains, and the flexible grammar allows the representation of general concepts. Moreover, knowledge from domain experts is very useful for data mining. The use of grammar allows the domain knowledge to be easily and effectively utilized. Furthermore, the user can specify the desirable rule format by composing a suitable grammar. This can increase the understandability and the usefulness of the discovered rules.

In many real-life situations, the available rules are general guidelines with many exceptional cases. The fitness function in the rule learning approach has been designed to learn such kind of knowledge. It compares the confidence factor of the rule with the average probability, so as to search for the patterns significantly deviated from the normal. Since one rule is insufficient to represent the complete knowledge, token competition has been used to learn as many rules as possible. This technique can effectively and efficiently formulate niches in the population, such that different rules are evolved in the same population. This rule learning approach can successfully construct rules from data. The rules can represent the regularities in the database and provide interesting knowledge to the users.

The data mining system has been applied to two real-life medical databases. The results can provide interesting knowledge as well as suggestion for refinements to the existing knowledge. We also have found unexpected results that have led to discovery of mistakes in databases. In the fracture database, the system automatically uncovered knowledge about the age effect on fracture, the relationship between diagnoses and operations, and the effect of diagnoses and operations on lengths of staying in the hospital. In the scoliosis database, we have discovered new knowledge about the classification of scoliosis and about the treatment. The discovered knowledge has led to refinements of the existing knowledge.

These experiments and the results demonstrate that LOGENPRO is a promising system for inducing knowledge from databases.

9.2. Future Work

In chapter 6, we have shown that LOGENPRO can successfully induce knowledge represented as logic programs from noisy datasets. We have also found that the noise handling ability of LOGENPRO is better than many existing ILP systems. Since training examples stored in everyday databases are usually imperfect, a very important research area in data mining is how to improve the noise handling mechanisms of our system.

One can use LOGENPRO on extracting knowledge from other datasets of the field. One can also combine LOGENPRO with other learning systems such as GOLEM (Muggletion and Feng 1990), LINUS (Lavrac and Dzeroski 1994), and mFOIL (Lavrac and Dzeroski 1994) to explore the possibility of further improvement on its learning ability.

Since the system is very flexible, different representations employed by other learning systems can be specified easily. It facilitates the integration of LOGENPRO with the latter. One approach is to incorporate the search operators of other systems into LOGENPRO. These operators include information guided hill-climbing (Quinlan 1990; 1991), explanation-based generalization (DeJong and Mooney 1986, Mitchell et al. 1986, Ellman 1989), explanation-based specialization (Minton 1989) and inverse resolution (Muggleton 1992). LOGENPRO can also invoke other learning systems as front-ends to generate the initial population. The advantage is that we can quickly find important and meaningful components (genetic materials) and embody these components into the initial population. Moreover, it has been found that LOGENPRO, when combined with other learning systems, has superior performance in learning logic programs from imperfect data as in the chess-endgame problem. The Darwinian principle of survival and selection of the fittest is a plausible noise handling method which can avoid overfitting and identify important patterns simultaneously. This superior noise handling ability is intrinsically embedded in LOGENPRO because it uses evolutionary algorithms as its primary learning mechanism.

For almost all applications of LOGENPRO, a huge amount of computation time is consumed in evaluating the fitness value of each program in the population since the genetic operators of LOGENPRO can be performed efficiently. Memory availability is another important problem of LOGENPRO because the population usually has a large number of programs. Moreover, since programs are represented as derivation trees of varying sizes, shapes, and structures. This representation method requires a lot of memory to store programs.

There is a relation between the difficulty of the problem to be solved and the size of the population. In order to solve substantial and real world problems, a population size of thousands and a longer evolution process are usually required. A larger population and a longer evolution process imply a larger number of fitness evaluations must be conducted and more memory is required. In other words, a lot of computational resources are required to solve substantial and practical problems. Usually, this requirement cannot be fulfilled by normal workstations.

Fortunately, these time-consuming fitness evaluations can be performed independently for each program in the population and programs in the population can be distributed among multiple computers. Thus, we plan to develop a parallel version of LOGENPRO.

Evolutionary algorithms have a high degree of inherent parallelism which is one of the motivation of studies in this field. In natural populations, thousands or even millions of individuals exist in parallel and these individuals operate independently with a little cooperation and/or competition among them. This suggests a degree of parallelism that is directly proportional to the population size used in evolutionary algorithms. There are different ways of exploiting parallelisms in evolutionary algorithms. We plan to study the possibility of parallelizing LOGENPRO using four different approaches. They are master-slave models, improved-slave models, massively parallel evolutionary algorithms, and island models.

The most direct way to implement a parallel evolutionary algorithm is to implement a global population in the master processor. The master sends each individual to a slave processor and let the slave to find the fitness value of the individual. After the fitness values of all individuals are obtained, the master processor selects some individuals from the population using some selection method, performs some genetic operations, and then creates a new population of offspring. The master sends each individual in the new population to a slave again and the above process is iterated until the termination criterion is satisfied.

Master-slave models can be improved easily using the tournament selection. Another direct way to implement a parallel evolutionary algorithm is to implement a global population and use the tournament selection. As described in chapter 3, the tournament selection approximates the behavior of ranking. Assume that the population size *N* is even and there are more than *N*/2 processors. *N*/2 slave processors are selected and are numbered from 1 to *N*/2. A processor selected from the remaining processors maintains the global population and implements an algorithm that controls the overall evolution process and the other *N*/2 slave processors. Each slave processor performs two independent *m*-ary tournaments. In each tournament, *m* individuals are sampled randomly from the global population. These *m* individuals are evaluated in the slave processor and the winner is kept. Since there are two tournaments, the two winners produced can be crossed in the slave processor to generate two offspring. The slave processor may perform further modifications to the offspring. The offspring are then sent back to the global population and the master processor proceeds to the next generation if all offspring are received from the *N*/2 slave processors.

Massively parallel evolutionary algorithms explore the computing power of massively parallel computers. To explore the power of this kind of computers, one can assign one individual to each processor, and allow each individual to seek a mate close to it. A global random mating scheme is inappropriate because of the limitation of the communication abilities of these computers. Each processor can select probabilistically an individual in its neighborhood to mate with. The selection is based on the fitness proportionate selection, the ranking, the tournament selection, or other selection methods proposed in the literature. Only one offspring is produced and becomes the new resident at that processor. The common property of different massively parallel evolutionary algorithms is that selections and mating are typically restricted to a local neighborhood.

Island models can fully explore the computing power of coarse grain parallel computers and distributed workstations. Assume that we have 20 high performance processors, such as the UltraSparc processors, and have a population of 4000 individuals. We can divide the total population down into 20 sub-populations (islands or demes) of 200 individuals each. Each processor can then execute a normal evolutionary algorithm such as LOGENPRO on one of these sub-populations. Occasionally, the sub-populations would swap a few individuals. The migration allows sub-populations to share genetic material (Whitley and Starkweather 1990, Gorges-Schlenter 1991, Tanese 1989, Starkweather et al. 1991).

Since there are 20 independent evolutionary searches occur concurrently, these searches will be different to a certain extent because the initial subpopulations will impose a certain sampling bias. Moreover, genetic drift will tend to drive these subpopulations in different directions. By employing migration, island models are able to exploit differences in the various subpopulations. These differences maintain genetic diversity of the whole population and thus can prevent the problem of premature convergence. We plan to exploit a number of variations of island models. These variations investigate the effects of subpopulations with different sizes or even dynamic sizes, asynchronous migration, dynamic number of migrating individuals, subpopulations with different fitness functions, adaptive migration methods, and cooperative/competitive co-evolution.

Appendix A

THE RULE SETS DISCOVERED

A.1. The Best Rule Set Learned from the Iris Database

```
1.   if petal width is between 0.08 and 0.77, then
     class is Iris-setosa.

     Fitness: 1.50
     Confidence: 100%;
     Support: 30%;
     Probability of consequent: 30%
2.   if petal length is between 1.98 and 4.97, and
     petal width is between 0.18 and 1.66, then
     class is Iris-vericolor.

     Fitness: 1.37
     Confidence: 100%;
     Support: 35%;
     Probability of consequent: 35%
3.   if sepal width is between 2.33 and 3.16, then
     class is Iris-virginica.

     Fitness: 0.43
     Confidence: 49.06%;
     Support: 26%;
     Probability of consequent: 35%
4.   if any, then class is Iris-virginica.

     Fitness: 0.35
     Confidence: 35%;
     Support: 35%;
     Probability of consequent: 35%
```

A.2. The Best Rule Set Learned from the Monk Database

A.2.1. Monk1

1. if jacket_color = 1, then positive.

   Fitness: 11.33
   Confidence: 100%;
   Support: 23.39%;
   Probability of consequent: 50%
2. if head_shape = 1 and body_shape = 1, then positive.

   Fitness: 9.93
   Confidence: 100%;
   Support: 7.26%;
   Probability of consequent: 50%
3. if head_shape = 2 and body_shape = 2, then positive.

   Fitness: 8.98
   Confidence: 100%;
   Support: 12.10%;
   Probability of consequent: 50%
4. if head_shape = 3 and body_shape = 3, then positive.

   Fitness: 8.59
   Confidence: 100%;
   Support: 13.70%;
   Probability of consequent: 50%
5. if any, then negative.

   Fitness: 0.51
   Confidence: 50%;
   Support: 50%;
   Probability of consequent: 50%

A.2.2. Monk2

1. if head_shape ≠ body_shape and is_smiling = 1 and holding ≠ 1 and jacket_color = 2 and has_tie ≠ 1, then positive.

   Fitness: 15.59
   Confidence: 100%;
   Support: 4.73%;
   Probability of consequent: 37.87%
2. if head_shape = 2 and body_shape ≠ 1 and is_smiling ≠ 2 and holding ≠ 1 and jacket_color ≠ 1 and has_tie ≠ 2, then positive.

   Fitness: 15.58
   Confidence: 100%;
   Support: 3.55%;
   Probability of consequent: 37.87%
3. if head_shape ≠ body_shape and is_smiling ≠ 1 and jacket_color = 1 and has_tie ≠ 1, then positive.

   Fitness: 15.58
   Confidence: 100%;
   Support: 2.96%;
   Probability of consequent: 37.87%
4. if body_shape ≠ 1 and is_smiling ≠ 1 and holding = 2 and jacket_color = 1 and has_tie ≠ 2, then positive.

   Fitness: 15.57
   Confidence: 100%;
   Support: 2.37%;
   Probability of consequent: 37.87%
5. if head_shape = 1 and is_smiling ≠ 2 and holding ≠ 1 and jacket_color = 3 and has_tie ≠ 1, then positive.

   Fitness: 15.56
   Confidence: 100%;
   Support: 1.78%;
   Probability of consequent: 37.87%

6. if body_shape = 1 and is_smiling = 1 and jacket_color = 3 and has_tie = 2, then positive.

   Fitness: 15.56
   Confidence: 100%;
   Support: 1.78%;
   Probability of consequent: 37.87%
7. if head_shape ≠ 1 and body_shape ≠ 1 and is_smiling ≠ 1 and holding = 3 and jacket_color = 1, then positive.

   Fitness: 15.56
   Confidence: 100%;
   Support: 1.78%;
   Probability of consequent: 37.87%
8. if head_shape = 1 and is_smiling ≠ 2 and holding ≠ 1 and jacket_color = 4 and has_tie ≠ 1, then positive.

   Fitness: 15.56
   Confidence: 100%;
   Support: 1.18%;
   Probability of consequent: 37.87%
9. if head_shape = 3 and body_shape ≠ 3 and is_smiling ≠ 2 and jacket_color ≠ 1 and has_tie = 2, then positive.

   Fitness: 5.05
   Confidence: 87.50%;
   Support: 4.14%;
   Probability of consequent: 37.87%
10. if head_shape ≠ body_shape and holding ≠ 1 and jacket_color = 2 and has_tie = 1, then positive.

    Fitness: 3.96
    Confidence: 70%;
    Support: 4.14%;
    Probability of consequent: 37.87%

11. if body_shape ≠ 1 and is_smiling ≠ 1 and holding = 2 and jacket_color ≠ 2 and has_tie ≠ 2, then positive.

    Fitness: 2.75
    Confidence: 75%;
    Support: 3.55%;
    Probability of consequent: 37.87%

12. if head_shape ≠ body_shape and is_smiling = 1 and holding ≠ 1 and jacket_color = 2, then positive.

    Fitness: 2.37
    Confidence: 91.67%;
    Support: 6.50%;
    Probability of consequent: 37.87%

13. if head_shape ≠ body_shape and holding ≠ 2 and jacket_color = 2 and has_tie = 1, then positive.

    Fitness: 1.35
    Confidence: 83.33%;
    Support: 2.96%;
    Probability of consequent: 37.87%

14. if body_shape = 1 and is_smiling ≠ 1 and jacket_color ≠ 1 and has_tie = 2, then positive.

    Fitness: 1.13
    Confidence: 50%;
    Support: 3.55%;
    Probability of consequent: 37.87%

15. if any, then negative.

    Fitness: 0.63
    Confidence: 62.13%;
    Support: 62.13%;
    Probability of consequent: 62.13%

A.2.3. Monk3

1. if body_shape ≠ 3 and is_smiling = 2 and jacket_color ≠ 4, then positive.

   Fitness: 11.46
   Confidence: 100%;
   Support: 22.30%;
   Probability of consequent: 49.59%
2. if head_shape ≠ body_shape and holding = 1 and jacket_color = 3, then positive.

   Fitness: 6.76
   Confidence: 100%;
   Support: 4.13%;
   Probability of consequent: 49.59%
3. if body_shape ≠ 3 and holding ≠ 2 and jacket_color = 2, then positive.

   Fitness: 6.06
   Confidence: 100%;
   Support: 12.40%;
   Probability of consequent: 49.59%
4. if head_shape ≠ 1 and holding = 1 and jacket_color = 3, then positive.

   Fitness: 4.51
   Confidence: 100%;
   Support: 4.13%;
   Probability of consequent: 49.59%
5. if body_shape ≠ 3 and jacket_color ≠ 4, then positive.

   Fitness: 2.68
   Confidence: 91.94%;
   Support: 47.10%;
   Probability of consequent: 49.59%
6. if body_shape ≠ 3 and jacket_color = 2 and has_tie ≠ 1, then positive.

   Fitness: 1.62
   Confidence: 100%;
   Support: 11.57%;
   Probability of consequent: 49.59%

7. if head_shape ≠ 2 and body_shape ≠ 3 and holding ≠ 3 and jacket_color = 2, then positive.

   Fitness: 0.87
   Confidence: 100%;
   Support: 10.74%;
   Probability of consequent: 49.59%
8. if any, then negative.

   Fitness: 0.51
   Confidence: 50.41%;
   Support: 50.40%;
   Probability of consequent: 50.40%

A.3. The Best Rule Set Learned from the Fracture Database

A.3.1. Type I Rules: About Diagnosis

1. Humerus
   if age is between 2 and 5, then diagnosis is Humerus.

   Fitness: 3.48
   Confidence: 39.75%;
   Support: 8.42%;
   Probability of consequent: 23.43%
2. Radius
   if sex is M, and age is between 11 and 13, then diagnosis is Radius .

   Fitness: 3.04
   Confidence: 51.43%;
   Support: 10.01%;
   Probability of consequent: 36.10%

A.3.2. Type II Rules: About Operation/Surgeon

1. Radius vs. CR+POP
   if age is between 0 and 7, and admission year between 1988 and 1993, and diagnosis is Radius, then operation is CR+POP.

   Fitness: 8.56
   Confidence: 50.61%;
   Support: 3.19%;
   Probability of consequent: 17.72%
2. Tibia vs. No Operation
   if age is between 1 and 7, and diagnosis is Tibia, then operation is Null (i.e. no operation).

   Fitness: 7.86
   Confidence: 74.05%;
   Support: 3.78%;
   Probability of consequent: 38.11%
3. Ulna vs. CR+POP
   if age is between 1 and 12, and admission year between 1989 and 1992, and diagnosis is Ulna, then operation is CR+POP.

   Fitness: 7.19
   Confidence: 47.37%;
   Support: 3.50%;
   Probability of consequent: 17.72%

   if diagnosis is Ulna, then operation is CR+POP.

   Fitness: 4.23
   Confidence: 36.17%;
   Support: 7.40%;
   Probability of consequent: 17.72%

4. Radius vs. CR+K-Wire
if admission year is between 1992 and 1994, and diagnosis is Radius, then operation is CR+K-Wire.

Fitness: 4.10
Confidence: 34.03%;
Support: 3.83%;
Probability of consequent: 16.23%

5. Humerus vs. CR+K-Wire
if diagnosis is Humerus, then operation is CR+K-Wire.

Fitness: 2.52
Confidence: 27.96%;
Support: 6.06%;
Probability of consequent: 16.23%

6. Ulna vs. OR
if age is between 11 and 15, and diagnosis is Ulna, then operation is OR.

Fitness: 3.24
Confidence: 33.20%;
Support: 3.25%;
Probability of consequent: 18.26%

7. Age vs. OR
if sex is M, and age is between 13 and 17, and admission year between 1985 and 1989, then operation is OR.

Fitness: 2.57
Confidence: 30.53%;
Support: 3.22%;
Probability of consequent: 18.26%

8. Age vs. No Operation
if age is between 0 and 7, then operation is Null (i.e. no operation).

Fitness: 1.08
Confidence: 43.33%;
Support: 16.22%;
Probability of consequent: 38.11%

A.3.3. Type III Rules: About Stay

1. Femur vs. Stay
   if admission year between 1985 and 1996, and diagnosis is Femur , then stay is between 8 and 2000 days. (i.e. stay 8 days or more, since 2000 is the maximum value of stay)

   Fitness: 21.99
   Confidence: 70.87%;
   Support: 3.14%;
   Probability of consequent: 10.24%

   if diagnosis is Femur , then stay is between 5 and 2000 days. (i.e. stay 5 days or more)

   Fitness: 18.70
   Confidence: 80.99%;
   Support: 3.30%;
   Probability of consequent: 19.22%
2. Tibia vs. Stay
   if age between 5 and 12, and diagnosis is Tibia, then stay is between 3 and 2000. (i.e. stay 3 days or more)

   Fitness: 8.93
   Confidence: 78.92%;
   Support: 5.05%;
   Probability of consequent: 39.15%

3. OR vs. Stay

if age between 2 and 14, and diagnosis is Humerus, and operation is OR, then stay is between 3 and 25 days.

Fitness: 8.86
Confidence: 75.57%;
Support: 3.52%;
Probability of consequent: 36.51%

if admission is between 1985 and 1987, and operation is OR, then stay is between 3 and 10 days.

Fitness: 6.99
Confidence: 65.52%;
Support: 3.47%;
Probability of consequent: 33.85%

if operation is OR, then stay is between 3 and 25 days.

Fitness: 6.13
Confidence: 64.90%;
Support: 12.22%;
Probability of consequent: 36.51%

4. No operation vs. Stay

if age is between 10 and 14, and admission year is between 1987 and 1996, and diagnosis is Radius, and operation is Null, then stay is between 0 and 1 day.

Fitness: 9.55
Confidence: 77.00%;
Support: 3.09%;
Probability of consequent: 35.65%

if operation is Null, then stay is between 0 and 1 day.

Fitness: 3.38
Confidence: 52.06%;
Support: 19.62%;
Probability of consequent: 35.65%

5. Radius vs. Stay
if age between 6 and 12, and admission year is between 1989 and 1992, and diagnosis is Radius, and operation is CR+POP, then stay is between 1 and 2 days.

Fitness: 6.01
Confidence: 81.11%;
Support: 3.22%;
Probability of consequent: 51.29%

if diagnosis is Radius, and operation is CR+POP, then stay is between 1 and 2 days.

Fitness: 5.49
Confidence: 78.57%;
Support: 10.22%;
Probability of consequent: 51.29%

if age is between 0 and 8, and diagnosis is Radius, then stay is between 0 and 3 days.

Fitness: 2.89
Confidence: 86.92%;
Support: 10.19%;
Probability of consequent: 71.30%

6. Humerus vs. Stay
if diagnosis is Humerus, and operation is CR+K-WIRE, then stay is between 2 and 5 days.

Fitness: 3.90
Confidence: 67.30%;
Support: 4.56%;
Probability of consequent: 47.16%

7. Year vs. Stay
if admission year is between 1985 and 1987, then stay is between 3 and 10 days.

Fitness: 2.58
Confidence: 46.98%;
Support: 8.65%;
Probability of consequent: 33.85%

A.4. The Best Rule Set Learned from the Scoliosis Database

A.4.1. Rules for Classification

A.4.1.1. King-I

1. if 1stMCGreater=N and 1stMCApex=T1-T8 and 2ndMCApex=L3-L4, then King-I.

   Fitness: 20.20
   Confidence: 100%;
   Support: 0.86%;
   Probability of consequent: 28.33%
2. if 1stMCGreater=N and 1stMCDeg=21-80 and 1stMCApex =T1-T12 and 2ndMCApex=L2-L3, then King-I.

   Fitness: 19.06
   Confidence: 96.67%;
   Support: 6.22%;
   Probability of consequent: 28.33%
3. if 1stMCGreater=N and L4Tilt=Y and 1stMCApex =T1-T10 and 2ndMCApex=L2-L5, then King-I.

   Fitness: 18.92
   Confidence: 96.15%;
   Support: 10.73%;
   Probability of consequent: 28.33%

A.4.1.2. King-II

1. if 1stCurveT1=N and 1stMCGreater=Y and 1stMCDeg=16-45 and 2ndMCDeg=28-54 and 1stMCApex =T4-T11 and 2ndMCApex=L2-L3, then King-II.

   Fitness: 16.63
   Confidence: 100.00%;
   Support: 1.07%;
   Probability of consequent: 35.41%
2. if 1stMCGreater=Y and L4Tilt=Y and 1stMCDeg=22-77 and 2ndMCDeg=19-54 and 1stMCApex =T1-T11 and 2ndMCApex=L2-L2, then King-II.

   Fitness: 12.85
   Confidence: 87.88%;
   Support: 6.22%;
   Probability of consequent: 35.41%
3. if 1stMCGreater=Y and L4Tilt=Y and 1stMCApex=T6-T10 and 2ndMCApex=L2-L5, then King-II.

   Fitness: 10.52
   Confidence: 79.76%;
   Support: 14.38%;
   Probability of consequent: 35.41%
4. if 1stMajorCurveGreater=Y and 2ndMCDeg=8-95 and 1stMCApex=T3-T11 and 2ndMCApex= T4-T10, then King-II.

   Fitness: 3.32
   Confidence: 52.17%;
   Support: 7.73%;
   Probability of consequent: 35.41%

A.4.1.3. King-III

1. if 1stCurveT1=N and L4Tilt=N and 1stMCApex=T1-T9 and 2ndMCApex=Null, then King-III.

   Fitness: 5.87
   Confidence: 25.87%;
   Support: 0.86%;
   Probability of consequent: 7.94%
2. if L4Tilt=N and 1stMCApex=T2-T6 and 2ndMCApex=T2-T11, then King-III.

   Fitness: 4.86
   Confidence: 25.71%;
   Support: 1.93%;
   Probability of consequent: 7.94%

A.4.1.4. King-IV

1. if 1stCurveT1=Y and 1stMCGreater=Y and L4Tilt=Y and 1stMCApex=L5-T10 and 2ndMCApex=T9-L5, then King-IV.

   Fitness: 11.10
   Confidence: 29.41%;
   Support: 1.07%;
   Probability of consequent: 2.79%
2. if 1stMCGreater=Y and L4Tilt=Y and 1stMCApex=T10-L5 and 2ndMCApex=T5-L4, then King-IV.

   Fitness: 6.02
   Confidence: 19.35%;
   Support: 1.29%;
   Probability of consequent: 2.79%

A.4.1.5. King-V

1. if 1stMCGreater=Y and L4Tilt=Y and 1stMCApex=T2-T5 and 2ndMCApex=T9-T11, then King-V.

   Fitness: 22.75
   Confidence: 62.50%;
   Support: 1.07%;
   Probability of consequent: 6.44%
2. if 1stMCGreater=N and 2ndMCDeg=37-70 and 1stMCApex=T4-T7 and 2ndMCApex=T2-T11, then King-V.

   Fitness: 19.98
   Confidence: 57.14%;
   Support: 0.86%;
   Probability of consequent: 6.44%
3. if 1stCurveT1=Y and 1stMCGreater=Y and L4Tilt=Y and 1stMCDeg=3-35 and 1stMCApex=T2-T6 and 2ndMCApex=T7-T9, then King-V.

   Fitness: 16.42
   Confidence: 50.00%;
   Support: 0.86%;
   Probability of consequent: 6.44%

A.4.1.6. TL

1. if 1stMCGreater=Y and 1stMCApex=T11-T12 and 2ndMCApex=Null, then TL.

   Fitness: 19.49
   Confidence: 41.18%;
   Support: 1.50%;
   Probability of consequent: 2.15%

A.4.1.7. L

1. if 1stMCGreater=Y and L4Tilt=N and 1stMCApex=L2-L5 and 2ndMCApex=Null, then L.

   Fitness: 26.32
   Confidence: 62.50%;
   Support: 1.07%;
   Probability of consequent: 4.51%

   if 1stCurveT1=N and L4Tilt=N and 2ndMCDeg=Null and 1stMCApex=L1-L3 and 2ndMCApex=Null, then L.

   Fitness: 21.59
   Confidence: 54.17%;
   Support: 2.79%;
   Probability of consequent: 4.51%
2. if 1stCurveT1=N and 1stMCApex=L2-L5 and 2ndMCApex=Null, then L.

   Fitness: 16.84
   Confidence: 45.45%;
   Support: 2.15%;
   Probability of consequent: 4.51%

A.4.2. Rules for Treatment

A.4.2.1. Observation

1. if Deg1=3-12 and Deg2 =Null and Deg3 = Null and Deg4 = Null, then Observation.

   Fitness: 7.59
   Confidence: 100.00%;
   Support: 1.93%;
   Probability of consequent: 62.45%

   if Deg1=5-27 and Deg2 =4-21 and Deg3 = 0-22 and Deg4 = Null and mens = 99, then Observation.

   Fitness: 7.55
   Confidence: 100.00%;
   Support: 1.07%;
   Probability of consequent: 62.45%

2. if Deg1=4-13 and Deg2 =2-29 and Deg3 = Null and Deg4 = Null, then Observation.

   Fitness: 6.8
   Confidence: 95.55%;
   Support: 6.01%;
   Probability of consequent: 62.45%

A.4.2.2. Bracing

1. if age = 2-12 and Deg1=20-26 and Deg2 =24-47 and Deg3 = 27-52 and Deg4 = Null, then Bracing.

   Fitness: 22.54
   Confidence: 100.00%;
   Support: 0.86%;
   Probability of consequent: 24.46%

2. if Deg1=21-28 and Deg2 =32-43 and Deg3 = Null and Deg4 = Null and RI = 3-4, then Bracing.

   Fitness: 15.18
   Confidence: 80.00%;
   Support: 0.86%;
   Probability of consequent: 24.46%

3. if Deg1=25-39 and Deg2 =21-42 and Deg3 = Null and Deg4 = Null and RI = 1-3, then Bracing.

   Fitness: 12.26
   Confidence: 71.43%;
   Support: 1.07%;
   Probability of consequent: 24.46%

Appendix B

THE GRAMMAR USED FOR THE FRACTURE AND SCOLIOSIS DATABASES

B.1. The Grammar for the Fracture Database

This grammar is not completely listed. The grammar rules for the other attribute descriptors are similar to the grammar rules 14 - 25

```
1:    start   ->    rule1.
2:    start   ->    rule2.
3:    start   ->    rule3.
4:    rule1   ->    [if], antes1, [, then], consq1, [.].
5:    rule2   ->    [if],antes1,[and],antes2,[,then],consq2 [.].
6:    rule3   ->    [if], antes1, [and], antes2, [and], antes3,
                    [, then], consq3, [.].
7:    antes1  ->    sex1, [and], age1, [and], admday1.
8:    antes2  ->    diagnosis1.
9:    antes3  ->    operation1, [and], surgeon1.
10:   consq1  ->    diagnosis_descriptor.
11:   consq2  ->    operation_descriptor.
12:   consq2  ->    surgeon_descriptor.
13:   consq3  ->    stay_descriptor.
14:   sex1              ->    [any].
15:   sex1              ->    sex_descriptor.
16:   sex_descriptor    ->    {sex_const(?x)}, [sex = ?x].
17:   admday1           ->    [any].
18:   admday1           ->    admday_descriptor.
19:   admday_descriptor       ->
          {day_const(?x)}, {day_const(?y)},
          [admission day between ?x and ?y].
20:   admday_descriptor       ->
          {month_const(?x)}, {month_const(?y)},
          [admission month between ?x and ?y].
21:   admday_descriptor       ->
          {year_const(?x)}, {year_const(?y)},
          [admission year between ?x and ?y].
22:   admday_descriptor       ->
          {weekday_const(?x)}, {weekday_const(?y)},
          [admission weekday between ?x and ?y].
23:   diagnosis1              ->    [any].
24:   diagnosis1              ->    diagnosis_descriptor.
25:   diagnosis_descriptor    ->    {disgnosis_const(?x)},
                                    [diagnosis is ?x].
      ...
```

B.2. The Grammar for the Scoliosis Database

This grammar is not completely listed. The grammar rules for the other attribute descriptors are similar to the grammar rules 8 - 16.

```
1:      start   ->      rule1.
2:      start   ->      rule2.
3:      rule1   ->      [if], antes1, [, then], consq1, [.].
4:      rule2   ->      [if], antes2, [, then], consq2 [.].
5:      antes1  ->      1stCurveT1, [and], 1stMCGreater, [and],
                        L4Tilt, [and], 1stMCDeg, [and], 2ndMCDeg,
                        [and], 1stMCApex, [and], 2ndMDApex.
6:      antes2  ->      age, [and], law, [and], deg1, [and], deg2,
                        [and], deg3, [and], deg4, [and], mens, [and],
                        ri, [and], tsi, [and], scoliosisType.
7:      consq1 ->       scoliosisType_descriptor.
8:      1stMCGreater    ->      [any].
9:      1stMCGreater    ->      1stMCGreater_descriptor.
10:     1stMCGreater_descriptor     ->      {boolean_const(?x)],
                                            [1stMCGreater = ?x].
11:     1stMCDeg                    ->      [any].
12:     1stMCDeg                    ->      1stMCDeg_descriptor.
13:     1stMCDeg_descriptor         ->
                    {deg_const(?x)}, {deg_const(?y)},
                    [1stMCDeg between ?x and ?y].
14:     1stMCApex                   ->      [any].
15:     1stMCApex                   ->      1stMCApex_descriptor.
16:     1stMCApex_descriptor        ->
                    {apex_const(?x)}, {apex_const(?y)},
                    [1stMCApex between ?x and ?y].

        ...
        ...
```

References

Abramson, H. and Dahl, V. (1989). *Logic Grammars*. Berlin: Springer-Verlag.

Agrawal, R. and Srikant, R. (1994). Fast Algorithms for Mining Association Rules. In *Proceedings of the 20th International Conference on Very Large Databases*, pp. 487-499.

Agrawal, R., Imielinski, T., and Swami, A. (1993). Mining Association Rules Between Sets of Items in Large Databases. In *Proceedings of the 1993 International Conference on Management of Data (SIGMOD 93)*, pp. 207-216.

Aho, A. V. and Ullman, J. D. (1977). *Principles of Compiler Design*. Reading, MA: Addison-Wesley.

Angeline, P. (1994). Genetic Programming and Emergent Intelligent. In K. E. Kinnear, Jr. (ed.), *Advances in Genetic Programming*, pp. 75-97. Cambridge, MA: MIT Press.

Angeline, P. (1993). *Evolutionary Algorithms and Emergent Intelligence*. Ph.D. Dissertation. The Ohio State University.

Angeline, P. and Kinnear, K. E. Jr., editor (1996). *Advances in Genetic Programming II*. Cambridge, MA: MIT Press.

Bäck, T. (1996). *Evolutionary Algorithms in Theory and Practice : Evolution strategies, Evolutionary Programming, Genetic algorithms*. New York, NY: Oxford University Press.

Bäck, T., Hoffmeister, F., and Schwefel, H. P. (1991). A Survey of Evolution Strategies. In *Proceedings of the Fourth International Conference on Genetic Algorithms*, pp. 2-9. San Mateo, CA: Morgan Kaufmann.

Baker, J. (1987). Reducing Bias and Inefficiency in the Selection Algorithm. In *Proceedings of the Second International Conference on Genetic Algorithms and their Applications*. Hillsdale, NJ: Lawrence Erlbaum.

Baker, J. (1985). Adaptive Selection Methods for Genetic Algorithms. In J. Grefenstette (ed.), *Proceedings of an International Conference on Genetic Algorithms and Their Applications*, pp. 101-111. Hillsdale, NJ: Lawrence Erlbaum.

Banzhaf, W., Nordin, P., Keller, R. E., and Francone, F. D. (1998). *Genetic Programming: An Introduction on the Automatic Evolution of Computer Programs and its Applications*. San Francisco, CA: Morgan Kaufmann.

Bergadano, F., Giordana, A., and Saitta, L. (1991). *Machine Learning: An Integrated Framework and its Applications*. London: Ellis Horwood.

Bergadano, F. and Gunetti, D. (1995). *Inductive Logic Programming: From Machine Learning to Software Engineering*. Cambridge, MA: MIT Press.

Blockeel, H., De Raedt, L., Jacobs, N., and Demoen, B. (1999). Scaling Up Inductive Logic Programming by Learning from Interpretations. *Data Mining and Knowledge Discovery*, **3**, pp. 59-93.

Booker, L., Goldberg, D. E., and Holland, J. (1989). Classifier Systems and Genetic Algorithms. *Artificial Intelligence*, **40**, pp. 235-282.

Bouckaert, R. R. (1994). Properties of Belief Belief Networks Learning Algorithms. In *Proceedings of the Conference on Uncertainty in Artificial Intelligence*, pp. 102-109.

Bratko, I. and King, R. (1994). Applications of Inductive Logic Programming. *SIGART Bulletin*, **5** (1), pp. 43-49.

Breiman, L., Friedman, J. H., Olshen, R. A. and Stone, C. J. (1984). *Classification and Regression Trees*. Belmont: Wadsworth.

Buchanan, B. G. and Shortliffe, E. H. editors (1984). *Rule-based Expert Systems The MYCIN Experiments of the Stanford Heuristic Programming Project. Reading*. Reading, MA: Addison-Wesley.

Carbonell, J. G. editor (1990). *Machine Learning: Paradigms for Machine Learning*. Cambridge, MA: MIT Press.

Cavicchio, D. J. (1970). *Adaptive Search Using Simulated Evolution*. PhD thesis, University of Michigan, Ann Arbor.

Cameron-Jones, R. and Quinlan, J. (1994). Efficient Top-down Induction of Logic Programs. *SIGART Bulletin*, **5**(1), pp. 33-42.

Cameron-Jones, R. and Quinlan, J. (1993). Avoiding Pitfalls when Learning Recursive Theories. In *Proceedings of the Thirteenth International Joint Conference on Artificial Intelligence*. San Mateo, CA: Morgan Kaufmann.

Cestnik, B. (1990). Estimating Probabilities: A Crucial Task in Machine Learning. In *Proceedings of the Ninth European Conference on Artificial Intelligence*, pp. 147-149. London: Pitman.

Cestnik, B. and Bratko, I. (1991). On Estimating Probabilities in Tree Pruning. In Y. Kodratoff (ed.), *Proceedings of the Fifth European Working Session on Learning*, pp. 151-163. Berlin: Springer Verlag.

Chakrabarti, S., Dom, B. E., Kumar, S. R., Raghavan, P., Rajagopalan, S. Tomkins, A., Gibson, D., and Kleinberg, J. (1999). Mining the Web's Link Structure. *IEEE Computer*, **32**(4), pp. 60-67.

Charniak, E. (1991). Bayesian Networks Without Tears. *AI magazine*, **12**(4), pp. 50-63.

Chen, M. S., Han, J., and Yu., S. (1996). Data Mining: An Overview from Database Perspective. *IEEE Transactions on Knowledge and Data Engineering*, **8**, pp. 866-883.

Cherkassky, V. and Mulier, F. (1998). *Learning from Data: Concepts, Theory, and Methods*. New York, NY: Wiley.

Chickering, D., Geiger, D., and Heckerman, D. (1995). Learning Bayesian Networks: Search Methods and Experimental Results. In *Proceedings of the Fifth Conference on Artificial Intelligence and Statistics*, pp. 112-128.

Chow, C. K. and Liu, C. N. (1968). Approximating Discrete Probability Distributions with Dependence Trees. *IEEE Transactions on Information Theory*, **14**, pp. 462-467.

Clark, K. (1978). Negation as Failure. In H. Gallaire and J. Minker (eds.), *Logic and Databases*, pp. 293-322. NY: Plenum Press.

Clark, P. and Boswell, R. (1991). Rule Induction with CN2: Some Recent Improvements. In Y. Kodratoff (ed.), *Proceedings of the Fifth European Working Session on Learning*, pp. 151-163. Berlin: Springer-Verlag.

Clark, P. and Niblett, T. (1989). The CN2 induction algorithm. *Machine Learning*, **3**, pp. 261-283.

Cohen, W. W. (1993). Pac-learning a Restricted Class of Recursive Logic Programs. In *Proceedings of the Tenth National Conference on Artificial Intelligence*, pp. 86-92. Cambridge, MA: MIT Press.

Cohen, W. (1992). Compiling Prior Knowledge into an Explicit Bias. In *Proceedings of the Ninth International Workshop on Machine Learning*, 102-110. San Mateo, CA: Morgan Kaufmann.

Colmerauer, A. (1978). Metamorphosis Grammars. In L. Bolc (ed.), *Natural Language Communication with Computers*. Berlin: Springer-Verlag.

Cooper, G. F. and Herskovits, E. (1992). A Bayesian Method for the Induction of Probabilistic Networks from Data. *Machine Learning*, **9**, pp. 309-347.

Cormen, T. H., Leiserson, C. E., and Rivest, R. L. (1990). *Introduction to Algorithms*. Cambridge, MA: MIT Press.

Davidor, Y. (1991). A generic Algorithm Applied to Robot Trajectory Generation. In L. Davis (ed.), *Handbook of Genetic Algorithms*, pp. 144-165. Van Nostrand Reinhold.

Davis, L. D. editor (1987). *Genetic Algorithms and Simulated Annealing*. London: Pitman.

Davis, L. D. editor (1991). *Handbook of Genetic Algorithms*. Van Nostrand Reinhold.

Dehaspe, L. and Toivonen, H. (1999). Discovery of Frequent DATALOG Patterns. *Data Mining and Knowledge Discovery*, **3**, pp. 7-36.

DeJong, G. F., editor (1993). *Investigating Explanation-Based Learning*. Boston: Kluwer Academic Publishers.

DeJong, G. F. and Mooney, R. (1986). Explanation-Based Learning: An Alternative View. *Machine Learning*, **1**, pp. 145-176.

DeJong, K. A. (1975). *An Analysis of the Behavior of a Class of Genetic Adaptive Systems*. PhD thesis, University of Michigan, Ann Arbor.

DeJong, K. A. and Spears, W. M. (1990). An Analysis of the Interacting Roles of Population Size and Crossover in Genetic Algorithms. In *Proceedings of the First Workshop on Parallel Problem Solving from Nature*, pp. 38-47. Berlin: Springer-Verlag.

DeJong, K. A., Spears, W. M. and Gordon, D. F. (1993). Using Genetic Algorithms for Concept Learning. *Machine Learning*, **13**, pp. 161-188.

De Raedt, L. (1992). *Interactive Theory Revision: An Inductive Logic Programming Approach*. London: Academic Press.

De Raedt, L. and Bruynooghe, M. (1992). Interactive Concept Learning and Constructive Induction by Analogy. *Machine Learning*, **8**, pp. 251-269.

De Raedt, L. and Bruynooghe, M. (1989). Towards friendly Concept-learners. In *Proceeding of the Eleventh International Joint Conference on Artificial Intelligence*, pp. 849-854. San Mateo, CA: Morgan Kaufmann.

Dietterich, T. G. (1986). Learning at the Knowledge Level. *Machine Learning*, **1**, pp. 287-316.

Dzeroski, S. (1996). Inductive Logic Programming and Knowledge Discovery in Databases. In U. M. Fayyad, G. Piatetsky-Shapiro, P. Smyth, and R. Uthurusamy (eds.), *Advances in Knowledge Discovery in Data Mining*, pp. 117-152. Menlo Park, CA: AAAI Press.

Dzeroski, S. and Lavrac, N. (1993). Inductive Learning in Deductive Databases. *IEEE Transactions on Knowledge and Data Engineering*, **5**, pp. 939-949.

Elder, J. F. IV and Pregibon, D. (1996). A statistical perspective on KDD. In U. M. Fayyad, G. Piatetsky-Shapiro, P. Smyth, and R. Uthurusamy (eds.), Advances in Knowledge Discovery and Data Mining, pp. 83-113. Menlo Park, CA: AAAI Press.

Ellman, T. (1989). Explanation-Based Learning: A Survey of Programs and Perspectives. *ACM Computing Surveys*, **21**, 163-222.

Eshelman, L. J., Caruna, R., and Schaffer, J. D. (1989). Biases in the Crossover Landscape. In J. D. Schaffer (ed.), *Proceedings of the Third International Conference on Genetic Algorithms*, pp. 10-19. San Mateo, CA: Morgan Kaufmann.

Fayyad, U. M., Piatesky-Shapiro, G., and Smyth, P. (1996). From Data Mining to Knowledge Discovery: An Overview. *AI magazine*, **17**(3), pp. 37-54.

Fogel, D. B. (1999). *Evolutionary Computation: Toward a New Philosophy of Machine Intelligence*. 2nd Edition. New York, NY: IEEE Press.

Fogel, D. B. (1994). An Introduction to Simulated Evolutionary Optimization. *IEEE Trans. on Neural Network*, **5**, pp. 3-14

Fogel, D. B. (1992). A Brief History of Simulated Evolution. In *Proceedings of the First Annual Conference on Evolutionary Programming*. La Jolla, CA.

Fogel, L., Owens, A., and Walsh, M. (1966). *Artificial Intelligence through Simulated Evolution*. New York: John Wiley and Sons.

Forrest, S. (1990). *A Study of Parallelism in the Classifier System and its Application to Classification in KL-ONE Semantic Networks*. London: Pitmann.

Frawley, W., Piatetsky-Shapiro, G., and Matheus, C. (1991). Knowledge Discovery in Databases: an Overview. In G. Piatetsky-Shapiro and W. Frawley (eds.), *Knowledge Discovery in Databases*, pp. 1-27. Menlo Park, CA: AAAI Press.

Ganti, V., Gehrke, J., and Ramakrishnan, R. (1999). Mining Very Large Databases. *IEEE Computer*, **32**(4), pp. 38-45.

Goldberg, D. (1989). *Genetic Algorithms in Search, Optimization, and Machine Learning*. Reading, MA: Addison-Wesley.

Goldberg, D. and Bridges, C. L. (1990). An Analysis of a Reordering Operator on a GA-hard Problem. *Biological Cybernetics*, **62**, pp. 397-405.

Goldberg, D. and Deb, K. (1991). A Comparative Analysis of Selective Schemes Used in Genetic Algorithms. In G. Rawlins (ed.), *Foundations of Genetic Algorithms*, pp. 69-93. San Mateo, CA: Morgan Kaufmann.

Goldberg, D. and Richardson, J. (1987). Genetic Algorithms with Sharing for Multi-modal Function Optimization. In *Proceedings of the Second International Conference on Genetic Algorithms*, pp. 41-49.

Gorges-Schleuter, M. (1991). Explicit Parallelism of Genetic Algorithms through Population Structures. *Parallel Problem Solving from Nature*, pp. 150-159. Berlin: Springer-Verlag.

Greene, D. P. and Smith, S. F. (1993). Competition-Based Induction of Decision Models from Examples. *Machine Learning*, **13**, pp. 229-257.

Grefenstette, J. J. (1986). Optimization of Control Parameters for Genetic Algorithms. *IEEE Trans. Systems, Man, and Cybernetics*, **16**, pp. 122-128.

Han, J. and Fu, J. (1995). Discovery of Multiple Level Association Rules from Large Databases. In *Proceedings of the 21st International Conference on Very Large Databases*.

Han, J., Lakshmanan, V. S., and Ng, T. (1999). Constraint-Based, Multidimensional Data Mining. *IEEE Computer*, **32**(4), pp. 46-50.

Heckerman, D. (1997). Bayesian Networks for Data Mining. *Data Mining and Knowledge Discovery*, **1**, pp. 79-119.

Heckerman, D. (1996). Bayesian Networks for Knowledge Discovery. In U. M. Fayyad, G. Piatetsky-Shapiro, P. Smyth, and R. Uthurusamy (eds.), Advances in Knowledge Discovery and Data Mining, pp. 273-306. Menlo Park, CA: AAAI Press.

Heckerman, D., Geiger, D., and Chickering, D. M. (1995). Learning Bayesian Networks: The Combination of Knowledge and Statistical Data. *Machine Learning*, **20**, pp. 197-243.

Hellerstein, J. M., Avnur, R., Chou, A., Hidber, C., Raman, V., Roth, T., and Hass, P. J. (1999). Interactive Data Analysis: The Control Project. *IEEE Computer*, **32**(4), pp. 51-59.

Herskovits, E. and Cooper, G. (1990). KUTATO: An Entropy-driven System for Construction of Probabilistic Expert Systems from Databases. Technical Report KSL 90-22, Knowledge Systems Laboratory, Medical Computer Science, Stanford Universtiy.

Holland, J. (1992). *Adaptation in Natural and Artificial Systems*. Cambridge, MA: MIT Press.

Holland, J. (1987). Genetic Algorithms and Classifier systems: Foundations and Future Directions.

Holland, J. and Reitman, J. S. (1978). Cognitive Systems Based on Adaptive Algorithms. In D. A. Waterman and F. Hayes-Roth (eds.), *Pattern-Directed Inference Systems*. London: Academic Press.

Holte, R. C. (1993). Very Simple Classification Rules Perform Well on Most Commonly Used Datasets. Machine Learning, **11**, pp. 91-104.

Hopcroft, J. E. and Ullman, J. D. (1979). *Introduction to automata theory, languages, and computation*. Reading, MA: Addison-Wesley.

Hoschka, P. and Klosgen, W. (1991). A Support System for Interpreting Statistical Data. In G. Piatetsky-Shapiro and W. Frawley (eds.), *Knowledge Discovery in Databases*. Menlo Park, CA: AAAI Press.

Janikow, C. Z. (1993). A Knowledge-Intensive Genetic Algorithm for Supervised Learning. *Machine Learning*, **13**, pp. 189-228.

Kalbfleish, J. (1979). *Probability and Statistical Inference, volume II*. New York, NY: Springer-Verlag.

Karypis, G., Han, E. H., and Kumar, V. (1999). Chameleon: Hierarchical Clustering Using Dynamic Modeling. *IEEE Computer*, **32**(4), pp. 68-75.

Kijsirikul, B., Numao, M., and Shimura, M. (1992a). Efficient Learning of Logic Programs with Non-Determinate, Non-Discriminating Literals. In S. Muggleton (ed.), *Inductive Logic Programming*, pp. 361-372. London: Academic Press.

Kijsirikul, B., Numao, M., and Shimura, M. (1992b). Discrimination-Based Constructive Induction of Logic Programs. In *Proceedings of the Tenth National Conference on Artificial Intelligence*, pp. 44-49. San Jose, CA. AAAI Press.

Kinnear, K. E. Jr. editor (1994). *Advances in Genetic Programming*. Cambridge, MA: MIT Press.

Kodratoff, Y. and Michalski, R. editors (1990). *Machine Learning: An Artificial Intelligence Approach, Volume III*. San Mateo, CA: Morgan Kaufmann.

Kowalski, R. A. (1979). *Logic For Problem Solving*. Amsterdam: North-Holland.

Koza, J. R. (1994). *Genetic Programming II: Automatic Discovery of Reusable Programs*. Cambridge, MA: MIT Press.

Koza, J. R. (1992). *Genetic Programming: on the Programming of Computers by Means of Natural Selection*. Cambridge, MA: MIT Press.

Koza, J. R., Bennett, F. H. III, Andre, D., and Keane, M. A. (1999). *Genetic Programming III: Darwinian Invention and Problem Solving*. San Francisco, CA: Morgan Kaufmann.

Lam, W. (1998). Bayesian Network Refinement Via Machine Learning Approach. *IEEE Transactions on Pattern Analysis and Machine Intelligence*, **20**, pp. 240-252.

Lam, W. and Bacchus, F. (1994). Learning Bayesian Belief Networks: An Approach Based on the MDL Principle. *Computational Intelligence*, **10**, pp. 269-293.

Langdon, W. B. (1998). *Genetic Programming and Data Structures : Genetic Programming + Data Structures = Automatic Programming*. Boston: Kluwer Academic Publishers.

Larranaga, P., Kuijpers, C., Murga, R., and Yurramendi, Y. (1996a). Learning Bayesian Network Structures by Searching for the Best Ordering with Genetic Algorithms. *IEEE Transactions on System, Man, and Cybernetics – Part A: Systems and Humans*, **26**, pp. 487-493.

Larranaga, P., Poza, M., Yurramendi, Y., Murga, R. and Kuijpers, C. (1996b). Structure Learning of Bayesian Network by Genetic Algorithms: A Performance Analysis of Control Parameters. *IEEE Transactions on Pattern Analysis and Machine Intelligence*, **18**, pp. 912-926.

Lavrac, N. and Dzeroski, S. (1994). *Inductive Logic Programming: Techniques and Applications*. London: Ellis Horword.

Leung, K. S., Leung, Y., So, L., and Yam, K. F. (1992). Rule Learning in Expert Systems Using Genetic Algorithms: 1, concepts. In *Proceedings of the 2nd International Conference on Fuzzy Logic and Neural Networks*, pp. 201-204.

Leung, K. S. and Wong, M. H. (1990). An Expert-system Shell Using Structured Knowledge. *IEEE Computer*, **23**(3), pp. 38-47.

Leung, K. S. and Wong, M. L. (1991a). Inducing and Refining Rule-Based Knowledge From Inexact Examples. *Knowledge Acquisition*, **3**, pp. 291-315.

Leung, K. S. and Wong, M. L. (1991b). Automatic Refinement of Knowledge Bases With Fuzzy Rules. *Knowledge-Based Systems*, **4**, pp. 231-246.

Leung, K. S. and Wong, M. L. (1991c). AKARS-1: An Automatic Knowledge Acquisition and Refinement System. In H. Motada, R. Mizoguchi, J. Boose and B. Gaines (eds.), *Knowledge Acquisition for Knowledge-Based Systems*. Amsterdam: IOS Press.

Leung, K. S., Wong, M. L., Lam, W., and Wang, Z. Y. (1998). Discovering Nonlinear Integral Networks From Databases Using Evolutionary Computation and Minimum Description Length Principle. In *Proceedings of IEEE International Conference on Systems, Man, and Cybernetic*, pp.2326-2331.

Levenick, J. (1991). Inserting Introns Improves Genetic Algorithm Success Rate: Taking a Cue From Biology. In R. K. Belew and L. B. Booker (eds.), *Proceeding of the Fourth International Conference on Genetic Algorithms*, pp. 123-127. San Mateo, CA: Morgan Kaufmann.

Lewis, H. R. and Rapadimitrion, C. H. (1981). *Elements of the Theory of Computation*. NJ: Prentice Hall.

Lloyd, J. (1987). *Foundation of Logic Programming*. 2nd edition. Berlin: Springer Verlag.

Louis, S. J. and Rawlins, G. J. E. (1991). Designer Genetic Algorithms: Genetic Algorithms in Structure Design. In R. K. Belew and L. B. Booker (eds.), *Proceeding of the Fourth International Conference on Genetic Algorithms*, pp. 53-60. San Mateo, CA: Morgan Kaufmann.

Mahfoud, S. W. (1992). Crowding and Preselection Revisited. *Parallel Problem Solving from Nature 2*, pp.27-36. Berlin: Springer-Verlag.

Mannila, H., Toivonen, H., and Verkamo, A. I. (1994). Efficient Algorithms for Discovering Association Rules. In *KDD-94: AAAI Workshop on Knowledge Discovery in Databases*.

Matthews, B. W. (1975). Comparison of the Predicted and Observed Secondary Structure of T4 Phase Lysozyme. *Biochemica et Biophysical Acta*, **405**, pp. 442-451.

Merz, C. J. and Murphy, P. M. (1998). *UCI Repository of Machine Learning Databases*. University of California, Irvine, Department of Information and Computer Sciences. URL: http://www.ics.uci.edu/~mlearn/MLRepository.html

Michalewicz, Z. (1996). *Genetic Algorithms Data Structures = Evolutionary Programs*. 3rd Edition. New York, NY: Springer-Verlag.

Michalski, R. J. (1983). A Theory and Methodology of Inductive Learning. In R. Michalski, J. G. Carbonell and T. M. Mitchell (eds.), *Machine Learning: An Artificial Intelligence Approach, Volume I*, pp. 83-134. San Mateo, CA: Morgan Kaufmann.

Michalski, R. S. (1969). On the Quasi-minimal Solution of the General Covering Problem. In *Proceedings of the Fifth International Symposium on Information Processing*, pp. 125-128.

Michalski, R. J., Carbonell, J. G., and Mitchell, T. M., editors (1983). *Machine Learning: An Artificial Intelligence Approach, Volume I*. San Mateo, CA: Morgan Kaufmann.

Michalski, R. S., Mozetic, I., Hong, J. and Lavrac, N. (1986a). The Multi-Purpose Incremental Learning System AQ15 and its Testing Application on Three Medical Domains. In *Proceedings of the National Conference on Artificial Intelligence*, pp. 1041-1045. San Mateo, MA: Morgan Kaufmann.

Michalski, R. J., Carbonell, J. G., and Mitchell, T. M. editors (1986b). *Machine Learning: An Artificial Intelligence Approach, Volume II*. San Mateo, CA: Morgan Kaufmann.

Michalski, R. and Tecuci, G., editors (1994). *Machine Learning: A Multistrategy Approach, Volume IV*. San Francisco, CA: Morgan Kaufmann.

Michie, D. Spiegelhalter, D. J., and Taylor, C. C. editors (1994). *Machine Learning, Neural and Statistical Classification*. London: Ellis Horwood.

Minton, S (1989). *Learning Search Control Knowledge: An Explanation-Based Approach*. Boston: Kluwer Academic.

Minsky, M. (1963). Steps Towards Artificial Intelligence. In E. Feigenbaum and I. Feldman (eds.), *Computer and Thought*. Reading, MA: Addison Wesley.

Mitchell, M. (1996). An Introduction to Genetic Algorithms. Cambridge, MA: MIT Press.

Mitchell, T. M. (1982). Generalization as Search. *Artificial Intelligence*, **18**, pp. 203-226.

Mitchell, T. M., Keller, R. M., and Kedar-Cabelli, S. T. (1986). Explanation-Based Generalization: A Unifying View. *Machine Learning*, **1**, pp. 47-80.

Montana, D. J. (1995). Strongly Typed Genetic Programming. *Evolutionary Computation*, **3**, pp. 199-230.

Mooney, R. J. (1989). *A General Explanation-Based Learning Mechanism and its Application to Narrative Understanding*. London: Pitman.

Morik, K. Wrobel, S. Kietz, J., and Emde, W. (1993). *Knowledge Acquisition and Machine Learning: Theory, Methods, and Applications*. London: Academic Press.

Muggletion, S. (1994). Inductive Logic Programming. *SIGART Bulletin*, **5** (1), pp. 5-11.

Muggletion, S. (1992). Inductive Logic Programming. In S. Muggletion (ed.), *Inductive Logic Programming*, pp. 3-27. London: Academic Press.

Muggleton, S. and Buntine, W. (1988). Machine Invention of First-order Predicates by Inverting Resolution. In *Proceedings of the Fifth International Conference on Machine Learning*, pp. 339-352. San Mateo, CA: Morgan Kaufmann.

Muggletion, S., Bain, M., Hayes-Michie, J., and Michie, D. (1989). An Experimental Comparison of Human and Machine Learning Formalisms. In *Proceedings of the Sixth*

International Workshop on Machine Learning, pp. 113-118. San Mateo, CA: Morgan Kaufmann.

Muggleton, S. and De Raedt, L. (1994). Inductive Logic Programming: Theory and Methods. *J. Logic Programming*, **19-20**, pp. 629-679.

Muggletion, S. and Feng, C. (1990). Efficient Induction of Logic Programs. In *Proceedings of the FIrst Conference on Algorithmic Learning Theory*, pp. 368-381. Tokyo: Ohmsha.

Muhlenbein, H. (1992). How Genetic Algorithms Really Work: I. Mutation and Hillclimbing. In R. Manner and B. Manderick (eds.), *Parallel Solving from Nature 2*. North Holland.

Muhlenbein, H. (1991). Evolution in Time and Space - The Parallel Genetic Algorithm. In G. Rawlins (ed.), *Foundations of Genetic Algorithms*, pp. 316-337. San Mateo, CA: Morgan Kaufmann.

Newell, A. and Simon, H. A. (1972). *Human Problem Solving*. Englewood Cliffs, NJ: Prentice Hall.

Ngan, P. S., Wong, M. L., Lam, W., Leung, K. S., and Cheng, J. C. Y. (1999). Medical Data Mining Using Evolutionary Computation. *Artificial Intelligent in Medicine, Special Issue On Data Mining Techniques and Applications in Medicine*. **16**, pp. 73-96.

Nilson, N. J. (1980). *Principles of Artificial Intelligence*. Palo Alto, CA: Tioga.

Park, J. S., Chen, M. S., and Yu, P. S. (1995). An Effective Hash Based Algorithm for Mining Association Rules. In *Proceedings of the ACM-SIGMOD Conference on Management of Data*.

Paterson, M. S. and Wegman, M. N. (1978). Linear Unification. *Journal of Computer and System Sciences*, **16**, pp. 158-167.

Pazzani, M. and Kibler, D. (1992). The Utility of Knowledge in Inductive Learning. *Machine Learning*, **9**, pp. 57-94.

Pearl, J. (1984). *Heuristics: Intelligent Search Strategies for Computer Problem Solving*. Reading, MA: Addison Wesley.

Pereira, F. C. N. and Shieber, S. M. (1987). *Prolog and Natural-Language Analysis*. CA: CSLI.

Pereira, F. C. N. and Warren, D. H. D. (1980). Definite Clause Grammars for Language Analysis - A Survey of the Formalism and a Comparison with Augmented Transition Networks. *Artificial Intelligence*, **13**, pp. 231-278.

Piatetsky-Shapiro, G. (1991). Discovery, Analysis, and Presentation of Strong Rules. In G. Piatetsky-Shapiro and W. Frawley (eds.), *Knowledge Discovery in Databases*. Menlo Park, CA: AAAI Press.

Piatetsky-Shapiro, G. and Frawley, W. J. (1991). *Knowledge Discovery in Databases*. Menlo Park, CA: AAAI Press.

Plotkin, G. D. (1970). A Note on Inductive Generalization. In B. Meltzer and D. Michie (eds.), *Machine Intelligence: Volume 5*, pp. 153-163. New York: Elsevier North-Holland.

Quinlan, J. R. (1992). *C4.5: Programs for Machine Learning*. San Mateo, CA: Morgan Kaufmann.

Quinlan, J. R. (1991). Knowledge Acquisition From Structured Data - Using Determinate Literals to Assist Search. *IEEE Expert*, **6**, pp. 32-37.

Quinlan, J. R. (1990). Learning Logical Definitions From Relations. *Machine Learning*, **5**, pp. 239-266.

Quinlan, J. R. (1987). Simplifying Decision Trees. *Int. J. Man-Machine Studies*, **27**, pp. 221-234.

Quinlan, J. R. (1986). Induction of Decision Trees. *Machine Learning*, **1**, pp. 81-106.

Ramakrishnan, N. and Grama, A. Y. (1999). Data Mining: From Serendipity to Science. *IEEE Computer*, **32**(4), pp. 34-37.

Rebane, G. and Pearl, J. (1987). The Recovery of Causal Poly-Trees From Statistical Data. In *Proceedings of the Conference on Uncertainty in Artificial Intelligence*, pp. 222-228.

Rechenberg, I. (1973). *Evolutionsstrategie: Optimienrung Technischer Systeme nach Prinzipien der Biologischen Evolution*. Stuttgart: Frommann-Holzboog Verlag.

Rissanen, J. (1978). Modeling by Shortest Data Description. *Automatica*, **14**, pp. 465-471.

Rouveirol, C. (1992). Extensions of Inversion of Resolution Applied to Theory Completion. In S. Muggletion (ed.), *Inductive Logic Programming*, pp. 63-92. London: Academic Press.

Rouveirol, C. (1991). Completeness for Inductive Procedures. In A. B. Lawrence and G. C. Collins (eds.), *Proceedings of the Eight International Workshop on Machine Learning*, pp. 452-456. San Mateo, CA: Morgan Kaufmann.

Sammut, C. and Baneji, R. (1986). Learning Concepts by Asking Questions. In R. Michalski, J. G. Carbonell and T. M. Mitchell (eds.), *Machine Learning: An Artificial Intelligence Approach, Volume II*, pp. 167-191. San Mateo, CA: Morgan Kaufmann.

Schaffer, J. D. (1987). Some Effects of Selection Procedures on Hyperplane Sampling by Genetic Algorithms. In L. Davis (ed.), *Genetic Algorithms and Simulated Annealing*. London: Pitman.

Schaffer, J. D. and Morishma, A. (1987). An Adaptive Crossover Distribution Mechanism for Genetic Algorithms. In *Proceedings of the Third International Conference on Genetic Algorithms*, pp. 36-40. San Mateo, CA: Morgan Kaufmann.

Schewefel, H. P. (1981). *Numerical Optimization of Computer Models*. New York, NY: Wiley.

Shapiro, E. (1983). *Algorithmic Program Debugging*. Cambridge, MA: MIT Press.

Shavlik, J. W. and Dietterich, T. G. editors (1990). *Readings in Machine Learning*. San Mateo, CA: Morgan Kaufmann.

Singh, M. and Valtorta, M. (1993). An Algorithm for the Construction of Bayesian Network Structures From Data. In *Proceedings of the Conference on Uncertainty in Artificial Intelligence*, pp. 259-265.

Smith, S. F. (1983). Flexible Learning of Problem Solving Heuristics Through Adaptive Search. In *Proceedings of the Eighth International Conference on Artificial Intelligence*. San Mateo, CA: Morgan Kaufmann.

Smith, S. F. (1980). *A Learning System Based on Genetic Adaptive Algorithms*. PhD thesis, University of Pittsburgh.

Spirtes, P., Glymour, C., and Scheines, R. (1993). *Causation, Prediction and Search*. Berlin: Springer-Verlag.

Srikant, R. and Agrawal, R. (1996). Mining Quantitative Association Rules in Large Relational Tables. In *Proceedings of the ACM SIGMOD Conference on Management of Data*.

Srinivasan, A. (1999). A Study of Two Sampling Methods for Analyzing Large Datasets with ILP. *Data Mining and Knowledge Discovery*, **3**, pp. 95-123.

Srinivasan, A. and King, R. D. (1999). Feature Construction With Inductive Logic Programming: A Study of Quantitative Predictions of Biological Activity Aided by Structural Attributes. *Data Mining and Knowledge Discovery*, **3**, pp. 37-57.

Starkweather, T., McDaniel, S., Mathias, K., Whitley, D., and Whitley, C. (1991). A Comparison of Genetic Sequencing Operators. In *Proceedings of the Fourth International Conference on Genetic Algorithms*, pp. 69-76. San Mateo, CA: Morgan Kaufmann.

Sterling, L. and Shapiro, E. (1986). *The Art of Prolog*. Cambridge, MA: MIT Press.

Syswerda, G. (1991a). A Study of Reproduction in Generational and Steady-State Genetic Algorithms. In G. Rawlins (ed.), *Foundations of Genetic Algorithms*, pp. 94-101. San Mateo, CA: Morgan Kaufmann.

Syswerda, G. (1991b). Schedule Optimization Using Genetic Algorithms. In L. Davis (ed.), *Handbook of Genetic Algorithms*, pp. 332-349. Van Nostrand Reinhold.

Syswerda, G. (1989). Uniform Crossover in Genetic Algorithms. In *Proceedings of the Third International Conference on Genetic Algorithms*, pp. 2-9. San Mateo, CA: Morgan Kaufmann.

Tanese, R. (1989). Distributed Genetic Algorithms. In J. D. Schaffer (ed.), *Proceedings of the Third International Conference on Genetic Algorithms*, pp. 434-439. San Mateo, CA: Morgan Kaufmann.

Tangkitvanich, S. and Shimura, M. (1992). Refining a Relational Theory with Multiple Faults in the Concept and Subconcepts. In *Proceedings of the Ninth International Conference on Machine Learning*, pp. 436-444. San Mateo, CA: Morgan Kaufmann.

Thrun, S. B., Bala, J., Bloedorn, E., Bratko, I., Cestnik, B., Cheng, J., DeJong, K., Dzeroski, S., Fahlman, S. E., Fisher, D., Hamann, R., Kaufman, K., Keller, S., Kononenko, I., Kreuziger, J., Michalski, R. S., Mitchell, T., Pachowicz, P., Reich, Y., Vafaie, H., Van de Welde, W., Wenzel, W., Wnek, J., and Zhang, J. (1991). The MONK's Problems: A Performance Comparison of Different Learning Algorithms. Technical Report CMU-CS-91-197, Carnegie Mellon University.

Whigham, P. A. (1996). Search Bias, Language Bias and Genetic Programming. In *Proceedings of the First Genetic Programming Conference*, pp. 230-237. Cambridge, MA: MIT Press.

Whitley, D. (1989). The GENITOR Algorithm and Selective Pressure. In *Proceedings of the Third International Conference on Genetic Algorithms*, pp. 116-121. San Mateo, CA: Morgan Kaufmann.

Whitley, D., Starkweather, T. (1990). Genitor II: a Distributed Genetic Algorithm. *Journal of Experimental and Theoretical Artificial Intelligence*, **2**, pp. 189-214.

Wirth, R. (1989). Completing Logic Programs by Inverse Resolution. In *Proceedings of the Fourth European Working Session on Learning*, pp. 239-250. London: Pitman.

Wong, M. L. (1998). An Adaptive Knowledge Acquisition System Using Generic Genetic Programming. *Expert Systems with Applications*, **15**(1), pp.47-58.

Wong, M. L., Lam, W., and Leung, K. S. (1999). Using Evolutionary Computation and Minimum Description Length Principle for Data Mining of Bayesian Networks. *IEEE Transactions on Pattern Analysis and Machine Intelligence*, **21**, pp.174-178.

Wong, M. L. and Leung, K. S. (1997). Evolutionary Program Induction Directed by Logic Grammars. *Evolutionary Computation*, **5**, pp. 143-180.

Wong, M. L. and Leung, K. S. (1995a). An Adaptive Inductive Logic Programming system Using Genetic Programming. In *Proceedings of the Fourth Annual Conference on Evolutionary Programming*. MA: MIT Press.

Wong, M. L. and Leung, K. S. (1995b). Inducing Logic Programs with Genetic Algorithms: The Genetic Logic Programming System. *IEEE Expert*, **9**(5), pp. 68-76..

Wong, M. L. and Leung, K. S. (1994a). Inductive Logic Programming Using Genetic Algorithms. In J. W. Brahan and G. E. Lasker (eds.), *Advances in Artificial Intelligence - Theory and Application II*, pp. 119-124. I.I.A.S., Ontario.

Wong, M. L. and Leung, K. S. (1994b). Learning First-order Relations From Noisy Databases Using Genetic Algorithms. In *Proceedings of the Second Singapore International Conference on Intelligent Systems*, B159-164.

Wu, Q., Suetens, P., and Oosterlinck, A. (1991). Integration of Heuristic and Bayesian Approaches in a Pattern-Classification System. In G. Piatetsky-Shapiro and W. Frawley (eds.), *Knowledge Discovery in Databases*. Menlo Park, CA: AAAI Press.

Zelle, J. M., Mooney, R. J., and Konvisser, J. B. (1994). Combining Top-down and Bottom-up Techniques in Inductive Logic Programming. Technical Report, Department of Computer Science, University of Texas.

Zytkow, J. M. and Baker, J. (1991). Interactive Mining of Regularities in Databases. In G. Piatetsky-Shapiro and W. Frawley (eds.), *Knowledge Discovery in Databases*. Menlo Park, CA: AAAI Press.

Index

Printed by Libri Plureos GmbH
in Hamburg, Germany